Elusive Promises

University of Plymouth
Charles Seale Hayne Library
Subject to status this item may be renewed
via your Primo account

http://primo.plymouth.ac.uk
Tel: (01752) 588588

DISLOCATIONS

General Editors: August Carbonella, *Memorial University of Newfoundland,* Don Kalb, *University of Utrecht & Central European University,* Linda Green, *University of Arizona*

The immense dislocations and suffering caused by neoliberal globalization, the retreat of the welfare state in the last decades of the twentieth century, and the heightened military imperialism at the turn of the twenty-first century have raised urgent questions about the temporal and spatial dimensions of power. Through stimulating critical perspectives and new and cross-disciplinary frameworks that reflect recent innovations in the social and human sciences, this series provides a forum for politically engaged and theoretically imaginative responses to these important issues of late modernity.

ELUSIVE PROMISES

Planning in the Contemporary World

Edited by

Simone Abram
Gisa Weszkalnys

berghahn
NEW YORK · OXFORD
www.berghahnbooks.com

First published in 2013 by

Berghahn Books

www.berghahnbooks.com

© 2013, 2016 Simone Abram and Gisa Weszkalnys
First paperback edition published in 2016

Library of Congress Cataloging-in-Publication Data

Elusive promises : planning in the contemporary world / edited by Simone
Abram, Gisa Weszkalnys.
  p. cm. — (Dislocations ; v. 11)
Includes bibliographical references and index.
ISBN 978-0-85745-915-2 (hardback) — ISBN 978-1-78533-213-5 (paperback)
ISBN 978-0-85745-916-9 (ebook)
1. City planning. 2. Urbanization. I. Abram, Simone. II. Weszkalnys, Gisa.
HT166.E467 2013
307.1'216—dc23

2012037851

British Library Cataloguing in Publication Data

A catalogue record for this book is available from the British Library

ISBN 978-0-85745-915-2 (hardback)
ISBN 978-1-78533-213-5 (paperback)
ISBN 978-0-85745-916-9 (ebook)

CONTENTS

ACKNOWLEDGEMENTS

Like many edited books, this volume has emerged from a long gestation, in which many people have had a helping hand. We would like to thank Catherine Neveu, Gwyn Williams, Jaume Franquesa, Sarah Pink, Anne Waldrop and Eeva Berglund for early input into the concept. We owe particular thanks to Åsa Boholm for enabling the contributing authors to refine and coordinate their chapters at a dedicated meeting in Gothenburg. We are immensely grateful that we had this opportunity, which brought us to the idea of the elusive promise as the frame for the volume, and in particular to Sandy Robertson, whose preliminary text on the philosophy of the promise was a guide and inspiration for our collective work.

We should also like to thank the three anonymous reviewers whose comments gave us much to think about as we reworked the volume, and the series editors for supporting the production of this volume.

Previous versions of chapters 3 (Sarah Lund), 4 (Deborah James), 6 (Richard Baxstrom) and 7 (Laura Bear) appeared in *Focaal*, Volume 2011, Number 61.

Visualising the temporality of planning. Image source © 2008 courtesy of the research consultancy Bureau-design+research, School of Architecture, University of
Sheffield

ELUSIVE PROMISES
Planning in the Contemporary World
An Introduction

Simone Abram and Gisa Weszkalnys

What does an anthropology of planning have to offer when the discipline's tools, notably ethnography, are becoming an increasingly common feature in a range of professions, including planning? Conversely, what can a sustained theoretical engagement with planning bring to anthropology? This volume aims to craft a response to these questions by demonstrating, first, that although anthropology's critical perspective rests in no small part on the ethnographic method, it cannot be reduced to it. Instead, ethnography produces a particular kind of critical insight through its capacity to grasp the contradictory and conflicting aspects that form an inherent part of the human social fabric, as well as through its increasingly sophisticated ways of connecting observations at the immediate level of the everyday to different, 'larger' scales of political, economic and cultural life. In addition, by putting planning in a broader comparative and conceptual framework and linking it to a set of anthropological concerns regarding the state, development, entitlement, agency and the imagination, an anthropology of planning can make a real contribution.

Second, we note that the significance of planning as a practice typical of state and market organizations across the globe has attracted relatively little attention in anthropology. Anthropological research has tended to focus on the more abstract concepts of 'the state' or 'politics', or on planning in the context of colonial or postcolonial government. Only a few detailed studies have explicitly addressed the problem of planning in democratic states (e.g., Robertson 1984). More generally, there is a widespread tendency either to demonize planning or to view it as too trivial and self-evident to deserve any sustained attention. Over the years, anthropologists have gradually begun to unsettle such perceptions, and the contributions to this volume continue in this spirit. They testify to the potential of anthropological analysis, giving us glimpses of the variety of state and non-state involvement in planning and the ways such involvement is locally apprehended and theorized. They offer ethnographic accounts from a wide range of contexts, from hypercomplexity in Sweden (Boholm) to land restitution in South Africa (James), urban invasions in Peru (Lund), the changing expectations of the welfare state (Vike), repeated evictions of the poor from desirable land in Brazil (Gledhill), river and port management in India (Bear), and virtual plans in contemporary Malaysia (Baxstrom). Between them, the chapters in this volume reveal the specific, and occasionally contradictory, temporalities and materialities articulated through planning in particular places and at particular times.

Planning is a form of conceptualizing space and time, and the possibilities that time offers space. It is something that most people do in various forms. We imagine the future – whether it be lunchtime, harvest, initiation or European interest rates – and then act on our desires for that future to take a particular shape. Of course, what exactly 'planning' signifies is not universal: the same word may apply to quite different practices, and similar practices may be described using different words (see Abram and Cowell 2004; Abu-Lughod 1975). In its most general sense of imagining the future and preparing in advance, planning entails a broad set of tactics, technologies and institutions to try to control the passage into the future, including practices and ideas that have spread across private and public organizations. At the state level, planning is a way of managing the present, of governing and organizing the relationships between the state, citizenry and other entities, whether non-departmental public bodies, non-profit agencies or commercial organizations. In our view, state planning practices continue to have a central influence on daily life. The 'local state' in particular – that is, the local agencies, bureaus, political party representations and councils through which most of us encounter the state on a daily basis (Gupta 1995) and through which the State exercises its most ordinary forms of power (Mitchell 1991) – is a planner par excellence. As we will show in this introduction, even at a time when state agencies' direct involvement in planning is being eroded, they continue to function as arbiters of planning activities. Forms of state-led planning usually have counterparts in private corporations; however, the planning activities of non-state organizations still enrol a range of private *and* public actors because of the need to abide by state and private planning and building regulations, conform to the categories of state welfare provision or organize financial affairs to the best advantage. In this volume, we are particularly interested in the institutionalized forms of planning found primarily in (nominally) democratic capitalist states. While planning occurs under different political and economic parameters, our aim is to pinpoint some of the common features and implications of taken-for-granted practices adopted by professionals, including town planners, architects, environmental consultants, and economists. These self-conscious experts in particular types of planning set budgets, envision new developments, and lay out schemes for welfare at both central and local levels of the state, and are called on to resolve objections and protests by a diverse range of interlocutors.

The authors in this volume share an understanding of planning as an assemblage of activities, instruments, ideologies, models and regulations aimed at ordering society through a set of social and spatial techniques. But they also highlight a characteristic tension produced by planning as an inherently optimistic and future-oriented activity. The future promised in plans seems always slightly out of reach, the ideal outcome always slightly elusive, and the plan retrospectively always flawed. This, in our minds, distinguishes the present volume from much fruitful work on planning and the state carried out by anthropologists and other scholars, for example, under a Foucauldian paradigm (e.g., Ferguson 1990; Rabinow 1989; Scott 1998). Studies inspired by Foucault have raised awareness of the subtle processes through which state power operates and of the apparatuses, technologies, discourses and practices of governmentality, many of which can be considered forms of planning as described in this volume. However, they have tended, on the one hand, to emphasize the spatial dimensions of these processes of ordering, regulating and controlling – both of national territories and of conceptual spaces of populations, assets, resources, and so on. On the other hand, these studies have generated an overly rationalistic and coherent sense of how planning operates as a technology of government. In this view, failure remains somewhat external to, rather than an integral and productive part of, the material practice of planning (Li 2005; Weszkalnys 2010). By contrast, in this introduction and the volume as a whole, we aim to move beyond the spatial and governmental focus, including notions of land use and spatial planning, partly inherited from Foucauldian analyses. Instead, we wish to include the messiness and contingency of different forms of planning. To do so, we emphasize the idea of the promise of a planned future at the heart of much planning activity, and examine the different and sometimes clashing temporalities at play in contemporary planning contexts.

The various forms of planning that we address have in common a concern with the transition through time between current and desired states. Planning, as a manifestation of what people think is possible and desirable, and what the future promises for the better, is a subject that ethnography can illuminate particularly well, with its capacity to capture the conflicting desires that plans attempt to control, and the contradictions between, and mutual accommodations of, what is promised and what is done. The notion of the promise also enables us to situate planning in a new historical perspective, as a particular formalization of the contract between state and citizen. Since the concept and practices of planning vary in detail between states and local contexts within them, we cannot start from a unified definition of planning. Instead, the promise provides us with a productive starting point from which the contributors explore issues of temporality, spatiality, complexity, agency, power and resistance implicated in the planning assemblage.

In this introduction, we draw on our own experiences of carrying out ethnographic research on planning in the UK, Germany, and Scandinavia, but we believe that these experiences point to issues of greater relevance. The rest of the introduction is organized as follows. First, in place of a conventional history of planning (covered in more depth by others[1]), we briefly identify some of the common features that have emerged in planning as a unified concept in democratic capitalist states. Second, we explore how the philosophy of the promise can be used to give us better purchase on notions of contemporary planning and outline the limitations of such a philosophical account. To understand the promise of planning, it is necessary to consider questions of historical specificity, materiality, politics and power that are not included in the philosophers' abstractions. In the third part of this introduction, we attend once more to the specificity of the contemporary condition – a condition often described as 'neo-liberal'. But instead of taking neo-liberalism at face value, we take seriously a caution uttered by Ferguson (2009) and others (e.g., Brenner and Theodore 2002) regarding the multiple ways in which neo-liberalism is produced and configured at the national and local levels. This is a point demonstrated powerfully by the ethnographies assembled in this volume. Lastly, we return to our original question of what an anthropology of planning has to contribute to the discipline more broadly and, more importantly, what shape it could take. Synthesizing a disparate set of literature and insights from the anthropology of the state, development, and beyond, we suggest a way forward for an ethnographic approach to planning that highlights ideas of time and space, materiality and imagination, and that – instead of posing abstract questions about institutions and legislation – turns to the actual work carried out by planners, citizens, and the plans themselves.

The Emergence of Planning

The story of planning told in the classic accounts of planning theory and planning history consolidates a notion of planning as the ordered, if contested, preparation of space for development, with its roots in modernity's invention of bureaucracy and the emergence of government as a problematizing activity (Rabinow 1989; Rose and Miller 1992). For many authors, planning as a mode of statist intervention found its ultimate expression in the Soviet planned economy, whose new cities were laid out to serve state ambitions (e.g., Alexander 2007; Sampson 1984). For others, planning arose as a response to failures of public hygiene (Boyer 1983), or more explicitly as the attempts of the state to organize the citizenry (Selznick 1949: 220). In this view, based on a welter of expert knowledge, plans arrange and distribute people, property, capital and resources in such a way that intervention becomes possible. However, while these forms of planning are clearly definable, they are certainly not unique to our historical moment. Neither attempts to organize citizenry nor the laying out of cities in an orderly manner commenced with European or American Late Modernity. Kalland (1996) points out that early Japanese cities were planned according to principles related to geomancy; and Lund (this volume) reminds us that Spanish colonists in the sixteenth century moved indigenous peoples into new cities precisely for the purpose of bureaucratic order. We might also refer to the order inscribed in ancient Greek or Aztec cities and note that architectural structure relied also on a particular social order.

Instead of retelling this story, we want to draw out four of the underlying problems for which planning has been offered as a response. These include, first, the contested relation between welfare and capital on one hand, and conflicts between capital and labour on the other. Second, in the context of colonial planning, this dual problematic was refracted by worries about race and the paramount goal of resource extraction. The other concerns to which planning seemed to offer an answer were, third, the effective exercise of state control over its citizens and territory, and fourth, what might be termed the comprehensiveness or holism of state provision. Together, the responses to these problems have given rise to forms of planning that are shared across capitalist states today. Planning regimes, or assemblages, have their own particular socio-historical trajectories and peculiarities, some of which we briefly trace in this section and through the book. We acknowledge that the emergence of planning sketched here is necessarily partial and selective. Rather than providing a chronology, however, we want to identify overlaps: for example, between state planning and philanthropic gestures, the organizational activities of monarchies and those of popular republics, or the patterns of state-organized welfare that arose in the late nineteenth century in response to the contradictions of capitalism.

A principal characteristic of contemporary democratic planning regimes is their role in mediating some of the central tensions in capitalist nation states. These tensions gave rise to a concern with the ways in which spatial and social order were to be made congruent, and attempts to create a better, more organized, healthy and productive society for capitalist production, epitomized in the ideal company village. US American planning, for example, grew out of a frustration among philanthropists with the increasingly appalling conditions in rapidly urbanizing American cities in the late nineteenth century (Boyer 1983). Urban 'improvers' sought social stability and the amelioration of insanitary conditions, while industrialists and capitalists sought a rapid turnover of potentially disposable cheap labour within easy reach of factories, docks and other workplaces, and easy access to raw materials. Urban planning in the United States thus arguably emerged as a contest between welfare and capital. Looking across the Atlantic, it is impossible not to hear in this the echo of Engels and Marx's agitation over the conditions of workers in the first great metropolitan industrial capitalist city of Manchester. Engels' concerns over the conditions of workers were shared in campaigning literature, in novels (notably those of Mrs Gaskell, who emphasized workers' desire for clean air and country walks) and in the political movements of the trade unions and Labour and Cooperative movements in the UK.

These did not work in isolation, though. Urban utopianism among Methodists and Quakers, inspired by associations between work and dignity in the face of the indignities of capitalism, brought the UK's first industrial ideal villages and towns: the company settlements at Rowntree in York and Cadbury in Birmingham, among numerous others. These were not the dollhouse ideal villages that helped to bring the aristocracy down (such as at Versailles), but earnest attempts to bring order and stability to the lives of working people. It would be wrong to romanticize their intentions – such projects were equally designed to ensure the stability of labour supply through company loyalty, and to maximize the working lives of their inhabitants in hours per day as much as years per life – but the role of religious motivation should not be underplayed. Ebenezer Howard's influential utopian garden cities (Howard 1902) similarly sought to undermine the conflict between capital and labour by capturing improvements in land value ('ground rents') from the landlords and redistributing it to the people in the form of residents' facilities and welfare. Though he was ultimately unable to entice landowners and investors into his project, Howard's programme of city planning was economically radical, reflecting contemporary concerns over the predominance of the gentry as landowners (see Ambrose 1986). Without the participation of those landowners, though, the ambitions of garden cities and suburbs were largely reduced to aesthetic-rational concerns, while the new towns of the early twentieth century were key to the campaigns that secured town planning as a core duty of local government in the UK and beyond.[2]

Second, planning in the colonial empires pursued a similar tactic regarding the alignment of economic development and welfare issues. At the same time, planning was used to tackle a set of different concerns arising in an intense exchange of models and practices between colony and metropolis (Rabinow 1989). The 'improvement' of conditions through planning, if it was a stated aim at all, was at most a highly selective and segregated exercise, pivoting on notions of putative racial and physiological difference (e.g., Kenny 1995). Better facilities and amenities were intended primarily for white colonial settlers, or were selectively implemented where increased profits were expected through the optimization of the labour force in agriculture and industry. 'Natives' were housed either in designated quarters or, increasingly, left to fend for themselves in spontaneous settlements on the outskirts of cities, for example, those springing up around mines (Ferguson 1999). In the African context in the late phase of British colonialism, this translated into worries about a perceived double problem of a rural peasantry largely disconnected from economic development, and a growing number of mobile labourers adding to a rapidly growing urbanized (and increasingly disorganized) population (cf. Stanner 1949). The types of responses developed in the colonial era, and the modes of spatial, economic and welfare planning they provoked, may be seen to reverberate in more recent, post-colonial planning exercises conducted, for instance, in the context of extractive industries or under the banner of corporate social responsibility (Peattie 1987; Rajak 2011).

A third, related major problem underlying planning concerns the effective exercise of state power and control. The movement for rational urban layout was not inspired by desires for improved hygiene and social conditions alone. Quite explicitly, the Hausmannization of Paris aimed to clear away the urban rabble. In his analysis of Hausmann's Paris, James Scott (1998) has highlighted the role of legibility, with the city best visible from above and embodied in models produced by planners representing the God's eye view. But this order was, of course, visible and effective not only from above. It also enabled intervention at street level. No more would the streets be so easily barricaded as they were during the 1789 revolution. That the opening up of public space to the military also made it available to protesting masses was perhaps inevitable, if inconvenient for the ruling classes. Well laid-out suburbs also eased the task of tax collection and surveillance. Thus, concerns with military control and the exercise of state powers mingled with worries about public health and hygiene, as well as the appropriate place for the different classes within the urban order. Across the centuries, such planning schemes have not only furthered spatial segregation along lines of race and class, and the displacement of the urban poor to the periphery (see also Baxstrom 2008; Caldeira 2000;

Holston 1989; Peattie 1987; Waldrop 2004). They have also made planning a formidable assistant to repression, civilization, militarization, accessibility, exclusion and exploitation, as chapters by both James and Lund demonstrate in this volume (see also Yiftachel 1998).

Following the Second World War, particularly in North-West Europe and Scandinavia, there emerged what was to become a fourth popular aim of planning in contemporary democratic states: an ideal of comprehensive holistic planning that integrates economic, welfare and spatial organization. Flourishing in the 1950s and 1960s, these planning regimes saw the state as a benign, quasi-parental force that sought to achieve quality of life for the whole population (see Vike 2004 and this volume). In the United States, rational planning was heralded as the future for efficient use of resources and democratic government (Lilienthal 1944). The famed Norwegian egalitarianism was built on a three-way compromise between the state, capitalists and trade unions, when all three recognized that by moderating their aims in respect of each other, they could all gain benefits (Barth, Moene and Wallerstein 2003). Allied with a pervading religious Puritanism and material modesty, Norway achieved a degree of social levelling unparalleled in Western Europe, echoed in architectural rationality and spatial accessibility. The written plans and drawings that secured the passage to ideal communities were strikingly humanitarian in contrast with British urban plans, for example.

Today more than ever, these central aims and assumptions that have accompanied the emergence and increasing professionalization of planning in the nineteenth and twentieth centuries influence the shape of planning assemblages. They include assumptions of a possible or idealized congruence between architectural and built form and the social order; attempted mediation between public and private interests and powers; efforts to improve forms of spatial control and regulation, with all their intended and unintended consequences; and finally, a rationalization and comprehensive integration of different elements of state provision to ensure the welfare of the greatest number. Importantly, state planning has also included the comprehensive regional economic development plans that contributed to the kinds of classical development failures and colonization attempts so widely recorded by Scott and others in the case of state-level development (see Brox 1966; cf. Ferguson 1990; Mosse 2005; Scott 1998).

Modern planning has thus become a primary mechanism for the colonizing tendencies of the contemporary state – chiefly, but not exclusively, the tendency to colonize internally. The public good is invoked as a key alibi of contemporary democratic government (particularly in welfare states) and also accounts for its colonizing effects, as democratic states try to govern more people and, increasingly, more things. Planning, in this sense, mobilizes a range of techniques, models and discourses, and contributes to the making and unmaking of shifting subjectivities of planners, citizens and other actors involved in the process. Our list of the underlying concerns equipping modern planning with its particular logic is not exhaustive; neither are all these elements always present, or present to the same degree, in any given planning project. More often than not, these underlying aims and assumptions have remained an unrealized ideal, a promise that is never fully met. This inherent contradiction between aimed-for and actually achieved forms and outcomes – what might be called planning as coordinated potential failure – is precisely what many of the contributions to this volume aim to show.

The Promise as Action

As noted earlier, planning is a key material practice through which we attempt to project ourselves into the future. Arguably, Foucauldian analyses have alerted us to the spatial formations involved in modern planning as well as the subtle operations through which the state acts, and is encountered and imagined on an everyday level. Using these insights as a springboard for our own analysis, we wish to bring out the important temporal aspects of such processes, including the desires and deferrals as well as the dreams and dilemmas that constitute actual practices of planning. The temporalities of planning have received only limited attention to date. We suggest that emphasizing the temporal and imaginative aspects of planning allows us to see it as a kind of compact between now and the future, a promise that may be more or less convincing to the subjects of planning, and more or less actualized. In doing so, we take our cue from philosophical investigations of performative linguistics to ask what a promise *does* and, in a similar way, ask what plans do as they make promises about the future.[3]

Linguistic philosophy has approached the promise as a particular kind of utterance, oral or written, with peculiar effects (Atiyah 1981; Austin 1962; Searle 1969). Promises are not merely statements. They do more than describe by expressing intention. Promising is a performance; it has effects and brings about an obligation on the part of the promisor. For example, when council planners (the promisors) present their visions for a material improvement of the built environment to a public of residents and citizens (the promisees), they create a strong expectation that this promise will be fulfilled. The plan becomes a kind of performative utterance that Austin (1962) characterizes as a total speech act: an utterance that is tied to both context and action and cannot be understood without an appreciation of the sociological conditions under which it occurs. From this perspective, the promise of planning is thus much more than 'just' speech: it produces a set of relations that should endure through time between promisor, promisee, and the thing or action promised.

Anthropological analyses of 'the magical power of words' in ritual performances similarly show that the context of speech is all-important (Tambiah 1985; Turner 1974); merely saying, 'I promise' is not sufficient to create a convincing effect. The performative effect of the promise (and of the plan) is achieved not by the utterance alone, but through its association with appropriate procedures, objects and circumstances under which the promise is invoked; certain feelings and intentions that are produced in the promisor; and the promisor's subsequent behavior in accordance with the promise. If these conditions remain unfulfilled, the utterance has not so much failed as misfired, or the process has been abused. Austin thus suggests that promissory utterances cannot be false. Rather, they can be unhappy – they can become 'infelicities' where a procedure is erroneous or mis-invoked. Promises are infelicitous when given in inappropriate circumstances, such as where the giver does not have the authority to make the offer, or where a procedure is not valid or does not extend to the particular case. Promises may be given using the wrong procedures, or may be offered without the action following. The complexity of planning promises, often involving a number of different institutional actors with different aims and agendas, offers much opportunity for such infelicity. A different kind of problem or infelicity emerges where the sincerity of the promisor is in doubt. Does the promisor intend to fulfil the promise? Is the promise made in what we might call 'good faith'? Or, as Searle (1969) asks, has the promisor been placed under an obligation to the promisee to do something that he or she would not have done anyway in the normal course of events? Only outside the ordinary scheme of events does the promisor have to make an effort to fulfil the promise, which then becomes a meaningful contract.

There are, however, some significant limitations to this philosophical rendering of the promise for an anthropology of planning (see also Born 2007). First, the philosophical accounts do not consider the important alternative dimensions of the promise, such as those made for rhetorical purposes, or for parody or other stage effects. Second, and more important for our purposes, philosophers have not explicitly considered the situation where promisor and/or promisee are corporations of sorts, rather than particular persons.[4] Third, there recurs in planning a kind of infelicity that is rarely theorized and that philosophers would find hard to trace, which stems from the obduracy of procedures, tools, and the very materiality of that which is to be reformed and transformed; it may positively refuse to be reshaped by the plan (Hommels 2005). In the following section, we will elaborate these points in order to translate the philosophy to the kind of promise that plans seem to hold out.

Planning as a Promise

As the ethnographies in this volume show, the promise entailed by planning can take varying degrees of institutionalization and concreteness. Planning can be a 'mere' expectation, an instruction, a policy, a project, an exercise of democracy, a blueprint, a law. It may not be a vow, but it always includes some element of moral obligation that ties the present to the future, and occasionally the past too. Questions of politics and power are critical to comprehending the precise ways in which the plan constitutes a promise. Before elaborating some important additional dimensions of the planning promise, we want briefly to note its historical specificity (as opposed to its abstract value as a philosophical or linguistic concept). The emergence of planning as a professional and state pursuit, sketched out earlier, took shape in a particularly turbulent period of conceptual realignment in the nineteenth century, a period that saw the adoption of managerial techniques such as the forecasting of trends by statistical means (see Hacking 1990). Barbara Adam (2005) suggests that new scientific prediction techniques accompanied a sense that the future had become an empty space amenable to being shaped by rational plans and blueprints.

This realignment is understood as part of the transition to modernity. This transition is often thought to be located in the emergence of specific institutions, such as the democratic nation state or liberal market economies, but such institutions did not appear consistently in different countries. As Wittrock (2000) argues, modernity's arrival may be better pinpointed, on the one hand, in the practices that marked the transformation into extensive capitalism, and on the other in a series of important conceptual changes constituted in the emergence of a type of promissory notes. The promissory notes that, according to Wittrock, heralded modernity 'point to desiderata that can be formulated about a range of achievements that may be reached by the members of a given community' (2000: 37). These were not vague desires, but explicit states of affairs implied by deeply held values, and they were expected to be met. They lent themselves as common reference points in public debate and as the basis for changing subjectivities, affiliations and institutional forms, founded on 'radically new presuppositions about human agency, historical consciousness, and the role of reason in forging new societal institutions' (Wittrock 2000: 39). This process also included a reformulation of the relationship between society, civil society and the body politic and new forms of enquiry into the constitution of society. Key categories formulated at the time to conceptualize society are among those we still use today, including the 'economic-rationalistic', assuming society to be a compositional collective; the 'statistical-inductive', where society is a systemic aggregate; the 'structural-constraining' and its corresponding image of society as organic totality; and finally the 'linguistic-interpretative', positing society as an emergent totality (Wittrock 2000: 45). These categories also set the parameters for the practices and techniques of increasingly professional planners and their concerns, and indeed for the promise of planning today.

It would not be stretching Wittrock's argument too far to suggest that plans constitute one such promissory document of the public domain. In this form they played a role in the regulation of the contradictions of capitalist development, the conceptual rearrangements of the nineteenth-century world and the formulation of 'the social' as a profoundly problematic realm (see also Rose 1999). Planning is a process that is documented in variously elaborated notes and pamphlets (e.g., Planning Guidance Notes, Forward Plans, Supplementary Planning Guidance). And as promissory notes, plans can be understood as meeting the broader demands of the promise as outlined in the philosophy discussed above: plans require a social context in which they can be produced, but they also require institutional structures under which they can be contested or enforced, and these reformulate the relationship between society, the body politic and what has been called civil society.

In this context, we suggest that the promise of planning may better be conceived as a performance involving actors who are more readily understood as corporate bodies rather than individuals. Robertson (2006a, 2006b) has pointed out that the corporation is the central principle on which both governments and commercial enterprises are constructed – the transcendent, metaphorized body that has been the making of modernity. By definition, a corporation is authorized by law to act as one individual, separate from the actions of its members. Corporations, institutions, administrative bodies and similar collectives need continually to convince us that they are effective, that they have some control over their and our collective futures, and that they exist in fact as well as in the eyes of the law. Plans are published, for example as the product of the council-as-corporation, and municipalities spend increasing amounts of time and energy promoting their ostensible individuality, both as distinct from other municipalities and as corporate entities. Faced with sustained attacks on their autonomy as a result of proliferating neo-liberal politics – an issue to which we return below – it has become increasingly imperative for municipalities to present themselves as though they were effective actors despite the threats to their autonomy and accountability. Such self-representation, therefore, may soon be the only means left of producing legitimacy in the eyes of both actual individual citizens and other corporate entities such as third-sector organizations, external businesses or contractors, as well as in relation to central government.

Ways of talking and practices of self-representation by both participants and their observers in the planning process may help this process, which is always shaped somehow by specific legal and political frameworks. By proposing a plan, and thus offering a kind of promise, the producers of the plan are constituting themselves through indexical self-reference: a performative act presumes performers, and by performing the act of 'I promise', they index themselves as that performative person (Benveniste 1966, cited in Lee 2001: 169). We are all familiar with the ways that various bodies, officers, politicians and advisors doing the planning are referred to as though they formed an undifferentiated entity ('the municipality', 'the state') with a personality of its own (Stapley 1996). The plan may be presented as a personalized product – such as in the Norwegian context, where documents produced by the administration are presented as the advice of the *Rådmann*, literally the council's advisor (who in the UK would be called a Chief Executive). Or the planner may lose their 'personality' altogether, as in the German 'construction plan' (*Bebauungsplan*) that, once approved by the relevant political agencies, becomes law 'persisting into eternity' (Weszkalnys 2010: 101). The process effectively elides the complex relations between planners, designers and different levels of local and state administration, public and private, that the construction plan involves.

The promisee of planning is often understood as the public or the citizenry – also rendered as a quasi-individual, resulting in processes of abstraction and reduction of varied populations that anthropologists and citizens themselves often find difficult to stomach (Abram 2011). In the context of democratic decision making and techno-scientific expertise, publics have an increasingly important legitimizing function (Nowotny, Scott and Gibbons 2001). The public is often treated as though it were an empirical entity with an a priori existence when it is better imagined as coming into being within the specific planning moment (cf. Gal and Woolard 2001; Warner 2003). Anthropological studies have shown that planning rarely takes account of actual people in their radical variety, and that detailed taxonomies of social groups are rarely used (see Abram 2002). When attempts are made to differentiate the public, they reveal how complex and unmanageable it really is. In this sense, planning schemes rarely provide an accurate description of current circumstances but rather adopt mechanisms to conjure worlds within their scope of action as promisor, using the conceptual body of the public as a promisee counterpart to its plans.

In other cases, the plan has been turned into a total linguistic act by drawing participants – potential consultees and advisors, municipal officials and elected representatives – into relations that are both social and material. These include, yet go beyond, the original promise; they have histories and constitute transactions with future implications in their own right. Indeed, they may exhibit 'hypercomplexity', as Boholm (this volume) outlines in the development of railway planning in Sweden. This scale of planning involves a high degree of 'inter-organizational communication, co-operation and co-ordination' between a multitude of public and private actors, decision makers, stakeholders, and members of the public, all bringing their own perspectives, values, beliefs and diverging interpretations to the negotiations, and each trying to second-guess the actions of the others. Importantly, in such hypercomplex processes, plans can also be an extraordinarily effective way of coordinating action, of achieving outcomes and of concretizing our imaginative fictions about the future.

The plan can thus be understood to take the place of the performative utterance of the promise with important material implications. This promise must be performed according to the correct procedures, produced at the right time, approved by the appropriate committees, announced according to adequate mechanisms and available to the proper kind of scrutiny; it also should ideally produce concrete and measurable effects. If it does not observe such procedural niceties, it lays itself open to challenge. If its content is not adequate or its ambitions are weak – for example, if it only offers to do what would happen anyway – then it might be criticized as 'just talk' (see Vike, this volume). If the context in which a plan is issued is considered incorrect or infelicitous, the actions arising from a plan can be challenged, either through due process or on the ground. Finally, if the promises it contains are not fulfilled, it might be considered invalid, adapted in retrospect to reflect the changing circumstances, or deemed altogether illegitimate (but when do we ever formally evaluate a forward plan made twenty years ago?).

Like the promise, a plan is thus much more than simply true or false, a success or a failure, and the temporality of the plan is not necessarily a straightforward move from present to future (Weszkalnys 2010). Vike (this volume) observes two distinct kinds of future time in the context of planning. The future of contemporary time is immediate and promises real solutions to problems now. Utopian time, by contrast, sees problems resolved in a future postponed, always out of reach. The temporality invoked by planning may thus be inherently irregular, and its outcomes continually deferred and materialized only in unfinished constructions (cf. Ssorin-Chaikov 2003). The promise conjures relations of obligation, which are themselves elements of more long-standing relationships that the promise may help maintain. However, for a plan to become a promise with an obligation on the part of the promisor, it needs sincerity. Baxstrom's study of Kuala Lumpur (this volume) is just one example where this sincerity seems to be missing: plans for urban restructuring appear to legitimize action in the present rather than to make a promise about the future, and their legitimacy is brought into question. Baxstrom goes so far as to suggest that in contemporary Kuala Lumpur, the plan functions as an 'instrument of momentary action' that, in effect, evacuates the future. This has a profoundly paradoxical effect on people's experience of time: in this city that is in constant flow, people's expectations are continually overturned while they try and keep up with the fast pace of change.

In sum, the contemporary promise of planning is a historically constituted compact, where promisor and promisee are largely configured in corporate form, be that the state and citizenry, or the council and the public. The conditions permitting such a compact include the emergence of new types of knowledge alongside a far-reaching reformulation of the relationship between society and the body politic in the nineteenth century, expressed in the peculiar artefact of the promissory note. The corporate promise of planning has, if anything, acquired more importance due to the persistent need for state bodies acting in corporate form to assert their agency, specifically in a context where their autonomy to plan seems increasingly encroached upon by private actors. The promise of planning thus produces a specific type of sociality, involving state and non-state actors, experts and lay people, planners, citizens, and private investors, as well as people who are and who are not party to the decisions and projects involved. It is not uttered in a vacuum; its exact shape in any specific locale is contingent upon a range of political, legislative and material factors. But while participants may insist that the concern to improve the human condition (which we discussed earlier) continues to lie at the heart of contemporary planning efforts, there remains considerable scope for unintended consequences, incompletion and breakdown, and for the ruses of power to play out.

Planning in a Neo-liberal World?

Present-day political transformations and changes to the model of the state – often gathered under the umbrella of the 'neo-liberal' – both accentuate and subdue, in occasionally paradoxical ways, the contrasting dimensions of the promise of planning we have outlined. Neoliberalism, as Ferguson (2009) notes, is a term used in ways that are both vague and demonizing. The Reagan and Thatcher governments' battle cries to unleash capital from the reign of 'red tape' have also reverberated in planning arguments for nearly half a century, as democratic states swing between favouring citizens and encouraging businesses. According to the free-market economists and politicians who have promoted the neo-liberal doctrine, the rise of planning regimes tied to welfare states in the post-war period led, by the 1970s, to citizen dependency and the inhibition of entrepreneurialism. The response has been an attempt to turn the tide against welfare, and planning regimes became a target of their fetishization of entrepreneurs and consumer capitalism. However, this increasingly dominant story overlooks the fact that there has rarely existed the kind of 'unfettered' free market that was then claimed to have been unduly restricted (Wittrock 2000: 34). Rather, state intervention has always been accepted, and it continues to be felt and cause considerable ambivalence in present planning regimes (Strom 2001: 6).

Beyond the general notion of the forms and effects of 'neo-liberalism', anthropologists and critical social theorists have offered a more differentiated picture of the current force of neo-liberal projects sweeping across the globe, presaged by Ferguson's (1990) critique of the disappearance of politics under managerialism (see also Mouffe 2000 for a theoretical critique). First, anthropologists have for some time called attention to how the practices gathered under the umbrella of neo-liberalism are made sense of locally, for instance, through narratives of illicit wealth and occult practices (West and Sanders 2003). They have also attended to the diverse strategies and effects through which neo-liberal formations take shape in different cultural and national contexts (Ong 2005; Zaloom 2009), thus adding a rich layer to analyses of the effects of neo-liberal tendencies across the globe. Similarly, critical theory has put forward a number of ways to move beyond a monolithic understanding of neo-liberalism. While Peck and Tickell (2002) suggest focusing on neo-liberal*ization* as a process rather than as a theoretical model or state of being, Brenner and Theodore (2002) argue that we should study 'actually existing neoliberalism'. Such critical accounts allow us to grasp what is happening on the ground rather than over-concretizing ideas of neo-liberalism, states and markets. Indeed, the kind of radical empiricism (Spencer 1997) that anthropologists have successfully applied to a number of our most taken-for-granted concepts has also been useful in unpacking neo-liberalism's supposedly unified and universal logic. They reveal differently enacted neo-liberal projects to be always shaped by the historical and cultural circumstances of their implementation (Abram 2007; Holston and Caldeira 2005; Latham 2006; Weszkalnys 2010). In this volume, James demonstrates how the neo-liberal repertoire of government may be less monolithic than has been assumed, especially in a transitional society such as South Africa, where it coexists, if uneasily, with contradictory expectations and forms of state and planning, as well as with non-governmental organizations. Indeed, as James points out, the same administrative staff move between state and non-state organizations, creating a range of continuities and discontinuities, tangled relations and paradoxical positions.

Nonetheless, we cannot but notice a set of political and economic modalities that seem to be gathering force across a range of sites whose boundaries are being renegotiated in the process. These modalities include, among others, significant shifts in the global distribution of capital, the increasing presence of non-state organizations in a profoundly reorganized public sector, the seemingly diminished role of state actors vis-à-vis private investors and developers, and the redrawing of lines of accountability. These shifts have palpable implications for planning, of which we would like to mention just four. First, at least since the 1980s, increasing amounts of capital have moved into global corporations beyond the reach of states. As global corporations have become increasingly willing to move their activities offshore, states have competed to attract investment. Within the European Union, the invention of new regional planning regimes has incorporated agencies dealing directly with supranational organizations, such as the regional governments applying for EU funding or the UK regional development agencies that compete to attract footloose capital, often to collapse once government incentives dry up. In their wake, citizens are often left with the detritus of industrial development, depleted resources, unemployment, monopolistic economies and welfare crises. In fact, the very conditions that provoked the invention of urban improvement in the nineteenth century seem to have returned in a moderately different order.

Second, one of the largest economic growth sectors has been in services and, in particular, in management consultancy. Once listed on the stock markets, some consultancy firms in need of new areas of expansion realized by the 1980s that the public sector promised just that potential. A massive expansion into the public sector materialized in the introduction of constant reorganization as a feature of public-sector management, under the banner of the introduction of privatization and outsourcing, and pursuit of the grail of marketization, in what came to be known as the new public management (see Ferlie 1996). Recent changes have demonstrated how far the bureaucratic procedures of planning can be removed to third parties, as state planning at different levels is increasingly contracted out to private agencies. In the 1990s, local authorities in the UK began to outsource their own local planning activities. More accurately, they outsourced the administrative activities that support the political choices made through planning. Paradoxically, as a result, a widely declared 'hollowing out' of the state has been paralleled by an increase in global bureaucratic apparatus.

Third, like many local government functions, planners face the task of regulating developments desired by large international corporations that, especially in the context of British Common Law, have the capacity to overpower small, relatively powerless and impoverished local government institutions.[5] Their methods in the UK have included threatening to launch expensive legal appeals of rejected planning applications that local authorities cannot afford to defend, and 'land banking' – acquiring ownership or options on large swathes of land for potential development. Even in national contexts where the state has remained in a comparatively more powerful position, such as Germany, there is a sense that it is increasingly not only government that is governing, and that governments are drawing back into weak regulatory modes while corporations pursue their own interests. Planners are still struggling to devise a response to these changing conditions for local planning, and to align their own and 'public' interests with those of developers. In this clash of two temporal trajectories, the modernist seeks ideal conditions and the capitalist seeks complete exploitation of the markets.

Fourth, while neo-liberal rhetoric might seem to make a focus on the state less relevant, neo-liberal discourses of minimal state, privatization, citizen-power, choice or participative government are themselves contradictory. Even highly 'shrunk' states where public services have been largely outsourced must govern these services, and the practices of audit may create a bureaucracy larger than that of a nationalized welfare state (Miller 2005; Strathern 2000). Several of the chapters in this book show how neo-liberal forms of governance tend to extend the reach of the state while simultaneously disengaging it from previous relations and ethics of accountability. They also show how the kind of democratically oriented, inclusive planning processes paradoxically endorsed by neo-liberal public management often fail to halt established competition over land, as Gledhill indicates for Brazil (this volume). Despite the promise of participative planning, it is still the poor who are displaced from the most valuable land.

Such changes prompt us to ask what exactly the roles of the state and of state-led planning are becoming. What effects do they have on the subjectivities of the actors involved? If a private commercial organization can be contracted to behave in a non-partisan way and produce the material documents that a permanently employed public service does (at least hypothetically), in what sense do the two forms differ? Bear (this volume) shows how, in fact, the role of public servants is radically transformed when they are no longer simply expected to carry out the regulations authored by state actors, but are obliged to adopt a transactionary role themselves. While we know that low-level bureaucrats have always had to embroider together the conflicting demands of organizational loyalty and personal ethics (see Lipsky 1980), in the new regime that Bear describes, they are free to redefine themselves as public entrepreneurs. Such changes affect not only the life of the public servant but the shape of the city too. Similarly, other studies of multinational organizations (Müller 2008), global networks (Riles 2000), consultancies and financial agents (Barry 2001) remind us that what we quaintly refer to as 'local' government is not locally bounded. This brings us considerably closer to understanding how planning practices and ideologies become global ideoscapes (Appadurai 1990) and how they participate in the arrangement and rearrangement of technological zones (Barry 2006). They move us from the old security of plans as the predictable and stable world of the state's regulatory framework to the new world of intergovernmentality, global flows and shifting relations between multinational organizations (public and private) and national and local states.

These changes raise difficult questions for the future of planning.[6] Where free trade includes the free movement of labour, how can housing be planned to account for unpredictable levels of demand? How far should plans be made to accommodate population change, or should the limited supply of buildings and services be used to regulate the flow of people? What kind of buildings should be produced to account for people's changing needs, including over the course of life (see Robertson 1991)? And how far should responses to such changes be planned at all? Such are the questions that trouble planners at different levels of the state when internationalism begins to undermine the apparent stability of national planning. Such questions further problematize what kind of promise planning is offering. From this perspective, the reach of neo-liberal ideology and global capital can easily appear infinite and very present, and planning a universal category. Yet in many cases this reach is limited: in territories that are not governed either by democratic rule or by states at all; or in movements that resist the message of good governance, transparency and democracy with counter pressures, conflicting views, and equally persuasive narratives. While the neo-liberalization of global institutions is often presented as a de facto description, ethnographic findings suggest that its manifold manifestations 'on the ground' are less clear-cut.

The Work of Planning

To comprehend the complex force field surrounding, and impinging on, the contemporary planning assemblage, we wish to unite disparate strands of anthropological research on the contemporary state, politics and development – that is, arenas in which planning has been visible but seldom explicitly theorized. By putting planning in the foreground, we also redirect the focus onto widely shared (if differently articulated) material practices, rather than on supposedly autonomous institutions or distinctive bodies of knowledge. Instead of posing abstract questions about the state, time and locality, the distinctly ethnographic approach taken in this volume turns to the actual work carried out by planners, citizens, experts, beneficiaries and victims of planning, and to the work carried out by plans themselves. Between them, the chapters highlight the temporally and materially constituted processes – drawing in a range of objects, technologies, discourses, expertise and forms of democratic participation – through which planning happens.

Such an approach expands on recent anthropological work that has explored the quotidian practices, rituals and discourses that together make up politics, policy, democracy and the changing forms of local government found in (multi)national states (Boholm 1996; Gupta 1995; Hansen and Stepputat 2005; Navaro-Yashin 2002; Shore and Wright 1997; for an earlier example see Richards and Kuper 1971). Anthropologists have not shied away from theorizing the state itself as a central organizing authority (Corbridge et al. 2005; Sharma and Gupta 2006), as well as political parties (Salih 2003; Shore 1990), central states or superstates (Abélès 1990; Bellier and Wilson 2000; Shore 2001) and state peripheries (Das and Poole 2004). But in doing so, they have demonstrated the interplay of everyday systems of power and resistance in which people find themselves implicated (cf. Abu-Lughod 1990). Such studies include the examination of the practices of citizenship (Neveu 2003), new participative practices in democratic states (Appadurai 2002; Holston 2008; Neveu 2007; Paley 2001), the design and management of spaces, public and private (Holston and Appadurai 1999; Rutheiser 1996), and environmental activism (Berglund 1998) and anticapitalist resistance (Williams 2008). From this work has emerged a focus on contemporary state planning that is only now being consolidated, in part through this volume itself.

In drawing on this literature, we have two further goals. First, we wish to blur the persistent boundary between, on the one hand, the planning and development that supposedly happens primarily in western states, and on the other hand, in what is generally glossed as Third World (or 'southern') development, or Development with a capital *D*. The rise of development studies from the 1960s onwards has partly led to a definition of Development as socio-economic development and as the transition to capitalist modernity (Robertson 1984: 43), and thus as distinct. Anthropological studies have forcefully argued against using 'the West' as a norm to which others should aspire (notably Escobar 1995), and scholars have turned their gaze towards the multifarious development processes happening in western countries day by day (e.g., Abram and Waldren 1998) and highlighted the important links, overlaps and imitations occurring between colonial, postcolonial and 'western' development as well as governmental and extra-governmental practices (Blundo and Le Meur 2009; Peattie 1987; Rabinow 1989; Robertson 1984). The approach taken here proceeds in that spirit, highlighting the commonalities as much as the differences between forms of planning in contrasting parts of the world.

Our second goal is to speak directly to current approaches outlined within planning theory itself, which tends to be most interested in the perspective of planning practitioners in either the private or public sector. We contend that despite an increasing number of studies offering nuanced insight into the world of planning professionals based on extensive participant observation (e.g., Flyvbjerg 1998; Forester 1989, 1999; Healey 1997), planning research remains largely wedded to normative concerns and frameworks (Alfasi 2003; Reade 1987; but see Bacqué, Rey and Sintomer 2005; Carrel et al. 2009; Rui 2004 for a contrasting account of French participatory democracy). As we hope to have made clear throughout this introduction, an anthropological examination of planning in the contemporary world cannot be reduced to the useful deployment of ethnographic tools, for example, to achieve the ends of participatory planning;[7] rather, it seeks to shed the same critical light by which anthropologists have illuminated other aspects of human life, to give insight into the conditions that make such forms of planning possible (or impossible) in the first place.

In this view, the ethnography of planning includes questions about inscription and reification, about authorship, authority and associated responsibility, and finally about the creativity and agency of the plan itself: how it compels other kinds of actions. Plans embody a promise for material and temporal order. First, there is the materiality of the space to be ordered, and the effects on the things and bodies of those for which order is attempted. But, as some of the essays in this volume show, the idealized orders that plans imagine are regularly disrupted through the interventions of people, through the obstinacies of landscapes and built forms, and through the obduracy of the written word, the calculation and the drawn line (see also Abram 2006; Hommels 2005). Second, all plans embody different temporalities of past, present and future. We are familiar with notions of progress and betterment embedded in the plan, and the parallel construal of the existing as 'outdated' and in need of overhaul. Importantly, instead of regurgitating this story of teleological progress and achievement that planning tells about itself, the chapters in this book point beyond the simple discrepancies between plan and action to the multiple temporalities at play, including the 'negative' temporalities of delay and failure (Weszkalnys 2010) and post hoc rationalization (see Flyvbjerg 1998).

This prompts us to ask what kind of work we can see the plan perform when it is clear that it is not a blueprint for the future. If, as Riles notes, 'documents are the paradigmatic artefacts of modern knowledge practices' (2006: 2), central to the production of knowledge about ourselves, then a plan may be considered a kind of document that both acts on that knowledge and, importantly, seeks to predict what will be knowledge in the future. As documents, plans may be seen to perform a particular kind of work, which frequently seems to be less about a specific content than the kind of conceptual orders that they lay out. The plan is perhaps the most explicitly future-directed and agentive document of all. Yet as the essays here show, the relationship between the spatio-temporal orders laid out by the plan and the actualities they engender is always fragile and multivalent; plans both encapsulate and exclude worlds of imagination and practice. One of the key factors responsible for the perceived discrepancies between plan and action may be the clash of technocratic and lived time performed in so many planning encounters. While modernist planning was characterized by a conception of social life as a generic and readily transposable totality, the chapters in this book note the ways in which planned development is more unstable, haphazard and fragile than often assumed. It is also more capable of accommodating existing and enduring forms and functions, including urban design, land use patterns or welfare institutions. What we see here are performances of time in the institutional, technological and social relations entailed in planning; and we ask how people do and experience these performances in political processes that take a long time themselves as well as conjuring a vision of time, with continuities and discontinuities, opening up the present moment into the future (cf. Wallman 1992).

Finally, rather than being incidental or exceptional, failures, mismatches, discrepancies and gaps appear to us a pervasive modality of planning. At all levels of state and local planning, gaps between what is designed and what is built, theory and practice, or what is said and what is done have tended to constitute a major object of concern for local actors and ethnographers alike. The ubiquity of certain practices, such as popular participation, audit and reporting, attests to this: they are practices intended to make these gaps visible. The elusiveness of the promise of planning seems to lie in these gaps, and nowhere is this more evident than in the new South Africa, where according to James (this volume), the utopian promise of land reform has floundered on the bureaucratic work of instituting land reform, and on the political confrontation with the conditions of foreign debt. The ambiguities of political change become visible as key people shift from role to role between state and non-state organizations, and as models of distributive and neoliberal politics rub along together. The 'gaps' between ideal, ideology and practice fill themselves with things unplanned, unexpected and inexplicable, and with things that get overlooked and forgotten. Instead of lamenting or simply noting them, the ethnographer's task is to chart how people deal with these gaps and mismatches, and to understand how they are significant to, and are occasionally elided by, the work of planning.

The Chapters

Halvard Vike's chapter addresses temporality in planning head-on, with a consideration of the changing temporal schemes of Norwegian welfare planning. Norwegian state planning is comprehensive, and land-use questions fall within a broader practice of short-, medium- and long-term planning at the local, regional and state levels. The context is that of one of the most robust welfare states of all democratic countries, representing something of a test case for political and social theories.

In analysing planning practices and reflecting on the development of the welfare state through the twentieth century, Vike observes that politics has come to revolve around the effective delivery of services. Service delivery, as it has come to be known, is now the medium of the contract between state and citizen. In this process, the temporal horizon of political legitimacy has shifted from a utopian future time, where comprehensive services were a goal one strived towards, to contemporary time, in which delivery is impatiently expected now. The kind of future welfare planning offers is thus altered, and Vike outlines how long-established patterns of participatory planning began to falter in the 1990s, leading to a changed public perception of plans as 'just words'. In the process, the ideal of planning appears to have been superseded by what Sørhaug refers to as the 'reforming organization', and Vike's core concern has been for the gender and class effects of this shift on the lowest-paid workers.

If the reforming organization arises out of a shift from clear distinctions between public and private sector to a world in which the public spirit that defines civil service is diverted into a range of agencies and companies, then this new framework can be captured by what Boholm calls hypercomplexity. Building on Luhmann's work on system planning and double contingency, she notes that planning includes the observation and anticipation of planning by others. In her chapter, Boholm notes that the multitude of potential consequences of policy decisions fuels heated local (and national) debates, in which conflicting interests and values are voiced. Complexity arises not only from this multitude of voices, but from the diversity of standpoints from which they are articulated, a diversity to which planners constantly struggle to adapt.

Major infrastructures, such as the railways that emerged in the nineteenth century, were built within a particular constellation of business and government that has radically altered since then. Railways are currently undergoing a moment of upheaval across Europe, with many countries experiencing both high-tech and high-speed expansion while much of the network moulders and old infrastructure gradually breaks down. Encouraged by a clear EU policy on rail network connectivity, the Swedish response has been a massive investment in new infrastructure and technology. By studying this at close quarters over a long period, Boholm reveals how the day-to-day working practices of different practitioners are mediated through 'meetings' in which temporal questions can pose intractable dilemmas, since planning for one future or another can have major effects on local conditions. Leaving options open, such as whether or not to build additional stations, might seem like an attempt not to foreclose on future possibilities, but it causes severe difficulties in the planning process itself. In other words, postponing proves to be deeply problematic for the present, while deciding future options now is likely to be problematic in the future. Thus the temporality of planning also becomes hypercomplex, as does the organization of planning in the present. Boholm demonstrates how collection action such as planning relies on layered reflexive communications, which can be observed through the 'flow' of social interactions.

Sarah Lund, on the other hand, looks at a kind of reverse temporality of planning. The promise of official planning approval for new settlements is still seen as desirable in Cuzco, Peru, but it grows out of a quite different constellation of powers, and a very different history of development. Lund argues that the state project's spatial vision of laying claim to territory becomes particularly apparent in the places marginal to the state. The peasant invasions of 'abandoned' lands in the 1970s posed, and continue to pose, significant challenges to bureaucratic practice as well as to the established imagery of a land divided between peasant mountains and civilized cities. While the Two Republic system of separate indigenous rule was abolished after independence in 1825, elements such as indigenous tribute reappeared in various guises into the twentieth century, highlighting the persistence of the idea of a dual state, of people with different status. Gradually, peasants and indigenous people gained access to citizenship – tied still to ownership of land in the countryside, and later transferred from collective to individual forms of citizenship, forms that persist in what Lund describes as the shared historical experience of people being both corporate and private persons.

Whereas planning histories emphasize the creation of new towns, conceived and then materialized according to planned policies, Lund describes urbanization in Peru as generated by land invasion. First, someone occupies a plot as part of a group, houses are built and, perhaps many years later, an individual might gain title to the property. Government planners and settlers must negotiate the status of ownership in a complex dance around illegalities, informalities and irregularities. Migration arising not only from rural poverty but also from political violence only enhanced the pressure on urban areas to house migrants, and little state activity prepared for these influxes. On the contrary, the process was driven by action, where necessity broke into settled zones in and around the city. Lund's chapter gives a nuanced account of the process of regularization and the gaining of title, while revealing the contested concept of the urban in Peru. Showing us different sides of the story of land invasion, and the different spatial sensibilities evident across the city, Lund argues for recognition of the deeply politicized nature of planning and the patchwork nature of state intervention, by showing us the role that planning has in the transformation of public lands into private property.

Deborah James considers a different form of the shift between public and private property. Her chapter explores the contradictory and contested but closely interlocking efforts of NGOs and the state in planning for land reform in South Africa. There, planning was a key tool for apartheid policy, with zoning, segregated development, and housing policy serving separation policies. In the post-apartheid era, claims that the poorest should have land are generally accepted, but defining who is among the poorest and who is deserving of land has been technically complex and politically tricky. As government policy has increasingly favoured people with the resources to become commercial farmers, the fate of the poor and dispossessed has become the remit of non-governmental organizations (NGOs). In this context, the question of how to deal with the labourers on white farms who would be rendered homeless if the farms were disbanded poses a real problem for policymakers. Should land reform be about tenure reform, and how can this be understood?

As James points out, NGOs have become involved in planning interventions not by replacing the state but by interacting with it. While it has been claimed that South Africa's new leaders embraced neo-liberal economics rather enthusiastically, James outlines the conditions for South African economic plans, and the changing relations between the state, market actors and NGOs. Recalling how the state poached staff from NGOs , she shows how many of these staff later resigned after disputes and confrontations. The turnover of staff has blurred the boundaries between the organizations, so that simplistic analyses of 'neo-liberal governmentality' are not adequate to understand the complexities of the relationship between NGOs and the state. Under apartheid, dialogue between African communities and white English-speaking middle-class activists resulted in hybrid models of ownership that filtered African ideas about landholding through European debates that contest private with public ownership. In the new state, territory and government had to be unified where before they had been in opposition, and this tension lies at the heart of land-planning difficulties in subsequent years. Whether land reform would lead to redistributed territorial rights, or to privatization of land and subsequent loss of rights has been tussled over, exposing divisive ideological justifications of positions held by the various NGOs. James, like Gledhill in the following chapter, weaves the political history into the lives of actors in the land reform process to show the complexity of state planning in practice, the temporal strands that policy makers and activists strive to unite, and the hopes and fears that heat the debates over what might, to the uninitiated, appear to be banal details of policy formation. A 'may' or a 'shall' in policy documents can have far-reaching and determinative effects.

Echoing James's call not to treat neo-liberal governmentality as unitary, in the next chapter Gledhill offers a detailed account of the forms of neo-liberalization being played out in Salvador, Bahia, Brazil, and asks whether they exacerbate class difference in urban development. Put quite starkly, he can be understood as asking what hope there is for the poor in participatory planning policy, in the face of increasingly securitized private developments built for developers, big businesses and those citizens with consumer power. Commentators are increasingly arguing that positive-sounding programmes of 'urban regeneration' that seek to improve urban conditions actually result in a retaking of the city for the middle classes. Gledhill points to cultural initiatives to raise self-esteem and foster 'black role models' that frame normative standards of desirable patterns of family life, for example, while property regimes condemn the working poor to the margins of urban land allocations. Yet Gledhill tells a revealing story of the reappropriation of planning processes by the very people who are the objects of governmentality, through a detailed historiographical account of the politics of land invasion and regularization. The struggle over the reappropriation of invaded land by private interests played out through the politics of the NGO world, direct action and youth mobilization, and was tied throughout the process to the politics of race. The process gave rise to new forms of grassroots organization, pressured by institutional political powers but exhibiting unlikely alignments of interest and unexpected consequences.

Gledhill highlights many of the issues we have nodded to in this introduction, including the role of documents and graphic plans, the subjectification of populations through planning policies, and the elusive promise that grassroots action and state plans hold out for those who have hopes for the future. His account confirms Lund's claim about the politicization of planning, demonstrating how planning is intimately tied into much broader questions of government. The 'problem of the favelas' has dogged Brazilian politics for decades, outlived countless government and NGO initiatives, and earned along the way a lively political profile as the focus of campaigns for a more participative form of government. Claims that the poor have a right to the city – made famous in the oft-cited work of Lefebvre – were recognized at the beginning of the twenty-first century in legislation that Gledhill characterizes as being from the neo-liberal era, but his account provides a detailed mapping of actual neo-liberalization that shows the diversity within neo-liberal structures, indicating that neo-liberalization is also a struggle, not simply a global sweep of change. While powerful actors can use plans to serve particular interests, a planning system also opens such plans up to contest. Where these openings are inadequate, other forms of resistance emerge.

In a situation that could certainly be characterized as an extreme exemplar of the late capitalist era, Baxstrom also distinguishes between plans and planning in his claims that plans function as virtual objects in the present. Grand strategic plans such as the '1Malaysia' plan fall into a pattern of Malaysian plans that are strong on slogans yet vague on specific goals and rarely lead to anything like the future imagined in them. Baxstrom thus points to the very elusiveness of the promises made in plans. His chapter challenges the notion of a plan as a vision of the future and a blueprint for a programme of future action, arguing that plans for what is sometimes called urban regeneration in Kuala Lumpur function effectively as a vehicle for action in the present. While plans gesture to 'the future', he argues that they do not need 'a future' to function. A lack of specificity leads Malaysian grand plans to appear to disavow the near present, while legitimating a range of actions now. The result is a city that Baxstrom describes as always moving fast but never actually going anywhere. How, then, can the future be imagined or planned in what feels like an infinite present?

Baxstrom has elsewhere recounted the daily experience of residents in a district of Kuala Lumpur undergoing rapid and unpredictable transformations, showing how plans legitimize radical changes to the built environment that can abruptly change the fortunes of small business owners, for example (Baxstrom 2008). He notes that plans can be not only problematic for the people who experience their effects, but also difficult for professional practitioners to deal with. A lack of procedure associated with plans can leave planners in weak positions themselves. When plans are materialized as documents, they can also become available to people not associated with their creation – and hence plans start to live a life of their own.

The changing role of public servants in the administration of different kinds of objectives that plans epitomize is the subject of Laura Bear's chapter. One of the characteristics we associate with neo-liberal govern-mentality is the ambiguity of relations between centres of power and lo-calities. While the discourses emphasize 'localism', the structures of state power are often increasingly centralized through a mechanism that del-egates budgets without delegating powers to control them or decide on the conditions associated with them. Bear notes that this results in contest and opacity in dialogues between bureaucrats and citizens, whose ne-gotiations result in outcomes quite different from those promised in the texts of state plans. She argues that this leaves low-level bureaucrats in a particularly compromised position, straddling the boundaries between state, public and non-state, private action. Seeing state plans as attempts to bring about promised futures, she echoes Adam and Groves's observation (2007) that these futures are by no means assured, showing that futures are imagined and practised differently by various participants in planning processes. By moving planning beyond the state, Bear argues, the Indian government produces a new form of planning, based on decentralized improvisation and speculation through networks of association, that strik-ingly alters the demands made on local bureaucrats while offering them legitimation for entrepreneurial schemes.

Bear's chapter offers a detailed description of the 'shadow state' of in-formal and exploitative activity that is drawn into the plans and revenues of the official state through the changing activities of Calcutta Port Trust of-ficials on the Hooghly River. She argues that what is happening in Kolkata is not that hybrid forms of the state are emerging, but that the separation between formality and informality is upheld by liberalization bureaucrats in India in the constant movement of plans, state tokens, officials and rev-enues between these domains. They are, she suggests, expanding an 'in-ner darkness of exclusion from rights' within the state. Plans thus have another level of action in this system: they legitimize local actions in the present, as Baxstrom indicates, but are also based on the personal prom-ises of bureaucrats, underpinned by patronage, friendship and religious imagery. To understand plans and planning, Bear is arguing, we must see plans in their wider context and through an ethnographic lens. What else are plans doing, how else are they used, and what other activities do they enable, other than the specific developments of which they ostensibly speak? Her masterful account of the intricacies of port life through the daily life and philosophies of Mr Bose in the Boat Registration Office show us the 'dark side' of planning as well as its many faces, differently shaded in the contemporary context of government and extra-governmental ac-tion. In Bear's account, we see the speculative promises of a wide range of state agencies played for all their worth among entrepreneurs and infor-malized labour.

Notes

1. Readers may want to refer to general and national histories of planning, e.g. Friedmann (1987), Sandercock (1998), or Hall (2002).
2. In fact, one might say that land-use planning became defined by a preoccupation with the correct layout of facilities and lost the ambition to reorder society more justly. The UK planning system thus remains a weak regulatory system that swings between favouring the 'environment' and 'development' (Murdoch and Abram 2002).
3. We are grateful for guidance from Sandy Robertson in our elaboration of this section.
4. For the importance of considering corporations, especially in relation to corruption, see Robertson (2006a, 2006b, 2009).
5. There are important differences in this regard between different national legislative contexts. For example, in a situation of common law, such as in the UK, private developers and investors have considerably more legal scope to challenge and overrule the decisions of state bodies than in civil law countries, such as Germany or Portugal, where private developers do not (yet) possess the same kinds of power.
6. Strategies of 'non-planning' observable, for example, in southern African metropolises may also be seen in this light as a way of dealing with such unpredictability (cf. Kamete and Lindell 2010).
7. This is not to say that such work is not important. Questions of the governance of change in the fabric of urban environments have also been addressed in architecture (e.g., Blundell-Jones, Petrescu and Till 2005), but the focus has been predominantly on participative design, rather than on participative governance or citizen-governing per se, although new research based in architecture schools is moving in this direction and using ethnographic techniques to do so (Berry-Chikhaoui and Deboulet 2007; Deboulet 2004).

References

Abélès, M. 1990. *Anthropologie de l'état*. Paris: A. Colin.

Abram, S. 2002. 'Planning and Public-Making in Municipal Government', *Focaal* 40: 21–34.

———. 2006. 'Bricks Coming Out of the Ground: Deconstructing Norfolk Park', in S. Macdonald (ed.), *Materializing Sheffield: Place, Culture, Identity*. HRI online. http://www.hrion line.ac.uk/matshef/abram/MSabram.htm

———. 2007 'Loyalty and Politics: The discourses of liberalisation' in S. Ardener and F. Moore (eds) *Professional Identities: Policy and Practice in Business and Bureaucracy*. Oxford: Berghahn: 87–107.

———. 2011. *Culture and Planning*. Aldershot: Ashgate.

Abram, S. and R. Cowell. 2004. 'Learning Policy: The Contextual Curtain and Conceptual Barriers', *European Planning Studies* 12(2): 209–228.

Abram, S.A. and J. Waldren. 1998. *Anthropological Perspectives on Local Development: Knowledge and Sentiments in Conflict*. London: Routledge.

Abu-Lughod, J.L. 1975. 'The Legitimacy of Comparisons in Comparative Urban Studies: A Theoretical Position and an Application to North African Cities', *Urban Affairs Review* 11: 13–35.

Abu-Lughod, L. 1990. 'The Romance of Resistance: Tracing Transformations of Power through Bedouin Women', *American Ethnologist* 17(1): 41–55.

Adam, B. 2005. 'Futures Told, Tamed and Traded'. *ESRC Professorial Fellowship: Futures*. Retrieved 17 May 2010 from http://www.cf.ac.uk/socsi/futures/ESRC PF Futures TTT.pdf.

Adam B. and C. Groves. 2007. *Future Matters: Action, Knowledge, Ethics*. Leiden: Brill.

Alexander, C. 2007. 'Soviet and Post-Soviet planning in Almaty, Kazakhstan', *Critique of Anthropology* 27(2): 165–181.

Alfasi, N. 2003. 'Is Public Participation Making Urban Planning More Democratic? The Israeli Experience', *Planning Theory and Practice* 4: 185–204.

Ambrose, P. 1986. *Whatever Happened to Planning?* London and New York: Methuen.

Appadurai, A. 1990. 'Disjuncture and Difference in the Global Cultural Economy', *Theory, Culture & Society* 7(2): 295–310

———. 2002. 'Deep Democracy: Urban Governmentality and the Horizon of Politics', *Public Culture* 14(1): 21–47.

Atiyah, P.S. 1981. *Promises, Morals, and Law.* Oxford: Oxford University Press.

Austin, J.L. 1962. *How to Do Things with Words.* Oxford: Oxford University Press.

Bacqué, M.-H., H. Rey and Y. Sintomer. 2005. *Gestion de proximité et démocratie participative, une perspective comparative.* Paris: La Découverte.

Barry, A. 2001. *Political Machines: Governing a Technological Society.* London and New York: Athlone Press.

———. 2006. 'Technological Zones', *European Journal of Social Theory* 9(2): 239–253.

Barth, E., K.O. Moene and M. Wallerstein. 2003. *Likhet under press: utfordringer for den skandinaviske fordelingsmodellen.* Oslo: Gyldendal akademisk.

Baxstrom, R. 2008. *Houses in Motion: The Experience of Place and the Problem of Belief in Urban Malaysia.* Stanford, CA: Stanford University Press.

Bellier, I.N. and T.M. Wilson. (eds) 2000. *An anthropology of the European Union: building, imagining and experiencing the new Europe.* Oxford, Berg.

Benveniste, E. 1966. *Problems in General Linguistics.* Miami: University of Miami Press.

Berglund, E.K. 1998. *Knowing nature, knowing science : an ethnography of environmental activism.* Cambridge, White Horse Press.

Berry-Chikhaoui, I., A. Deboulet and L. Roulleau-Berger. (eds). 2007. *Ville internationales, entre tensions et réactions des habitants.* Paris: La Decouverte.

Blundell-Jones, P., D. Petrescu and J. Till. 2005. *Architecture and Participation.* London: Spon Press.

Blundo, G. and P.-Y. Le Meur. (eds) 2008. *The Governance of daily life in Africa : ethnographic explorations of public and collective services.* Leiden: Brill.

Boholm, Å. (ed.) 1996. *Political Ritual.* Gothenburg: Institute for Advanced Studies in Social Anthropology.

Born, G. 2007. 'Future-Making: Corporate Performativity and the Temporal Politics of Markets', in D. Held and H. Moore (eds), *Cultural Politics in a Global Age: Uncertainty, Solidarity and Innovation.* London: Oneworld: 288–296.

Boyer, M.C. 1983. *Dreaming the Rational City: The Myth of American City Planning.* Cambridge, MA: MIT Press.

Brenner, N. and N. Theodore. 2002. 'Cities and the Geographies of "Actually Existing Neoliberalism"', in N. Brenner and N. Theodore (eds), *Spaces of Neoliberalization: Urban Restructuring in North America and Western Europe.* Oxford: Blackwell, pp. 2–32.

Brox, O. 1966. *Hva Skjer i Nord-Norge? En studie i norsk utkantpolitikk.* Oslo: Pax Forlag.

Caldeira, T.P.R. 2000. *City of Walls: Crime, Segregation and Citizenship in Sao Paulo.* Berkeley: University of California Press.

Carrel, M., C. Neveu and J. Ion. (eds) 2009. *Les intermittences de la démocratie: formes d'action et visibilité citoyennes dans la ville.* Paris: L'Harmattan.

Corbridge, S., G. Williams, M. Srivastava and R. Veron. 2005. *Seeing the State: Governance and Governmentality in India.* Cambridge: Cambridge University Press.

Das, V. and D. Poole. 2004. *Anthropology in the Margins of the State.* Oxford: Oxford University Press.

Deboulet, A. 2004. Entre reconstruction et dé-construction, la négociation locale des projets à Beyrouth. *Urbanisme* 336: 34–36.

Escobar, A. 1995. *Encountering Development: The Making and Unmaking of the Third World.* Princeton, NJ: Princeton University Press.

Ferguson, J. 1990. *The Anti-Politics Machine: 'Development', Depoliticization, and Bureaucratic Power in Lesotho.* Cambridge: Cambridge University Press.

———. 1999. *Expectations of Modernity: Myths and Meanings of Urban Life on the Zambian Copperbelt.* Berkeley: University of California Press.

———. 2009. 'The Uses of Neoliberalism', *Antipode* 41(S1): 166–184.

Ferlie, E. 1996. *The New Public Management in Action.* Oxford: Oxford University Press.

Flyvbjerg, B. 1998. *Rationality and Power: Democracy in Practice.* London: University of Chicago Press.

Forester, J. 1989. *Planning in the Face of Power.* Berkeley: University of California Press.

———. 1999. *The Deliberative Practitioner: Encouraging Participatory Planning Processes.* Cambridge, MA, and London: MIT Press.

Friedmann, J. 1987. *Planning in the Public Domain: From Knowledge to Action.* Princeton, NJ: Princeton University Press.

Gal, S. and K.A. Woolard. 2001. 'Constructing Languages And Publics: Authority and Representation', in S. Gal and K.A. Woolard (eds), *Languages and Publics: The Making of Authority.* Manchester: St. Jerome Publishing, pp. 1–12.

Gupta, A. 1995. 'Blurred Boundaries: The Discourse of Corruption, the Culture of Politics, and the Imagined State', *American Ethnologist* 22(3): 375–402.

Hacking, I. 1990. *The Taming of Chance.* Cambridge: Cambridge University Press.

Hall, P. 2002. *Cities of Tomorrow: An Intellectual History of Urban Planning and Design in the Twentieth Century.* Oxford: Blackwell.

Hansen, T.B. and F. Stepputat. 2005. *Sovereign Bodies: Citizens, Migrants, and States in the Postcolonial World.* Princeton, NJ: Princeton University Press.

Healey, P. 1997. *Collaborative Planning: Shaping Places in Fragmented Societies.* Basingstoke: Macmillan.

Holston, J. 1989. *The Modernist City: An Anthropological Critique of Brasília.* Chicago and London: University of Chicago Press.

———. 2008. *Insurgent Citizenship: Disjunctions of Democracy and Modernity in Brazil.* Princeton, NJ, and Woodstock: Princeton University Press.

Holston, J. and A. Appadurai. 1999. 'Introduction: Cities and Citizenship', in J. Holston (ed.), *Cities and Citizenship.* Durham, NC: Duke University Press, pp. 1–18.

Holston, J. and T. Caldeira. 2005. 'State and Urban Space in Brazil: From Modernist Planning to Democratic Interventions', in A. Ong and S.J. Collier (eds), *Global Assemblages: Technology, Politics, and Ethics as Anthropological Problems.* Oxford: Blackwell, pp. 393–416.

Hommels, A. 2005. 'Studying Obduracy in the City: Toward a Productive Fusion between Technology Studies and Urban Studies', *Science, Technology & Human Values* 30(3): 323–351.

Howard, E. 1902. *Garden Cities of To-morrow* (2nd edition of *To-morrow: A Peaceful Path to Real Reform*). London, S. Sonnenschein.

Kalland, A. 1996. 'Geomancy and Town Planning in a Japanese Community', *Ethnology* 35(1): 17–32.

Kamete, A.Y. and I. Lindell. 2010. 'The Politics of "Non-Planning" Interventions in African Cities: Unravelling the International and Local Dimensions in Harare and Maputo', *Journal of Southern African Studies* 36(4): 889–912.

Kenny, J.T. 1995. 'Climate, Race, and Imperial Authority: The Symbolic Landscape of the British Hill Station in India', *Annals of the Association of American Geographers* 95(4): 694–714.

Latham, A. 2006. 'Berlin and Everywhere Else: A Reply to Allan Cochrane', *European Urban and Regional Studies* 13(4): 377–379.

Lee, B. 2001. 'Circulating the People', in S. Gal and K.A. Woolard (eds), *Languages and Publics: The Making of Authority.* Manchester: St. Jerome Publishing, pp. 164–181.

Li, T.M. 2005. 'Beyond "the State" and Failed Schemes', *American Anthropologist* 107(3): 383–394.

Lilienthal, D.E. (1944). *TVA: Democracy on the March.* Harmondsworth: Penguin.

Lipsky, M. 1980. 'Street-Level Bureaucracy: Dilemmas of the Individual in Public Services', New York: Russell Sage Foundation.

Miller, D. 2005. 'What Is Best Value?' in P. du Gay (ed.), *The Values of Bureaucracy*. Oxford: Oxford University Press, pp. 233–256.

Mitchell, T. 1991. 'The Limits of the State: Beyond Statist Approaches and Their Critics', *American Political Science Review* 85(1): 77–96.

Mosse, D. 2005. *Cultivating Development: An Ethnography of Aid Policy and Practice*. London: Pluto Press.

Mouffe, C. 2000. *The Democratic Paradox*. London: Verso.

Müller, B. 2008. *The Anthropology of International Institutions*. European Science Foundation workshop LAIOS Paris, 27–29 March 2008. http://www.iiac.cnrs.fr/laios/sites/laios/IMG/pdf/ESF_programme.pdf

Murdoch, J. and S.A. Abram. 2002. *Rationalities of Planning*. Aldershot: Asghate.

Navaro-Yashin, Y. 2002. *Faces of the State: Secularism and Public Life in Turkey*. Princeton, NJ: Princeton University Press.

Neveu, C. 2003. *Citoyenneté et espaces public. Habitants, jeunes et citoyens dans une ville du Nord.* Villeneuve d'Ascq: Presses Universitaires de Septentrion.

——— (ed.). 2007. *Culture et pratiques participatives: perspectives comparatives*. Paris: L'Harmattan.

Nowotny, H., P. Scott and M. Gibbons. 2001. *Re-Thinking Science: Knowledge and the Public in an Age of Uncertainty*. Cambridge: Polity Press.

Ong, A. 2005. 'Ecologies of Expertise: Assembling Flows, Managing Citizenship', in A. Ong and S.J. Collier (eds), *Global Assemblages: Technology, Politics, and Ethics as Anthropological Problems*. Malden, MA: Blackwell, pp. 337–353.

Paley, J. 2001. *Marketing Democracy: Power and Social Movements in Post-Dictatorship Chile*. Berkeley: University of California Press.

Peattie, L.R. 1987. *Planning, Rethinking Ciudad Guayana*. Ann Arbor: University of Michigan Press.

Peck, J. and A. Tickell. 2002. 'Neoliberalizing Space', *Antipode* 34(3): 380–404.

Rabinow, P. 1989. *French Modern: Norms and Forms of the Social Environment*. Chicago and London: University of Chicago Press.

Rajak, D. 2011. *In Good Company: An Anatomy of Corporate Social Responsibility*. Stanford, CA: Stanford University Press.

Reade, E. 1987. *British Town and Country Planning*. Milton Keynes: Open University Press.

Richards, A.I. and A. Kuper. 1971. *Councils in Action*. Cambridge: Cambridge University Press.

Riles, A. 2000. *The Network Inside Out*. Ann Arbor: University of Michigan Press.

——— (ed.). 2006. *Documents: Artifacts of Modern Knowledge*. Ann Arbor: University of Michigan Press.

Robertson, A.F. 1984. *People and the State: An Anthropology of Planned Development*. Cambridge: Cambridge University Press.

———. 1991. *Beyond the Family: The Social Organization of Human Reproduction*. Berkeley and Los Angeles: University of California Press.

———. 2006a. 'The Anthropology of Grey Zones', *Ethnos* 71(4): 569–573.

———. 2006b. 'Misunderstanding Corruption', *Anthropology Today* 22(2): 8–11.

———. 2009. 'Corporate Greed'. ASA Globalog. Retrieved 10 September 2009 from http://blog.theasa.org/

Rose, N. 1999. *Powers of Freedom: Reframing Political Thought*. Cambridge: Cambridge University Press.

———. and P. Miller. 1992. 'Political Power Beyond the State: Problematics of Government', *British Journal of Sociology* 43(2): 173–205.

Rui, S. 2004. *La Démocratie en Débat*. Paris: Armand Colin.

Rutheiser, C. 1996. *Imagineering Atlanta: The Politics of Place in the City of Dreams*. London: Verso.

Salih, M.A.M. 2003. *African Political Parties: Evolution, Institutionalisation and Governance*. London: Pluto.

Sampson, S.L. 1984. *National Integration through Socialist Planning: An Anthropological Study of a New Romanian Town*. Boulder, CO: East European Monographs.

Sandercock, L. (ed.). 1998. *Making the Invisible Visible: A Multicultural Planning History*. Berkeley and London: University of California Press.

Scott, J.C. 1998. *Seeing Like a State: How Certain Schemes to Improve the Human Condition Have Failed*. New Haven, CT: Yale University Press.

Searle, J.R. 1969. *Speech Acts: An Essay in the Philosophy of Language*. Cambridge: Cambridge University Press.

Selznick, P. 1949. *TVA and the Grass Roots: A Study in the Sociology of Formal Organization*. New York: Harper Torchbooks.

Sharma, A. and A. Gupta. 2006. *The Anthropology of the State: A Reader*. Oxford: Blackwell.

Shore, C. 2001. *European Union and the Politics of Culture*. London: Bruges Group.

———. 1990. *Italian communism: the escape from Leninism: an anthropological perspective*. London, Pluto.

———. and S. Wright (eds). 1997. *Anthropology of Policy: Critical Perspectives on Governance and Power*. London and New York: Routledge.

Spencer, J. 1997. 'Postcolonialism and the Political Imagination', *Journal of the Royal Anthropological Institute* 3(1): 1–19.

Ssorin-Chaikov, N. 2003. *The Social Life of the State in Subarctic Siberia*. Stanford, CA: Stanford University Press.

Stanner, W.E.H. 1949. 'Observations on Colonial Planning', *International Affairs* 25(3): 318–328.

Stapley, L. 1996. *The Personality of the Organisation: A Psycho-Dynamic Explanation of Culture And Change*. London: Free Association Books.

Strathern, M. (ed.). 2000. *Audit Cultures: Anthropological Studies in Accountability, Ethics, and the Academy*. London: Routledge.

Strom, E.A. 2001. *Building the New Berlin: The Politics of Urban Development in Germany's Capital City*. Lanham, MD, and Oxford: Lexington Books.

Tambiah, S.J. 1985. *Culture, Thought, and Social Action: An Anthropological Perspective*. London: Harvard University Press.

Turner, V.W. 1974. *Dramas, Fields, and Metaphors: Symbolic Action in Human Society*. Ithaca, NY, and London: Cornell University Press.

Vike H. 2004. *Velferd uten grenser : den norske velferdsstaten ved veiskillet* [Welfare without limits: The Norwegian welfare states at the crossroads]. Oslo: Akribe.

Waldrop, A. 2004. 'Gating and Class Relations: The Case of a New Delhi Colony', *City & Society* 16(2): 93–116.

Wallman, S. (ed.). 1992. *Contemporary Futures: Perspectives from Social Anthropology*. London: Routledge.

Warner, M. 2003. 'The Mass Public and the Mass Subject', in M.A. Elliott and C. Stokes (eds), *American Literary Studies: A Methodological Reader*. New York: New York University Press, pp. 243–263.

West, H.G., and T. Sanders. 2003. *Transparency and Conspiracy: Ethnographies of Suspicion in the New World Order*. Durham, NC: Duke University Press.

Weszkalnys, G. 2010. *Berlin, Alexanderplatz: Transforming Place in a Unified Germany*. Oxford: Berghahn Books.

Williams, G. 2008. *Struggles for an Alternative Globalization: An Ethnography of Counterpower in Southern France*. Aldershot: Ashgate.

Wittrock, B. 2000. 'Modernity: One, None, or Many? European Origins and Modernity as a Global Condition', *Daedalus* 129(1): 31–60.

Yiftachel, O. 1998. 'Planning and Social Control: Exploring the Dark Side', *Journal of Planning Literature* 12: 395–406.

Zaloom, C. 2009. 'How to Read the Future: The Yield Curve, Affect, and Financial Prediction', *Public Culture* 21(2): 245–268.

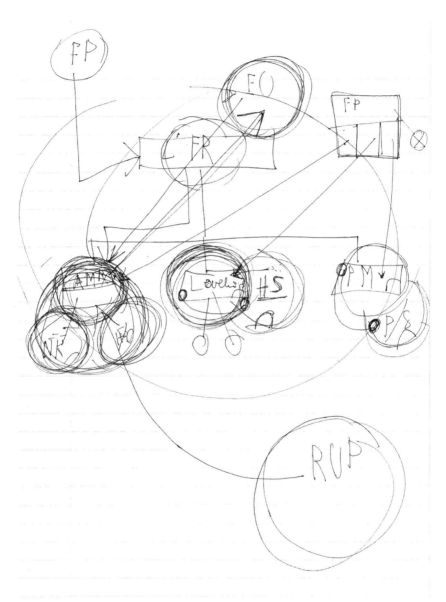

A documentary record of a county planner's explanation of democratic, inclusive and consensus-oriented planning. In attempting to explain the logic of the process, he demonstrated the complexity of planning bureaucracy. Source: Halvard Vike

– Chapter 1 –

Utopian Time and Contemporary Time
Temporal Dimensions of Planning and Reform in the Norwegian Welfare State

Halvard Vike

Introduction

> The eighteenth century bequeathed to us a dual legacy of reason and democracy. Reason meant trust in the capacity of the mind to grasp the orderly processes of nature and society, and to render them intelligible to us. Democracy meant trust in the capacity of ordinary people for self-governance. It presupposed a capacity for reasoning in all of us. (Friedmann 1987: 3)

In his monumental book on planning, *Planning in the Public Domain: From Knowledge to Action* (1987), John Friedmann optimistically calls for a form of planning that mobilizes people and makes use of their ideas, knowledge and energy in deliberative processes that may realize the common good. In his Enlightenment vision, it is essential to establish a popular counterweight to the technocratic tendencies that so often are generated by the institutions of modernity – science, expertise and management.

Norwegian politics, which has been the focus of my research for about two decades now, is an interesting test case for the kind of democratic involvement Friedman calls for. In this chapter, I will describe the major change over the last couple of decades in how planning is conceived and used in public policy in Norway. Arguing that the Enlightenment vision of participatory planning – planning as mobilization and democratization, and as a broad deliberative process through which goals for the future are formulated and the means to achieve them are identified – has been a key element of how democracy is conceptualized, I will try to show how and why characteristically organizational and managerial versions of neo-liberal planning have become dominant, and point to some of the implications that, in the context of Norwegian politics, follow from this.

While by no means an original hypothesis or unique tendency, the change I describe here seems to have been particularly rapid and, moreover, heavily influenced by the universal ambitions characteristic of the Norwegian welfare state. Thus a paradox is involved. It has been commonly believed that the 'de-commoditization' (full public responsibility) of welfare rights and services – which are conventionally seen as the prototypical 'common good' in modern democracies – has led to a greater interest in public politics and a decrease in citizens' alienation (Esping-Andersen 1998, 1999). However, the fall of participatory planning in Norway may prove to be an unintended outcome of an exceptionally strong and widespread idea that politics in an ambitious welfare state like Norway is fundamentally about delivering the right type and amount of services at the right time. Politics, in this context, is conceived as a contract between the state and the individual user-citizen – a relation that leaves local democratic institutions with a specialized function as service producers.

This is especially evident in a peculiar temporal shift in the conceptualization of politics: the transformation of what I call *utopian time* (or gaze, if you will) into *contemporary time.* This conceptual distinction is inspired by sociologist Michael Pusey (1998: 56ff.), who in a critique of what he sees as an 'attack' on civil society in Australia speaks about a 'shift in the modality of time from public time to market time', which 'is experienced as the shrinking horizon of meaningfully anticipated futures'. While the former allows for the anticipation of the future on the basis of what is experienced as meaningful here and now, the latter tends to come 'at' us as a set of functional requirements to which we need to adapt. Pusey explores a number of interesting implications of this shift, the most important of which concerns trust. Drawing on Niklas Luhmann, he emphasizes that reformers (in the market and in the public sector) tend to treat trust as something that 'is only required if a bad outcome would make you regret your action' (1998: 58).

I find Pusey's perspective highly fruitful and have chosen to adapt it for the purpose of throwing light on my own observations. In my own conceptualization, utopian time is to be seen as the horizon of the possible, a temporal framework within which a collective movement along a path approaches a set of goals – goals that motivate, provide hope, and consequently tend to make people willing to sacrifice something on the way. Most importantly, in my perspective, is that utopian time may install a degree of patience (services that are not available now will be available soon), and at the same time (at least ideally) a mutual obligation on the part of the interests that have achieved the compromises necessary to establish it. Such obligations, for instance of the kind that prevent strikes, sabotage, resignation, institutional fragmentation, and so on, are predicated on trust and may generate more trust (Tilly 2005). Contemporary time, by contrast, is the temporal mode of the market transaction, that is, the logic of immediate return, chosen trust, and functional, pragmatic adaption to 'reality'. Cognitively, contemporary time is equivalent to 'utopia now'. In Norwegian politics, contemporary time is the temporal horizon within which universal welfare becomes individual rights guaranteed by the state – to be fulfilled here and now. As I will show, this transformation has massive implications, and it mirrors a major centralization of welfare politics in Norwegian society. This centralization is largely left unnoticed in political discourse in Norway, and on the surface it seems to rest on an overwhelming consensus. The 'structural dilemma' inherent in this is that individual welfare guarantees – more services and better quality for more people at lower cost – gives rise to a major overload problem on the part of the state. Although the overload problem as such is not new, 'utopia now' definitely is. The pressure on service-providing institutions and professions to operate within the horizon of contemporary time means, in principle, that there is neither room for patience nor the kind of trust generated by the notion that proper planning allows measures to be taken to secure more and better services in the future. In this perspective, contemporary time can be seen as an essential element of neo-liberal governance, as analysed with particular clarity (with reference to the British case) by Carrier and Miller in their discussion of 'virtualism' (1998), and Shore and Wright in their chapter on 'coercive accountability' in Strathern's edited volume *Audit Cultures* (2000). Both these contributions deal with the way managerial technologies are put to work to make service providers responsible for more than their actual capacity allows them to provide, thus undermining their autonomy. One of the extensive implications is spelled out in the introduction to this book: the '"gaps" between ideal, ideology and practice fill themselves with things unplanned, unexpected and inexplicable, and with things that get overlooked and forgotten'.

The Norwegian Context

Looking back at the division of labour between the central state and the municipalities a few decades ago, it is clear that the latter played an important part in formulating goals for the future. Local politicians had their own source of legitimacy to draw on and enjoyed considerable institutional autonomy (Baldersheim and Rose 2000; Engelstad, Selle and Østerud 2004; Fimreite 2003). Now, in their attempts to provide according to the standards set by the central state, they are primarily concerned with coping with their overwhelming responsibilities, not with negotiating terms — that is, negotiating the relationship between power and responsibility (Vike, Haukelien and Bakken 2009). Hence they are seen to prioritize the task of getting more things done for less money, in pursuit of which a very strong pragmatic attitude has emerged.

As I will illustrate later in this chapter, the majority of the local politicians I encountered in my varied fieldwork in Norway were utterly hostile to 'visions' and 'abstract goals'. Consequently, they focused on retaining some degree of freedom of action in the short run by seeking ways to reform the organization and employees they were set to govern. When directing their attention to such tasks, they frequently seemed to develop certain suspicions, which were almost always confirmed by 'evidence'. There is always money to be saved by doing things more efficiently, just as there are always employees who waste resources, and users who demand too much. A similar attitude has emerged regarding the political role itself. There are always politicians and party members who naively think the municipality can keep doing things 'the old way' and demand more resources from the central state. Such views of the kind of competence and political participation that is really needed would imply that not only institutions, procedures and employees, but political participants, too, are in need of reformation. It seems that the horizon of contemporary time, reserved for them by the central state, has been embraced. In this cognitive universe, the meaning of planning becomes identical with vitalism: reforming and transforming people in order to maximize output. At its heart is flexibility. But since the flexibility needed in the municipal organization is so hard to achieve by formal reorganization alone, it is desirable to turn to its roots: identities and attitudes among the workforce.

In the Nordic countries, the idea of planning played a major role in modernization and democratization. Ideologically it served as a normative vision of how to push forward towards something better collectively, and as a method – a way to do things politically. As the authors of *The Cultural Construction of Norden* (Sørensen & Strådth 1997) and many others (Barnes 1954; Graubard 1986; Heidar 2004) have pointed out, in these countries participatory democracy developed in ways that made *politics* into a much more heroic activity and category than in most other Western countries, and political institutions became highly legitimate. Large parts of the population came to see organizational membership political activity as a means of improving one's own life conditions, protecting one's interests and collectively seeking to transform society for the better in the long run. The idea of politics and political influence took shape through a specific combination of the pragmatics and practicalities of local decision making at the municipal level, on the one hand, and utopian visions of ultimate freedom and the good society on the other. In Norway, the pattern seems particularly clear. The country's old elites were exceptionally weak, and modern, democratic political institutions were developed from below, as it were, with a high degree of popular representation. Grounded in Europe's most liberal constitution, these institutions became consolidated during the 1800s as platforms for a nationalist awakening against Swedish hegemony and for independence. Political modernization during the 1800s came to be very heavily anchored in Enlightenment visions, strongly guided by the idea that through literacy, participatory competence (cultivated in schools and especially in voluntary associations, most of which were characteristically idealist but at the same time explicitly political and national in orientation) and social mobility, democracy and freedom could be realized to the extent that class dominance could be transcended (Eikås & Selle 2003; Sejersted 1993; Slagstad 1998).

In the decades following independence from Sweden in 1905, national, democratic political institutions demonstrated that they could make a significant difference. Among other achievements, waterfalls were nationalized, universally oriented welfare reforms were conceptualized and partly implemented, minimum prices on fish and agricultural produce were guaranteed for fishermen and farmers, workers' rights became institutionalized and the prospects of overcoming deep class divisions and conflicts through parliamentary compromise seemed real. After the German occupation during the Second World War, the idea that political institutions and the popular energy that was channelled into them constituted the main source of most good things – social integration, growth, progress and optimism – was strongly reinforced (Furre 1991). All this was about planning. The extraordinary changes people experienced, and the idea that not only could desirable improvements be brought forth by technology, but also the social organization of hope and social energy – politics – could be instrumentally applied to anticipate the future, helped to generate a feeling of freedom in a double sense. First, it was seen as freeing people from scarcity and dependence, and second, it fostered a sense that through political activity of a particular kind – planning – it was possible not only to anticipate the future, but also to form it democratically.

The idea of planning in the West is intimately intertwined with Enlightenment ideas and especially with the idea of 'the economy' (Friedmann 1987: 5–8). Keynesian economics was a major breakthrough insofar as it became the reference point for the (partial) political domestication of 'the economy'. Until the 1930s, economic policies had been largely under the sway of liberal, normative ideology. Political interference in the monetary system had generally been seen as morally wrong because this system constituted a major pillar in the institutional set-up of the liberal state. However, from the point of view of the new realism in economic theory, the traditional perspective appeared as 'fiction economics' (Berg & Pharo 1987). The political atmosphere in the 1930s had allowed for some experimentation with this new cultural technology. The ideological ground upon which it was carried out was the vision that a proper conceptualization of 'the economy' could, in fact, materialize as a bridgehead from which the organization of society could be made possible in a new way. This not only added new legitimacy to the Labour Party and the state; it transformed 'the economy' from a moral category 'outside' politics into a tool in the hands of those in power and those in control of scientific reason. As such, it strongly reinforced the idea that economic knowledge bestows upon policymaking agents a new freedom from 'political slogans and dogmas', as a leading Norwegian economist has formulated it (Østerud 1972: 34).

Although ideas of participatory planning were never important in the overwhelmingly technocratic atmosphere that characterized the immediate pre– and post–Second World War eras, nor were they completely marginalized. It is essential to bear in mind here that local democracy in Norway – based on local representation and a division of labour between state and municipalities that gave the latter a major role in welfare policy and welfare provision in particular – has a long history and is exceptionally well established. Ideas of participatory planning increasingly found their way into municipal and regional politics in the 1960s. To make a long history short, the Enlightenment-inspired vision of local and regional planning as a way to mobilize for real participatory democracy remained – roughly speaking – alive and quite strong until some time during the 1990s but now seems to be in a state of dramatic decline and crisis (Sørhaug 2003; Vike et al. 2009). Clearly, this is related to the responsibility overload at the municipal level, which has put a premium on efficient service provision at the cost of participation (Wolfe 1977). At the regional level, however, things took a different direction. As the problem of coordinating the rapidly growing and very complex public sector grew, and the need to reintegrate it with business and civil society became a prioritized issue, the regional level (the counties) was defined as the appropriate arena for planning. Thus, regional democracy has served as the hallmark of the Enlightenment vision of democratic planning in Norway since the 1970s. The county plan was, and formally still is, the arena in which all national policies and local (municipal) needs are supposed to be integrated and coordinated through broad participation. While studying the county planning process in 1995, which turned out to be the last of the generation of comprehensive plans based on a holistic approach and broad participation, I realized that participants from the municipalities were deeply sceptical. They, and others who read the plan for the purpose of finding ways to 'use' it, were unsure whether the plan was mainly a participatory exercise, a strategy for action, a tool, or simply some kind of bad poetry.

The Telemark County Plan

In 1995 I made an official evaluation of the Telemark County Plan (Vike 1996). The purposes of the county plan were to secure political legitimacy, ensure administrative coordination and build and develop society. On a more practical level, its purpose was to contribute to the coordination of regional policies. To succeed, the county administration needed the co-operation of the seventeen municipalities in Telemark, which have the primary responsibility for policymaking within their own boundaries. Therefore, it was considered essential that the planning process be as inclusive as possible. Legitimacy was seen as inseparable from broad participation. The process took three years and involved numerous politicians and administrators at the county level and from the municipalities, along with representatives from various regional state agencies and voluntary associations (approximately 200 taking part in the milestone conferences, 50 in the working groups).

As recently as 2005 in Norway, the county plan was given high priority as a coordinating device at the regional level, and it is supposed to carry out the most pressing tasks in the development of society: secure democratic function through broad participation in the development of the plan, develop visions for the future, integrate the various fields of policy and administration, and secure *helhet* ('wholeness', 'the totality'). As a local political process closely regulated and monitored by the state, the Telemark County Plan illustrates the politics of planning in the welfare state.

The plan, titled *Arbeid, Mangfold, Trivsel* (Work, Variety, Well-being) was very ambitious. Five themes made up the content of the document: infrastructure, environment, living conditions for the young, preventive measures, and trade and industry. Each of these was developed by a mixed working group. Although these groups did not coordinate their work during the process, they were all subject to the requirement of thinking *helhetlig* ('taking the whole into consideration'). Afterwards, the results of the work done by the five groups were linked together and integrated. The second element in the plan was the 'goal structure'. The work was organized as a process where overriding goals – 'visions' – were to be translated into strategies and concrete policies – *tiltak* ('measures'). The document took shape according to this logic. First, *situasjonen* ('the situation') was described, and then *utfordringer* ('challenges') and *overordna mål* ('superior goals') were followed by *strategier* ('strategies') and *tiltak.*

Literally speaking, the plan was full of words. I make this ironical comment because on many occasions, both county and municipal plans have been criticized for their lack of 'concreteness'. The current plan, however, was supposed to be both visionary and practical.

In interviews with participants, municipal contact persons and observers to the planning process, I was struck by the deep scepticism towards the lack of precision in the plan. Several mayors in the county, for instance, simply thought the plan useless. Its goals were too broad and unrealistic, they said, and the plan did not present any credible strategy for achieving goals. The formulation 'The plan is a marketplace of good ideas, I suppose' was hardly a celebration of its quality; neither was the expression 'the plan seems to live its own life'. One of the mayors of Telemark stressed that the plan contained 'too much beating about the bush (*utenomsnakk*)', was 'too Christmas card-like' and had little substance. The goals were somehow free-floating and 'unrealistic'. This was reflected in the experience of the participants in the working groups. Regarding the problem of preventive measures (*forebygging*), one of them lamented: 'We struggled enormously with the goal hierarchies. What are goals and what are means? At the end it became completely impossible to define the goal structures and apply them. We couldn't make out what was what.'

Goal hierarchies are like 'taxonomic trees': they consist of primary goals that are supposed to be specified by lower-order ones. Means are to be strictly separated from these goals but are, of course, at the same time essential for their realization. As the above statement indicates, several participants found this apparatus hard to think with. However, no one criticized it explicitly, and they seemed to accept its relevance.

The primary goals of the Telemark County Plan were formulated as follows:

Infrastructure:
Telemark shall develop efficient, secure and environmentally sensitive (*miljø-vennlige*) communications and pleasant places (*gode steder*) in both urban and rural areas and create improved conditions for prospering business and industry, cultural pluralism and nice (*trivelige*) living conditions.

Environment:
To secure an ecologically justifiable consumption of natural resources in order to maintain a stable environment with biological diversity for the generations that follow us.

Living conditions for the young:
All children and youth shall grow up in a positive social, cultural and physical environment characterized by care, security and well-being (*trivsel*). Their

personal growth and development shall be stimulated so that they acquire self-confidence and belief in the future and are stimulated to make an effort for society. Their county shall make them love their community and acquire a sense of belonging (*heimeglade og rotfeste*).

Preventive measures (Forebygging):
To improve the social and cultural, physical and ecological environment for the inhabitants by measures that generate good living conditions for each individual and in society.

Trade and industry:
Increased sales of goods and services out of the county and reduced purchase of goods and services from the outside are strategically important for the development of business and industry for two reasons. This will increase incomes in both the private and the public sector. This increase is a precondition for a higher level of public and private services in the county. In addition to this, an export-oriented and import-competitive (*importkonkurrerende*) industry will secure existing jobs and become the foundation of new ones.

The set of overarching goals was formulated in a self-reflexive manner that was supposed to make them visionary and concrete at the same time. Their basic legitimation was that they were to be realizable. In my interviews (primarily with municipal representatives), however, it became evident that the goals were considered rather foolish because they were not sufficiently 'realistic'. The critique was particularly harsh when it came to living conditions for the young and preventive measures. While the goal formulations in the trade and industry chapter, for instance, were supplied with a large number of concrete plans and measures to increase profitability, these two areas suffered from an almost total lack of *tiltak* ('measures'). Because of this, many informants said, the goals were only *ønsketenking* ('wishful thinking').

When visionary ideas are subjected to measurement and a kind of rational logic that generates an expectation that political goals – when structured as hierarchies – are supposed to serve as 'tools', utopian ambivalence seems necessarily to follow. Many participants in the planning process in Telemark County were well aware of this problem, but ambivalence was nevertheless treated in a very uniform way. None of my informants had much utopian energy left, as it were, and thus they did not consider the possibility of further developing the poetics of utopian formulations through a heavier concentration on crafting goals that might be more enthusiastically applauded. Instead, even though several members of the work groups stressed that they had a very hard time following the rigid logic of hierarchical, goal-oriented reasoning, there was broad recognition that what needed to be improved was the link between means and goals. This is an interesting conclusion, it seems to me, because of the striking similarity between the source of the problem and its solution.

The main characteristic of the above goal formulations is not that they signify a desire for utopian transformation. Rather, they portray a state that is supposed to be the result of *improvement*. The overall message of the plan is a request to continue doing the things that have been done but do them better and more consistently. If this is accomplished within each of the areas in the county plan, *helhet* ('overall integration', 'holism') will be secured. Ambitions of this type seemed to constitute a major source of disappointment among the participants and the commentators. While in the early phase of planning the planners were severely criticized for being too high-flown in their formulations, the result was not well received because it was seen as trivial. A striking aspect of this criticism was that the goals, and the strategies by which they were supposed to be achieved, were not primarily treated as a problem of values and social change, but rather as a meta-political problem of searching for means that might improve things. This seems to be why many informants turned to the chapter on trade and industry. Here, the logic of means and ends is more consistent, and there is potential for the surplus needed in order to stimulate general improvement.

Many – especially municipal commentators – levelled massive criticism against word overload. The plan documents were too long, and too many words, by failing to connect to people's motivations and prescriptions for action, become 'merely words'. As one leading politician in Skien put it: 'The county plan is like a mediocre essay about how the world is and how it ought to be. It seems as though the bureaucrats write for each other. We are not opposed to planning, but it has to relate to the world in which we live.' For this politician and many others, the problem was that the words were formulated by the wrong kinds of people and without concern for the overall purpose of *doing something concretely* with them. For them, concrete measures were generally much more interesting than goals. The critical attitude towards language, particularly high-flown words put together in what one of the municipal mayors called 'essay-like ways' (too many words, lacking precision), was summed up in another leading politician's complaint: 'I'm so tired of plans.'

In 1995, local politicians in Telemark – as in the rest of Norway – probably had good reasons to be 'tired' of plans of this type. They had reached a point where the problem of dealing with large numbers of participants, spending time discussing 'visions' at seminars and conferences, and working with abstract formulations about moving forward seemed increasingly anachronistic and a waste of time. Their concern was to solve pressing problems and find solutions to problems that demanded more than political interest of an 'ideological' nature, and a different kind of knowledge or expertise. Their political interest was linked to action, efficiency and results, and it led them to concentrate on what they identified as the very foundation of political action: cognitive order and administrative efficiency.

The county plan is the hallmark of the vision of participatory, holistic planning, and as such it reflects Norwegian political culture's strong emphasis on egalitarianism, broad representation, consensus and compromise. A plan whose concept aimed at integrating mass participation with a design that demanded not only clear-cut relations between goals at various levels and specified means, but also visionary ideas, and that moreover was supposed to integrate state policies, regional concerns and municipal interests within a heterogeneous region (the county) – landed with a thud, regarded by many as useless. In the municipality of Skien, by far the biggest of the eighteen municipalities in Telemark County, critics were especially harsh, arguing that the plan lacked realism. Realism, in their view, had to do with what can actually be done, which demands strategic insight or some other kind of expertise relating to the institutions that can actually achieve something, and to the specific resources they possess. 'The problem is how to get things done', they often told me. Most often, the search for the tools needed to get things done was considered far more important than the debate over the political ideas. 'Ideological talk' was often frowned upon, and political 'realism' was often explicitly contrasted with 'wishful thinking'. As one Labour Party leader expressed it: 'We can pass tons of resolutions, but it won't help a bit.' Another formulation, often aired (in one version or another) in political meetings and aimed at characterizing politicians who wasted energy on high-flown talk, was *Politikere som driver politikk med følelsene* ('politicians who engage themselves emotionally in politics'). 'We do not lack the visions', the most influential politician in Skien, B. Johansen, assured me. In his eyes the vital question was 'how to get from talk to practice'.

The search for a greater 'realism' reflects a gradual change in Norwegian politics that at this point manifested itself as a deep frustration with the idea that politics is about mobilization, participation and legitimacy. Finding ways to get things done had become the main concern, and with this shift, leading politicians developed a much clearer sense among of being in charge of big organizations – of being leaders. Thus it is no coincidence that 'the fall' of the county plan 'happened' during this period. But what came in its stead? Over the following decade, the county plan was gradually transformed into a set of more purpose-oriented partnership arrangements between the county administration and the municipalities, in both Telemark and the rest of the country. An aspect deserving special attention is the emphasis on politics and planning as something that takes place in a hierarchical world, and as a relationship between designers of reform on the one hand, and the objects of reform on the other. Revitalizing communities and organizations was seen as a potent way of increasing value through creativity and responsibility, and the art of managing such processes became a focus for both managers and politicians.

Assisting People in Becoming Themselves

In 1996 I followed a project called Community Mobilization in Telemark (Bolkesjø and Vike 1997). Carried out cooperatively by the county administration and the regional state authorities (*Fylkesmannen*), it aimed to spur small district communities 'to take the future into their own hands' by generating projects that could create employment. It had a broader vision, however, based on the assumption that employment may come as a spin-off effect of community work in a broad sense. Thus the project, which was inspired by the slogan 'When the Community itself is allowed to decide', supported various initiatives that sought 'to bring the community together', thus stimulating self-confidence, good ideas, community spirit and entrepreneurship.

Community Mobilization in Telemark was, to be sure, not a political project. Perhaps for that reason, its premises were universally accepted. The project managers, a group of administrators from the *Fylkesmannen* and Telemark County, supplemented by one politician and a couple of municipal business consultants (*næringskonsulenter*), clearly saw this, in line with government guidelines, as an opportunity to equip people in peripheral communities in Telemark with the tools to become more independent and take responsibility for themselves. The project included six communities, which were given a total sum of NOK 300,000 over a three-year period on condition that they followed their project's plan, organized the project properly, reported back to the project managers and, indeed, were able to establish a broad participatory foundation. In addition, it was required that the projects be carried out on a voluntary basis, although the vision also included the hope that the umbrella project would help overcome the barrier between voluntary enthusiasm and the formal, municipal sector.

The project managers were very enthusiastic about the project. On the whole, they saw it as a chance for the communities to rid themselves of their problems. In particular, tension and conflict, lack of risk orientation, lack of community spirit and suspicion – particularly detrimental to successful innovation (*jantelovmentalitet*) – and what some of them called *høvdingmentalitet* ('big man mentality', or 'boss mentality') were identified as main problems. By eliminating such factors and stimulating creativity, innovation and the ability to 'lift together', the community would, it was assumed, be able to realize its true and natural potential. It would be more goal-oriented, qualitatively better and more united. The project managers carefully monitored the mobilization process according to this vision and intervened whenever it seemed to take an uncontrolled course.

A major dilemma in the business of controlling the mobilization process was the question of how, and when, to transfer responsibility from the project management group to the participants themselves. One member of the management group evoked the metaphor of raising a child, which to me seemed fairly representative of how the relationship was conceptualized. The members of the management group knew that if people in the communities were to 'establish ownership' over the process and 'assume responsibility', control would have to be indirect and progressively looser. The most telling aspect of this metaphoric construction of community mobilization seems to be the idea that the management group would have to be patient enough to observe people carrying out experiments and making mistakes but not intervene, thereby assisting them in becoming, as it were, full-grown participants. As one member reflected, regarding her role as a supervisor: 'Am I a good mother? What is a good mother supposed to be?' In my interviews with the members of the management group, I was struck by the way they took a diagnostic meta-view on the communities involved, for instance comparing them according to the extent of their history of passivity, of letting influential 'big men' (or the municipality) do the job, or of destructive conflict. This process was all the more difficult because the group saw its work as part of a more encompassing task that was not supposed to be explained and transmitted to the communities: to 'help people get off their sofas and become involved in the community'.

In terms of shared ambitions, cooperation and positive attitude, the project was a major success. This was not because a large number of new jobs were created, but because – as all project committees in the six communities enthusiastically reported – it did in fact contribute to more participation, creativity and unity. This, in turn, was of course premised on the fact that the participants, mostly unconditionally, adopted the understanding of what 'community mobilization' was supposed to be, as formulated by the management group. Based on the evaluation report (Bolkesjø and Vike 1997), the following finding epitomizes this understanding: most participants reported that now, as opposed to in the past, a shared understanding, more unity and a 'cosier' atmosphere had been established in their community. This relates to an assumption that local culture – which, though not a term used by the participants themselves, was evoked time and again by other terms ('mentality', etc.) – had been changed from something destructive and habitual to something creative, attractive and to some extent controlled. As one participant formulated the idea: 'There was no big discussion or disagreement. We have worked towards shared solutions that everyone could support.' Furthermore, in accordance with the experience of proving that they could rid themselves of their own problems – for instance, 'the mentality of suspicion' (*jantelovmentalitet*) – they reported that they had strengthened their 'self-confidence' and learned to 'assume responsibility'. As to the problem of responsibility, some participants took the same view of other participants that the project group held of the six communities: they expressed concern that some failed to understand what it means to be cooperative and take responsibility.

Another dimension in the participants' experience of the community mobilization project was the relationship between the informal life of the communities and the municipalities, which were represented on all community committees. The management group emphasized very clearly that the project was to draw primarily on voluntary enthusiasm, not on municipal initiative, since the latter would prevent the community from becoming aware of its potential and what it means to form its own future. In particular, the group expected informal processes to re-create the local *ildsjel* ('community enthusiast') and *dugnadsånd* ('work party spirit') in the communities, a combination that was expected to transcend the mental and practical limitations that tend to curb formal organizations' creativity more than is desirable. Throughout the project period, the members of the management group were acutely aware of the importance of informality, and they used it as one of their main criteria of evaluation. For instance, one of the projects was criticized for having a municipal bureaucrat (the chief administrator in the municipal agriculture department) as its committee leader, and for being too caught up in ordinary municipal political processes, thus reinforcing existing hierarchies, expectations and interactional patterns. Yet at the same time, the group ensured that procedures for organizing the projects and accounting for the steps taken were strictly enforced. One of the project group members was somewhat ambivalent about this, being used to much better and more efficient report routines. 'I'm not used to being as kind as this', he pointed out.

The Community Mobilization in Telemark project was premised on the idea that bureaucratic management, in alliance with consumer society, has resulted in a passive attitude in peripheral communities. However, under the assumption that these communities had a natural potential for self-realization, regeneration of this potential was sought by stimulating them to become themselves. According to the development discourse in the management group, by appealing to the enthusiastic spirit already present beneath the surface, the integrated 'community' could be re-established as a corporate unit devoid of destructive factionalism and mutual suspicion.

As pointed out above, the idea of community development formulated by the project managers was well received, and the projects must be seen as a success. Reports from the community committees and the extensive questionnaire turned in by their members hold no indication that the participants rejected the ideas in the project. On the contrary, they saw the project as a way of realizing their own ambitions and reported that it had helped them cleanse themselves of negative attitudes, conflicts and passivity. They grasped the idea of strengthening their informal networks and were acutely aware that their potential to become viable communities rested on their ability to transform these networks into entrepreneurial success in the market.

Seen in a historical light, the community mobilization programme represents a strongly revised version of planning, focused primarily on how to reform people and their culture so as to make them 'compatible' with what is conceptualized as today's society and its needs and challenges. The need to develop new subjects, values and social forms is seen primarily as a way to get the involved people and communities in touch with their own potential, their true selves and their 'natural' inclinations – that is, as a way of purifying them. This is presumably why those involved in the programme did not perceive it as something forced upon them that threatened their autonomy, dignity or sense of self. In this regard it presents a striking contrast to what we may call the politics of the centre-periphery relation in Norway. In comparative terms the Norwegian periphery has been exceptionally strong politically and highly sensitive to policies that fail to take citizens' autonomy and values (such as language) seriously and thus are seen as reflecting the interests of urban elites. Participants in the community mobilization programme, however, did not regard the need for improvement or the form of assistance they received on the way as a 'generous betrayal'.

Reforming Organizations, Institutions and Persons

As a way to achieve transformation, reform of organizations, institutions and persons has proved to be much more attractive than planning. While there seem to be many reasons for this, the shift from utopian to contemporary time may throw some light on the matter. First, the idea of reform has an important vitalist element. Reforms carry with them the promise that those involved are not caught in a zero-sum game, but rather in a project that sets energies free and transforms them into common goods. In one sense, then, reforms have a moral element: they instil a sense of responsibility for being reformed. Planning, for instance in the form of a Norwegian county planning process, primarily contributes to forming subjects and identities by establishing contexts for actors, so logically the success or failure of such plans must be attributed to aspects of their design or the willingness, on the part of actors who have decided to take part in them and support them, to keep their promise (Vike 1997). This moral aspect of the art of reforming can thus be seen as an aspect of contemporary time. Above, I conceptualized contemporary time as a temporal framework that elites and managers can apply to create a double bind for subordinates: whereas their job is to meet standards set here and now, the overall political responsibility to provide resources, adjust overly demanding standards and so on takes the future as its point of reference and is fundamentally conditional (Shore and Wright 2000). Reforms are supposed to be carried through regardless of the normal capacity of those being reformed, and reformers can often be observed advancing the desired result. Whatever reforms bring forth, the desired result is conditioned by the ability of those being reformed to internalize is and become transformed. If for some reason the targets of reform feel they may fail, the burden of proof tends to be on them. If they fail to become what they ought to become, they are guilty, not of having done something wrong but of being inadequate. They are always somehow incomplete, which in the eyes of the reformers explains why organizations and institutions fail – in other words, why good policies do not always produce the desired outcome.

In an imaginative and critical appraisal of planning – *From Planning to Reform: The Great Shift in Governance* – Tian Sørhaug (2003) argues that a rationality shift has taken place in Norwegian politics. Whereas plans typically originate from the need to achieve a long-term balance and coordination between growth and redistribution based on some kind of overarching political value that reflects the utopian desire to achieve qualitative, societal transformation, reforms can be seen as 'a social mechanization of politics' (Sørhaug 2003: 47). Reforms tend to be carried through swiftly, apparently reflecting the ambition to get things done rather than secure the involvement of concerned interests, which may block or delay them. Reforms are utopian in a different manner than plans, particularly because they involve promises of more and better value. To secure this extra value, they are typically designed from a distance and made to work through self-monitoring by the objects of reform. This mechanism allows for a major shift of emphasis regarding participatory planning and its utopian horizon. While such planning tends to allow for failure and a certain tolerance for the non-perfect, reforms are predicated on leaders' power to advance the extra value promised, and to place the responsibility for failure on those who were given the task of reforming themselves.

A large part of what earlier was a part of the politics of planning is now 'outsourced' to become a daily part of administrative and professional work in institutions that are more or less continually reformed. Indicators are developed to facilitate this process, but also to be easily 'readable' and serve as tools for action – again, from a distance. This tends to produce a dynamic that Michel Foucault famously labelled 'government of government', which in this particular context generates a process that serves to undermine the discretion, adaptability and legitimacy of the grassroots levels of the state. As this erodes the kind of trust generated by the ability to negotiate the terms of responsibility sharing, government of government tends toward self-reinforcing spiral movement: it needs to continuously intensified to make up for the lack of trust (Power 1994; Shore and Wright 2000).

Over the last couple of decades, forceful voices have repeatedly demanded reform of the welfare state, and indeed, several big reforms have been implemented. The results are hotly debated, and the discrepancy between the promises the reforms carried and the actual performance capacity of the reformed organizations has provoked considerable frustration. As Sørhaug indicates, it is highly significant that the idea that reforms are desperately needed is most often voiced by those whose vision is shaped by their position at the top of hierarchies. In other words, whereas the public tends to be dissatisfied with the welfare state's inability to fully keep its own promises, political elites are much more concerned about the way things are done (Gregory 2003). Political elites tend to respond to popular demands by inflating promises and reforming institutions. This response does not target what the public generally experiences as the main problem; there is no deep sense that welfare services are bad or inappropriate, but only that they are too few and that access is sometimes insufficient. Rather, it reflects a concern specific to the elites themselves: their need to re-create their own freedom of action and avoid being overwhelmed by responsibility, which tends to undermine flexibility.

Local politicians have a pressing need to maintain some sort of freedom of political action, some sort of flexibility. The only way of achieving that – or so it seems – is by maximizing value. Sufficient resources are unlikely to be found externally (i.e., through better financial support from the state), so they must be found within, via reformation of the organization and its personnel. Thus planning becomes organizational reform. The gaze is turned inwards, inspiring a political gaze that looks for better ways of doing things organizationally and above all seeks information that may be of strategic and practical use in reformation work. As the bulk of municipal responsibility concerns primary education and especially primary health and care for the elderly, these services constitute the focus of attention.

Local politicians assume responsibility for what the central state has guaranteed the users of services as individual rights, but they have the option of pushing their dilemma further down the ladder to the service providers. In Norway, as in the rest of Scandinavia, service providers – teachers, social workers of various kinds, nurses, assistant nurses and non-skilled personnel – are overwhelmingly women. Their work, in contrast to all other professions (in the private and public sector alike) is characterized by a fundamental lack of control over boundaries. They have very limited control over factors that influence the amount of responsibility they assume and thence the quality of their work. It is service providers' relative inability to reject arbitrary increases in their workload that allows the ambitious welfare state to decentralize its dilemma (ambitions/rights vs. actual capacity).

In the last decade, a group of colleagues and I studied the consequences of state policies at the local, municipal level as they affect identities, discourses and practices among local politicians and grassroots bureaucrats, to use Michael Lipsky's terminology (Lipsky 1980). What we found was the state elites' overwhelming tendency to decentralize dilemma and to separate formal responsibility from practical responsibility. From 2006 to 2009 we investigated welfare policy and the organization and provision of elderly care services in four municipalities on the Western coast (Vike et al. 2009). Fieldwork among care personnel revealed that as the municipal welfare sector was reformed, their responsibilities and workloads increased, and correspondingly, their time to coordinate their work, discuss and develop standards, and so on gradually diminished. The professional infrastructure needed to secure quality of service was dramatically threatened. At the same time, their superiors introduced users' guarantees and encouraged users to complain when services were insufficient.

This is how an element of 'virtualism' is introduced (Miller 2002, 2003). The 'virtual' reality of formal standards and guarantees is much more than a symbolic entity: it underlies a discourse of quality involving the central state, the audit agencies and the municipal leadership exchanging information on the state of quality within the horizon of contemporary time. Thus it seems evident that reformation transforms the promise inherent in utopian time – making the future better together, and accepting the less than perfect here and now – in three ways. First it is made virtual. Standards of quality and output are abstracted and modelled, serving as a benchmark to which real services are expected to conform. This virtual reality is 'monopolized' by those who manage concrete work processes from a distance, in the sense that they alone enjoy the privilege of referring to the future and to ideals/values in order to justify decisions made here and now. Second, the promise inherent in utopian time is injected into or transported to contemporary time. Third, contemporary time is reserved for lower organizational levels, in particular service providers. The task of dealing with the welfare state's major dilemma – the gap between ambitions and rights on the one hand, and actual capacity on the other – is their responsibility here and now. In this way, service providers have to adapt to the reality of scarce resources and real priorities, but are made accountable according to the standards set by utopian time. Together, these transformations constitute a major source of power and may partly explain the hold that promises made within the mode of new public management seem to have on the Norwegian welfare state. Above all, they facilitate the reintegration of value and fact, both at the level of policymaking and in the art of management.

Conclusions

Utopian time may be seen as the temporal dimension relevant to participatory planning, as this form of planning was known and practised in Norway in full scale from about the 1960s through the 1990s. It created a democratic, epistemological and relational temporality that seemed well adjusted to what may be called optimistic expectations and the maintenance of generalized trust. Yet it gave rise to deep frustration because given the new, fundamental dilemmas of the welfare state and the pressure it put on local democratic institutions, it could not deal with basic concerns. As a result, the planning gaze turned inwards to focus on organizational reform and the production of increased value within established institutional and financial frames. Borrowing a poignant phrase from Clifford Geertz (1963), the process emanating from this can be called organizational *involution*. Contemporary time, in this context, means two things. First, it denotes a process whereby local politicians direct their attention to what seems pragmatically possible, which for all practical purposes means more value for less money. In this capacity, local politicians enter the domain of administration and take the role of organizational leaders. More fundamentally, however, contemporary time must be taken to mean the temporal structuring of a dilemma they, as local politicians, are more or less forced to face and deal with. The central Norwegian state – that is, the National Assembly and the Government – has created a major overload. Under utopian time this problem could be dealt with by referring to an anticipated, improved future: Services that could not be delivered today could be tomorrow. Such plans installed a degree of patience, making most actors trust that improvements would materialize.

Since the 1980s or so, however, welfare policies have increasingly taken the form of individual rights, thus directly linking the central state to the receivers of service. Held hostage to binding promises, municipalities are permanently guilty of inability to deliver sufficient quality and quantity. Negotiating the terms of the relationship between power and responsibility with the central state no longer seems an option. To be able to balance budgets, local politicians therefore seek resources where they are available. In their eyes, it seems evident that politics as mobilization is not deeply relevant – and indeed, may become a nuisance – to their identity as managers of complex organizations. Municipal planning, which under these conditions has increasingly taken the form of reformation of relations and selves, designed and managed from a distance, is carried through by managers and local politicians who desperately seek to maintain their freedom of action, and seems to have found a new prototypical form. This clearly undermines participatory planning and the democratic, mobilizing potential it entails, or entailed. As I have tried to show in this chapter, this is partly explained by a specific contextual organization of utopian and contemporary time, respectively, that allows the reintegration of value and fact at the level of policymaking and management.

References

Baldersheim, H. and L. Rose (eds). 2000. *Det kommunale laboratorium. Teoretiske perspektiver på local politikk og organisering*. Bergen: Fagbokforlaget.
Barnes, J. 1954. 'Class and Committees in a Norwegian Island Parish', *Human Relations* 7: 39–58.
Berg, T. And H. Pharo (eds.) 1987. Vekst og velstand. Norsk politisk historie 1945–1965. Oslo: Universitetsforlaget.
Bolkesjø, T. and H. Vike. 1997. 'Mobilisering som bygdeutviklingsstrategi', *Landbruksøkonomisk Forum* 3: 49–62.
Carrier, J. G. and D. Miller (eds.) 1998. *Virtualism: A New Political Economy*. Oxford: Berg.
Eikås, M. and P. Selle 2003. 'Voluntary Organizations and The Norwegian Welfare State: From Mutual Trust to Contracting', in N. Götz and J. Hackmann (eds), *Civil Society in the Baltic Sea Region*. Aldershot: Ashgate, pp. 107–118.
Engelstad, F., P. Selle and Ø. Østerud. 2003. *Makten og demokratiet. En sluttbok fra Makt- og demokratitutredningen*. Oslo: Gyldendal Akademisk.
Esping-Andersen, G. 1998. *Welfare States in Transition: National Adaptations in Global Economies*. London: Sage.
———. 1999. *Social Foundations of Postindustrial Economies*. New York: Oxford University Press.
Geertz C. 1963. *Agricultural Involution. The Process of Ecological Change in Indonesia*. Berkeley, Los Angeles and London: University of California Press.
Graubard, S.R. (ed.). 1986. *Norden: The Passion for Equality*. Oslo: Scandinavian University Press.

Fimreite, A.L. 2003. *Der hvor intet er, har selv keiseren tapt sin rett! : Om lokalt folkestyre og rettigheter* (rapport 8). Bergen: Rokkansenteret.

Friedmann J. 1987. *Planning in the Public Domain: From Knowledge to Action.* Princeton, NJ: Princeton University Press.

Furre, B. 1991. *Vårt hundreår. Norsk historie 1905–1990.* Oslo: Samlaget.

Gregory, R. 2003. 'Transforming Governmental Culture: A Sceptical View of New Public Management', in T. Christensen and P. Lægreid (eds), *New Public Management: The Transformations of Ideas and Practice.* Aldershot: Ashgate, pp. 231–261.

Heidar, K. (ed.). 2004. *Nordic Politics: Comparative Perspectives.* Oslo: Universitetsforlaget.

Lipsky, M. 1980. *Street-Level Bureaucracy: Dilemmas of the Individual in Public Services.* New York: Russell Sage Foundation.

Power, M. 1994. *The Audit Explosion.* London: Demos.

Pusey, M. 1998. 'Between Economic Dissolution and the Return of the Social: The Contest for Civil Society in Australia', in J. Alexander (ed.), *Real Civil Societies: Dilemmas of Institutionalization.* London: Sage, pp. 40–66.

Sejersted, F. 1993. *Demokratisk kapitalisme.* Oslo: Universitetsforlaget.

Shore, C. and S. Wright. 2000. 'Coercive Accountability: The Rise of Audit Culture in Higher Education', in M. Strathern (ed.). *Audit Cultures: Anthropological Studies in Accountability, Ethics and the Academy.* London: Routledge, pp. 57–89.

Slagstad, R. 1998. *De nasjonale strateger.* Oslo: Pax.

Sørensen Ø. and B. Stråth (eds). 1987. *The Cultural Construction of Norden.* Oslo: Scandinavian University Press.

Sørhaug, T. 2003. 'Fra plan til reformer: Det store regjeringsskiftet', in I. Neumann and O. J. Sending (eds), *Regjering i Norge.* Oslo: Pax.

Telemark County (1994). *Telemark County Plan 1994-1997.* Skien: Telemark fylkeskommune.

Tilly, C. 2005. *Trust and Rule.* Cambridge: Cambridge University Press.

Vike, H. 1996. *Conquering the Unreal: Politics and Bureaucracy in a Norwegian Town.* Oslo: Department of Social Anthropology.

———. 1997. 'Reform and Resistance. A Norwegian Illustration', in C. Shore and S. Wright (eds), *Anthropology of Policy.* London, Routledge, pp. 195–216.

———, H. Haukelien and R. Bakken. 2009. *Kompetanse- og faglig infrastruktur i helse- og omsorgstjenestene* (rapport no. 252). Bø, Telemark: Telemarksforsking.

Wolfe, A. 1977. *The Limits of Legitimacy: Political Contradictions of Contemporary Capitalism.* London and New York: Macmillan.

Østerud, Ø. 1972. *Samfunnsplanlegging og politisk system. En analyse av samfunnsplanlegging som politikk og ideologi.* Oslo: Gyldendal.

Building the Norge-Väner link at Bohus. Source: Trafikverket

– Chapter 2 –

FROM WITHIN A COMMUNITY OF PLANNERS
Hypercomplexity in Railway Design Work

Åsa Boholm

Introduction

Planning decisions about zoning, land use and the localization and build-ing of large-scale facilities (e.g., transportation infrastructure for road, railway and air traffic; plants for energy production and distribution; waste disposal and mining facilities) have broad and lasting societal im-pact, and high public and media visibility. Consequently, they also have a host of political implications (Saint, Flavell and Fox 2009). A key tension addressed in the literature on facility siting (for an overview see Boholm and Löfstedt [2004]) concerns interactions between planning communities made up of decision makers interconnected within a complex institutional framework, and affected local populations and stakeholders (Boholm 2008). While policy makers, regulators and experts are expected to take into account costs, negative externalities, risks and benefits, those affected by planning decisions focus on issues of identity and place attachment, public participation, trust and fairness (Boholm and Löfstedt 2004).

The multitude of actual and possible, unforeseen and expected conse-quences of policy decisions on land use and facility siting provides rich nourishment for heated local debate centred on the voicing of conflicting interests and values, demands and wishes regarding the uses and mean-ings of land and landscape (Boholm and Löfstedt 2004; Boholm 2008; Ko-nopasek, Stöckelova and Zamykalova 2008; Stoffle et al. 2004). Ultimately, the legitimacy of power over the local environment is at stake (Binde and Boholm, 2004; Boholm 2008; Corvellec, 2001; Saint et al. 2009). However, the complexity attending these decisions is not due to the sheer number of issues and perspectives alone. Knowledge of any of the relevant issues is necessarily knowledge from a certain standpoint (van den Hove 2006), and standpoints diverge, sometimes quite dramatically. Given the 'coexistence of irreducible standpoints' (van den Hove 2006: 11), one wonders how facility siting projects become realized at all. This chapter addresses a possible explanation: the establishment of a hegemonic position vis-à-vis all other standpoints (Laclau and Mouffe 1985). Following this lead I examine infrastructure planning from the inside by focusing on the organizational dynamics within a community of planners working together to implement state infrastructure transport policy. The case study involves the planning of a double-track railway line in western Sweden. Taking a deliberate inside perspective on the interactions, working methods and understandings within a community of railway planners, this essay looks at railway planning and project management as a social practice situated within a community of planners (both public and private organizational agents). The question raised is how the community of planners established managerial hegemonic positions (Flyvbjerg 1998; Räisenen and Linde 2004) on ways of implementing the railway line.

Theoretical inspiration derives from practice-based approaches to knowledge and social action in anthropology (Hobart 1993; Ingold 2000; Lave 1988, 1997) and philosophy (Bratman 1992, 1999; Gilbert 2006). These approaches understand cognition as a social activity embedded in practices and ongoing social relationships rather than as comprising only mental phenomena, mental (cultural) models and representations (Ingold 2000; Lave 1988, 1997). The situatedness of knowledge and thought in practical real life (Lave 1988; Lave and Wenger 1991), accompanied by a focus on the 'social actor in action in the lived-in world' (Lave 1988: 13), is at the core of this theoretical stance.

Backgrounding Past and Future Railway Modernization

In nineteenth-century Europe, aspiring nation states expended tremendous effort to plan and build railways in accordance with a 'powerful, liberating and disturbing vision of what technology offered' (Harrington 2000: 229). The railway emerged as the emblem par excellence of modernity (Carter 2001). It was associated with the wonders of technical engineering, the advent of a new order of bureaucratic management, the expansion of the dominion of the nation state and a cosmopolitan outlook. Unsurprisingly, attitudes towards this first 'mass transit system' of the modern age (Harrington 2000) were ambivalent. Seen as promising a mixture of economic and social progress, democracy, liberty and technological benefits, it meanwhile was also understood to bring danger and disaster, social disorder and violence, and the destruction of landscape and rural values (Beaumont and Freeman 2007; Harrington 2000).

In 1853, the Swedish government decided to build a national, publicly funded network of railway lines. The first national railway line was inaugurated in 1856, the same year the government authority Swedish State Railways was founded to organize railway infrastructure and traffic. The number of lines increased quickly, and by 1879 the country had a well-developed railway network punctuated by stations and adhering to a single timetable. The Swedish government continued developing the network up to the end of the Second World War. In the post-war era this trend declined, and numerous local railway lines were closed down, deemed uneconomic and inefficient because of the increasing role of private transportation by car. Adhering to a standardized timetable and operating on iron tracks nailed into sleepers laid on the ground, the railway had become obsolete. It was supplanted by another modern transport technology, the private car, which let the individual driver go anywhere whenever he or she desired.

In the aftermath of the oil crises of the 1980s, however, the post-war expansion of road traffic and private car ownership and use, fostered by new road infrastructure, was being reconsidered in policy and planning. Negative side effects of road traffic, such as accidents causing fatalities and injuries, environmental degradation, pollution and traffic congestion, were increasingly recognized, as was the limited nature of petroleum resources. Railway transportation was now viewed as a viable alternative to road traffic. Substantial investments went towards modernizing and upgrading the Swedish railway network in preparation for both high-speed, long-distance train traffic and increasing commuter traffic (Falkemark 2006). Several new mega-projects, such as the West Coast Railway line, including the Hallandsås Tunnel (Boholm 2000) and the Bothnia Railway in the north, were conceived in the mid 1980s.

Today, the issue of global climate change is prompting new investments in railway infrastructure, since railways are portrayed as a 'green', climate-friendly mode of transportation. One telling example of the current political emphasis on new railway infrastructure is a September 2009 government investigation determining that by 2025, Sweden should have continental-style express trains (with speeds up to 320 km/h) connecting Stockholm with Sweden's second- and third-largest cities at a cost of SEK 125 billion (EUR 12.5 billion). This largest-ever Swedish infrastructure investment promises reduced travel times and better regional development and economic growth (Statens offentliga utredningar [SOU] 2009: 74).

Hopes are indeed high for railway in the future. Nonetheless, considerable distance separates a *planned* piece of railway infrastructure and its existence as an 'engineering artefact' (Suchman 2003: 189) situated on firm ground. The numerous legal, technical, political, economic, spatial and temporal restrictions on the planning process require protracted cooperation by a number of governmental authorities, consultants and experts. The modern planning and construction of a railway line require specialized knowledge of many matters: geology, hydrogeology, groundwater, ecology, wildlife, landscape, legislation, politics, construction, technical design, traffic, local society. Successful implementation of national transport infrastructure policy resulting in the built structures envisioned in the initial (state-designed) policy programme therefore requires a high degree of joint commitment among decision makers. As the public administration literature notes, implementation draws on communication, cooperation and coordination between administrations and organizations (O'Toole 2003; Pressman and Wildavsky 1973; Winter 2003) and, not the least, experts of many brands.

Presenting the Case: The Norway–Väner Link and the 'Upland' Non-station

In 1994, the Swedish government decided to invest SEK 10 billion (approximately EUR 1 billion) in upgrading the road and rail capacity of the Norway–Väner Link north of Göteborg in western Sweden by making the existing single-track railway into a double-track line dimensioned for high-speed trains. The new railway line promises reduced travel time, shorter intervals between departures, commuter stations and environmental benefits. Among several sub-projects is a route south of the city of Trollhättan comprising approximately 14 kilometres of double-track rail, including three tunnels ranging from 124 to 200 metres long and a 400-metre-long bridge.[1] The route traverses rural farmland and mountainous areas covered with dense pine forests and passes through two rural communities, each with just over 500 inhabitants. The area is rich in both archaeological and historic heritage and natural conservation sites, including a river running through a spectacular canyon. The passage through forested hills and mountains also calls for several tunnels and deep mountain cuttings. The local communities and municipality of Trollhättan generally favour the project and the selected route. Some individual citizens and affected landowners, however, are critical, mostly regarding portions of the project that affect their properties.[2]

The government investment to upgrade the Norway–Väner Link has several policy objectives. The new railway line, which is justified by environmental and traffic safety concerns, is projected to promote economic growth, regional development and efficient public transport. The investment in the new line is embedded in a policy vision of regional economic growth, expanded and more efficient commuter traffic and better traffic safety. To accommodate commuter traffic, the railway line must have stations allowing travellers to access the trains. The route will bypass Upland[3], a small community of approximately 500 inhabitants. The railway investigation report noted that Upland would have to grow in order to justify its having a commuter station.[4] According to the calculations of the regional public transport company (West Traffic), the projected number of commuters is far too low to justify constructing a train station in Upland, and stopping the train there would unacceptably extend the travel time. A station in Upland is therefore not deemed economically viable.[5]

> Today Upland has too few travellers for the regional trains to make a stop. ... West Traffic has the goal of creating a traffic supply that foster growth reaching an optimal number of travellers. A stop in Upland would prolong travel time between Göteborg and Trollhättan. That would cause travellers to choose to go by car or simply exclude work or education options that entail commuting by train. ... The population of Upland should at least double or triple to make a train stop economically feasible. (author's translation)[6]

The railway investigation report further stated that the planning of the new railway line passing Upland should allow for the possibility of building a station with platforms there in the future. Some of the specifications of the station have been determined; for example, the platforms must be accessible to physically handicapped people, and bicycle lanes should link to the platforms.[7] The future commuter station in Upland was one of several issues attracting public interest at consultation meetings held in September 2005 for the railway investigation.[8] Of particular concern were the location of any future station (i.e., in the centre or outside of Upland), the fact that the entire project is pointless if people cannot travel by train, and the opinion that the alternative route passing Upland at some distance is preferable, since absent a station there is no advantage in having the railway line so near Upland's population centre.

Multi-sited ethnography (Marcus 1995) has been used to follow planning of the railway route as it unfolds in the lived-in world of planners and project management. I observed planning work among a community of planners for a railway line on the Norway–Väner route for one and a half years by participating in various planning meetings, including both internal project meetings and meetings with external stakeholders and authorities.

Railway Planning at Work:
Regulatory and Organizational Context

In Sweden, railway infrastructure is state owned and the national government decides about investing in new lines and upgrading or closing down existing lines. The National Rail Administration (NRA), a government authority and a successor of the Swedish State Railways, is responsible for the railway system, including provision of the rail tracks, signal system and electricity for trains, while the trains themselves are run by companies that lease rail capacity from the NRA. Railway planning is regulated by the Railway Building Act (Svensk författningssamling [SFS] 1995: 1649) and the Environmental Code [SFS] 1998: 808) and involves several government authorities and stakeholders in protracted consultation processes.

Formally, a railway planning process is structured sequentially in administrative stages. The *railway investigation* identifies and weighs alternative routes for the proposed line. This phase includes consultation with the regional county board, municipalities, public authorities, stakeholder organizations and members of the public together with an environmental impact assessment conducted in accordance with the Environmental Code. The *railway planning* stage comprises detailed planning, both of the railway line location within the chosen corridor and of its various construction features and impacts on the environment, landscape and land use. Consultations with landowners, municipalities, regional boards and other authorities are essential in formulating the railway plan. The Railway Building Act requires that the plan be made public if it will substantially impact the environment, public health or nature resource use, or encroach on private property. After promulgation, the NRA board can approve the railway plan on condition that the regional county board[9] has no objections to it.

In planning the Upland railway line, Division South of the NRA contracted with the firm Rail Administration Consulting (RAC) to formulate the railway plan and all investigations required for it. In all, the NRA's railway plan project involved fifty consultants with various types of expertise, who were responsible for the economic aspects and time plan of the proposed rail line, under the leadership of the RAC project leader (a specialist in the comprehensive planning of construction projects, licensing and legal issues). Other NRA officials taking part in the project included experts on, for example, economics, environmental monitoring, quality control, information, purchasing, safety and traffic. The competencies of the NRA specialists covered technical coordination, environmental impact assessment and real estate and land management.

Trust and Joint Commitment

Sweden has a long history of consensus-style regulation in which elite stakeholders negotiate and make agreements without the judicial interference or other adversarial procedures that are common in the United States (Karlsson 2010; Kelman 1981; Löfstedt 2005; Lundqvist 1980; Vogel 1986). Consensus-style regulation builds on social trust. It includes a limited set of organizational agents and elite stakeholders (such as industry, lobby organizations, trade unions, experts and government officials) by means of informal, closed meeting spaces. Flexibility in decision making, the weighing and taking into account of interests and a strong motivation to form an agreement among those concerned characterize this managerial culture.

The consensual regulatory style among the community of planners attributes critical importance to continuity of individual planners at work. Planners tend to be anxious about the maintenance of staff continuity, which is regarded as crucial to a 'smooth' planning process. When a planner, especially one who is an office holder, leaves his or her post in the organization, uncertainty arises among the other planners as to the validity of the organization's joint commitment, which must be reinforced and stabilized by the successive office holder. The planners must be able to trust that joint commitments are valid and that the actions and intentions of co-planners are aligned (Bratman 1992, 1999; Gilbert 2006). Deviations from what was agreed on earlier change the conditions for the other planners and are thus perceived as making work more difficult. The planners strive to foresee how the other planners are thinking, so that they can adjust their own planning and, if necessary, negotiate and establish a joint agreement on some new line of action. They therefore need to be continuously updated on each other's plans, since these will likely affect the conditions for their own planning.

Meetings as a Mode of Operation

Railway planners spend a great deal of their working time at meetings of various sizes and degrees of specialization. In the studied case, the project meetings were generally held once a month and fulfilled several functions: coordinating planning, detecting critical issues by including a broad range of competencies in discussions, and serving as a means for the NRA project leader to control and supervise the planning process in terms of an administrative logic of time, cost and deliverables from consultants.

The roles of buyer (*beställare*), namely, the NRA, and executor (*utförare*), namely, the RAC main consultant and his or her sub-consultants, were to some extent spatially indicated at the meetings, since the two groups tended to sit opposite each other around the conference table. Other participants grouped themselves more freely, although NRA officials tended to cluster around the NRA project leader's side of the table, the consultants being on the opposite, 'consultancy' side. The atmosphere was a mixture of formality and informality, and meetings often opened with small talk referring to everyday matters and job-related issues concerning absent people or shared contacts. There was also some turnover of meeting participants as some left for new jobs. Consultants often gave the impression of being extremely diligent, referring to working on weekends and tight deadlines. The group was mixed in terms of gender, with several women in leading roles.

The project meetings were led by the NRA project leader and the RAC leader of the commission. Each meeting had an agenda that was sent out with the invitation to the meeting. A project meeting normally included the NRA project leader, the NRA land negotiator, the NRA environment assessment co-coordinator, and occasionally other 'in-house' NRA experts with competency in other fields relevant to the project. Also attending were consultants from the head consultancy firm, RAC, and sub-consultants the RAC contracted from its own consultancy firms. The consultants were experts in, for example, geology, hydrogeology, tunnel engineering, railway building technology, environmental impact and risk assessment.

The meetings were structured by formal agendas, provided by the RAC leader of the commission and consisting of numerous action points and issues to deal with. A secretary recorded minutes to be distributed with the agenda for the next meeting. The meetings covered a wide range of perspectives: practical, technical, theoretical, political, administrative, organizational, legal and informational. Extremely diverse issues were taken up, including road building, road status, tunnel building, bridge construction, flora and fauna, wild animals and their behaviour, landscape characteristics and values, geological investigations of ground conditions, conditions for farming and agriculture, individual stakeholders and safety of future traffic. Apart from the project meetings, many other, smaller meetings of various specialized planning groups took place.

Another type of meeting – the reference group meetings – included representatives of authorities and stakeholders, as well as the NRA project leader, the NRA environmental impact assessment coordinator, the NRA land negotiation specialist, the RAC project leader and the RAC commission leader. Members were the regional county board, the municipality in whose jurisdiction the railway is planned (represented by a senior official from the technical and physical planning administration and officials from the environmental administration, responsible for environmental protection and biodiversity), the regional public transportation company (West Traffic) and the Road Administration. While the regional county board and the municipality attended every reference group meeting during the study period, the regional public transportation company and the Road Administration only participated on occasion. The reference group meetings were chaired by the NRA official who had been the project leader of the pre-investigation study of the project line. This official assumed the role of the 'living memory' of the past of the project, occasionally reminding the planners of concerns and aims that had been relevant in earlier stages of planning.

Each meeting started with a review of the minutes of the previous meeting, and sometimes the minutes were revised if someone thought that what was written was not entirely accurate. The minutes were not considered official protocols but semi-official documentation for internal use that 'fixed' the status of project matters. The minutes documented the various actors' positions and concerns regarding the many issues discussed at the meetings, such as converting the old line into a cycling route, addressing the matter of central Upland and the area near the planned (but not projected) railway station, gaining access to local bathing lakes, organizing the storage of superfluous excavated landfill, organizing the transport of such material on local roads and designing under- or overpasses for local roads. The minutes spelled out the future status of various local values, which were described and given tangible form: railway station, bathing lake, cycling lane, or potentially hazardous transport of landfill in heavy vehicles. They recorded and confirmed promises, articulating what had been agreed on and from what horizon the future was envisaged.

In the reference group, there was outspoken consensus on the value of coordinated strategies between the municipality, the county board, the NRA and the RAC project team(s) to ensure that the planning process proceeded effectively. The reference group made no decisions but served as an arena for sharing information and discussing the project in which the main official stakeholders and public authorities were represented. Its members made decisions in their own organizations (i.e. the municipality, county board or NRA), and what was discussed at the reference group meetings could inform and influence these decisions. The rationale for the reference group was that it gave official public stakeholders an opportunity for direct access to project development information. They could thus address any concerns or queries they might have to the NRA/RAC leaders, who could then in turn adjust their planning to accommodate concerns of, for example, the municipality or the county board.

Six Months of Station Planning

In the railway planning stage, the NRA was responsible for planning to facilitate a future commuter station in Upland but lacked the mandate to plan for the actual building of such a station. Consequently, the NRA lacked economic means to legally resolve land use issues in the potential station area or compensate landowners. Stations, as part of the rail traffic infrastructure, are the responsibility of the regional public transport company (West Traffic), which, as noted, is to plan for an Upland station only if its estimates indicate demand is sufficient for a profitable train stop in Upland. The railway investigation's mention, and conditional 'promise', of an Upland station came to present a planning problem in the subsequent railway planning stage. The planners had to plan for both the non-station in the railway plan and a possible future station in the real world. We will now, through glimpses into six months of railway planning, follow how railway planners addressed the ambiguous issue of the station (simultaneously a non-station in the near future and an envisioned station in the more distant future) at project meetings and reference group meetings.

At a project meeting on 26 June 2007, the station was brought up for discussion by the RAC project leader, who thought the issue needed to be discussed at a reference group meeting since any future station had a bearing on land use issues. Her planning problem concerned what to do with private land in the potential station area, which was also, she said, a question for the municipality and its general and detailed physical planning of the area.

NRA project leader:	We have to be clear. It is uncertain whether it is going be a station.
RAC project leader:	This will be actualized at the public consultation meeting. We need a sketch of the area in question.
Geological expert:	The municipality has the initiative.
RAC project leader:	We need to prepare this for the consultation meeting. It is important that the municipality participate and can answer questions.

The planners recognized that the municipality had a crucial role regarding planning in Upland, since it had the mandate to make physical land use plans, according to the Planning and Building Act (SFS 1987: 10). Detailed planning identifies specific land uses, such as industry, recreation, housing, community functions, transport infrastructure, cultivation or burial grounds, which are then legally binding. The zoning of land for various uses is legally connected with building permit regulations and legislation regarding specific types of land and land use according to the

Environmental Code. The railway planners identified a need to cooperate with the municipality in planning the public consultation meeting, since they acknowledged that the municipality, through the Planning and Building Act, could influence the construction of any future station. They realized that because of the municipality's central role in any future station, cooperation with the municipality had to be established before facing the local public at the public consultation meeting about the railway plan.

Two months later, on 22 August 2008, the station was again on the agenda when the environmental impact assessment and upcoming public consultation process were discussed at a project meeting. The need for cooperation with the municipality regarding the station area was again emphasized, and the NRA project leader noted that negotiations with the municipality regarding the management of contaminated land were in order. A month later, on 12 September, when discussion of the environmental impact assessment and public consultation meetings was resumed, the question of the station again arose, now in connection with planning the reference group meeting the following week. The railway planners aimed to present plan drawings of the station area at this meeting but did not have final drawings. The NRA project leader said that the reference group members would understand that what was presented at the meeting was work in progress. The RAC commission leader suggested that preliminary sketches of the station area be presented together with a proposal. The NRA project leader emphasized that 'We should plan for things that can be done'. The discussion then moved on to the public consultation meeting and what would be said there. The NRA project leader recommended that 'As little as possible must be said about the station at the consultation meetings – West Traffic does not want any talk of a station'. Nobody questioned this instruction to omit mention of the station in deference to the wishes of the regional transportation company. At this project meeting, the railway planners agreed that the station should not be mentioned in public communications.

This agreed-upon position of silence, however, proved problematic at the reference group meeting a week later (18 September), when the NRA chair noted that the station was mentioned in the railway investigation, that it was in the public mind and that stakeholders (in this case, landowners) were concerned. 'How will it be presented?' he asked. 'We have to agree on how this issue will be dealt with and how we will express ourselves.' The chair then turned to the official from the municipality, the head of the technical and physical planning administration, and asked, 'What do you think?' She answered that planning at this stage should make a future station possible, and continued: 'We will adapt the railway line so that it is possible to build a station – this is what we should say.

People do not care that much.' Some members of the project group, how-ever, strongly disagreed, saying, 'Landowners care – a lot!' The NRA land negotiation specialist then asked whether land would be bought, and the RAC project leader asked how landowners who were going to be affected by a station should be dealt with. The NRA chairman asked whether this could be dealt with voluntarily, and the NRA land negotiation specialist pointed out that land issues had to be discussed with the landowners in advance.

The discussion proceeded to touch on the landowners and properties that would actually be affected by a future station. It was noted that it was problematic that real estate matters could not be regulated in the railway plan, since no station was actually planned. According to the NRA project leader, 'We cannot put the station into the railway plan. We do not have the money to pay for the land needed.' The NRA chairman objected: 'But we cannot sweep this part of the process under the carpet. We need to come to a full stop. We must be clear. We must address this issue later, on but we must be conscious of what we are doing. The only thing that we do know is that West Traffic is "holding the door open".' Then the meeting moved on, from how to manage the non-station when facing the local public, to how to advance towards actualizing the station by means of municipal physical planning intended to influence the planning of the regional transport company. A map with a station location indicated on it was spread out on the table and examined. One problem discussed was a certain highly critical stakeholder's ownership of land adjacent to, or even encroaching on, the future station location. The county board official suggested that 'Maybe it would be best if we kept a low profile'. The chair intervened: 'This is important – the railway investigation had sketches of what the station might look like.' The municipal official then declared the municipality's intentions on this planning issue:

> The municipality will make a detailed plan of the area, and then West Traffic will believe that the municipality believes that Upland will grow. The munici-pality does not actually believe that, but it can make a detailed plan in order to make West Traffic plan for a station in Upland. Times are changing. West Traffic is thinking too much about big cities. Different regional traffic companies have different cultures.

The official then compared West Traffic with another regional public transport company that she believed had a less pronounced urban/sub-urban bias.

After some discussion of crossings between roads and the railway line, the county board official wanted to make a point. He said that a mes-sage he had from the regional county board chief executive Göran Bengtsson was giving 'a clear signal regarding the Trollhättan package, that the county board would be supportive and adaptable. We are the long arm of the state. Göran Bengtsson has spoken to the Department (of Industry). This does not have to be in any notes'. With this statement, the county board official signalled to the group that the county board did not intend to make trouble, that is, did not intend to veto the railway plan. This interjection conveyed the county board's commitment to joint action (Bratman 1992; Gilbert 2006).

The public consultation meeting on 23 October was well attended, attracting approximately 100 local residents who came to learn about the railway plan. The NRA project leader mentioned the station in passing in her introduction to the meeting, which explained the aim of the consultation meeting and the objectives of the railway project. She pointed out that a double-track railway would make it possible to increase railway traffic and raise speeds up to 250 km/h, that it would take just thirty or even twenty-five minutes to go by train from Trollhättan to Göteborg, and that safety would be improved by flyover crossings between road and railway. Then she mentioned the timeline, finances and legal licensing of the project and explained the main arguments in favour of the chosen corridor: Upland was going to grow, the chosen corridor would produce less noise disturbance than the other alternatives, it would have no barrier effect on the community, it would limit the catastrophic consequences of railway accidents, and it would facilitate access to a future station. The station, however, was not mentioned any further.

At the reference group meeting a month later, on 30 November, discussion of the station continued. The municipal official said that the physical general plan in Upland was going to be revised in 2008.

> The local building committee will take up the question of the detailed plan for the station area. We will clearly show West Traffic that Upland is going to grow and that we are serious. This is what they did in Small town.[10] The climate questions ... Much is happening now.... We should go in and buy land right now. Land will be cheaper as long as there is no detailed plan.

The municipal official here referred again to the strategy of trying to influence West Traffic indirectly through planning actions on zoning intended to influence the planning actions of the regional public transportation company. In attempting to influence West Traffic, however, the municipality did not explicitly express its intentions – that is, the municipality did not tell West Traffic that it would promote population growth in Upland and wanted West Traffic to start planning for a station. Instead, it used an indirect strategy – zoning planning (consisting of overview plans and detailed plans) – to display the municipality's belief in a scenario of future population growth in Upland. The municipality understood that such a demonstration might sway West Traffic to effect changes in its plans that would 'open the doors' for the station.

The Planning of Planning:
Hypercomplexity in Social Interaction

The concept of 'double contingency' in social interaction (see Vanderstraeten 2002), originally introduced by Talcott Parsons and Edward Shils (1951), has been further developed by Niklas Luhmann (1995). Double contingency captures the circumstance in which social actors are dependent on each other as reflective subjects, with the effect that 'each actor is *both* acting agent and object of orientation *both* to himself and to the others' (Parsons 1968: 436). Social interaction therefore has fundamental inbuilt uncertainty: not only can future actions not be predicted with absolute certainty, but observed actions cannot be interpreted with certainty. Social interaction therefore has two contingencies: 'the contingency of what an actor actually does in the context of an elementary interaction situation and the contingency of the other's reaction to what is being done' (Vanderstraeten 2002: 80).

The double contingency of social interaction prompts several basic questions relating to the coordination of collective action in societal planning. How do actors understand and relate to each other, and how does this understanding influence their planning? What expectations do they have of each other, and how do such expectations guide their actions? Double contingency is therefore directly relevant to the planning and coordination of collective action in that it opens up opportunities for secondary observations. As Luhmann points out, planning comprises both first-order planning and observations of planning: 'System planning necessarily produces hypercomplexity. Planning … will plan itself and its effects together. Thus budget planning creates exaggerated reports of needs, and the one who is planning can take this into consideration' (Luhmann 1995: 471). Such reflexive planning of planning stems from the uncertainties of the relational and directed subjectivities of the actors, who relate to each other as both agents and observed objects.

Luhmanns's (1995: 471) idea of hypercomplexity addresses the circumstance that system planning includes observations of planning undertaken by others. Planners take into account how their planning will be observed, interpreted and understood by other planners. As this railway planning case indicates, expectations as to the intentions, interpretations and actions of others (e.g., which co-planners or stakeholders might be affected by planning decisions) constitute a crucial (social) dimension of planning. The Upland railway line reference group became an arena for hypercomplex system planning and the coordination of actors in which they were able, as Luhmann would put it (1995: 471), to 'observe' each other's planning agendas so that they could adjust their own agendas to those of others.

The ethnographic glimpses of six months of various institutional actors' railway planning work concerning the Upland station issue sheds light on some of the social dynamics of hypercomplexity in planning. Various planners plan their own planning based on interpretations and understandings of the other planners' intentions and strategies. They also try to influence each other by means of planning actions, conveying intentions and strategies to which they foresee other planners responding in certain ways. The Upland station case illustrates cooperation between the municipal administration and the NRA in which the municipality assumes a central role. By means of zoning planning, the municipality hoped to induce West Traffic to plan for the building of a station in Upland. This shows that hypercomplexity is not mere reactive anticipation but a proactive attitude, since planners – in this case the municipality – actively, although implicitly, seek to influence the planning of other planners, such as the regional transport company West Traffic, by communicating belief and intentionality. The municipality used physical planning (i.e., designating areas for housing, roads, schools, a railway station, etc.) to convey a visionary promise about the future of Upland. In doing so, the municipality hopes to induce West Traffic to invest in a station in Upland, which will eventually promote community growth.

Concluding Discussion

Throughout the process, the Upland station had two planning contexts – the railway investigation and the railway plan – that were simultaneously continuous (in terms of planning sequencing) and discontinuous (in terms of planning substance). The railway investigation framed the station in the context of broad transportation policy goals aimed at increasing commuting and regional growth. The station was part of a vision of regional commuter train traffic. In the subsequent railway planning stage, the task was to address a real-world local context where a station in a small community in the remote Swedish countryside was not deemed economically viable by the public transport company assigned the task of organizing regional traffic based on market conditions. This contrast between broad policy visions and the actual organization of the conditions for regional public transport made planning the railway station quite problematic. The planners responded to the ambiguity of the station issue by planning with foresight, anticipating what other key actors might do, and trying to influence other planners' intentions so as to achieve their goals.

Communication between planners is vital to the planning process, since planners must continually review and ensure the validity of the mutual responsiveness, commitment and support that condition their joint efforts (Bratman 1992, 1999). Meetings are thus the modus operandi of railway planning: they enable the coordination of planning and action to ensure that stakeholders and experts reach a working agreement. At meetings, planners can express reservations and demands, making their viewpoints and positions transparent in a semi-public space. Meetings are arenas where planners observe each other, build expectations about other planners' disposition to plan and, on the basis of such observations, interact and coordinate to accomplish joint plans by establishing of managerial hegemonic positions (Räisenen and Linde 2004).

The unfolding of the cooperative planning of a railway station of ambiguous ontology, in which planning encompasses both a 'non-station' (that will not be built) and a promised station (that might be built in the more distant future), has shown how crucial joint commitment and personal trust are within the community of railway planners (Bratman 1992, 1999; Gilbert 2006). The case highlights how the planners – NRA officials, consultants, officials from the municipality and the county board – formed a community of planners, bound by a commitment to joint action (Bratman 1992, 1999), to plan a new railway line. This community of planners built solidarity to advance the project's realization, for example, in relation to private stakeholders who might want to hinder or stop it. Private stakeholders were sometimes discussed at the meetings, and information was disseminated about problematic individuals and their possible plans to appeal the railway plan. Other such identified planners who did not share the commitment to joint action vis-à-vis the railway plan were handled by means of joint planning strategies, so as to achieve 'smooth' and hegemonic planning.

As this case illustrates, a crucial difference between individual and collective action is that in collective action, individual actions and their effectiveness depend on the actions of others (Pierson 2000). As we have seen, planning is not a result of isolated planned actions but of the layered reflexive communication of intentions and beliefs, within a community of planners bound by a joint commitment to facilitate the coming into existence of a new railway line. A social anthropological perspective can offer a neutral (i.e., non-normative) standpoint for the 'viewing of views' (Ingold 2000: 15) in researching the interaction between and 'commerce' of perspectives and situated action in planning. Following Strathern's (2000: 285) recommendation to focus on the flow of social interaction and understanding, the 'balancing' of action and accounting, (doing and saying), this ethnographic account has aimed for a comprehensive approach to intentionality and contextuality.

Notes

1. Dnr F07-2988/SA20, 2007-03-13.
2. Building was planned to commence in 2009, and the project was scheduled to be finished in 2012. The railway investigation report was completed in June 2006 and the National Rail Administration submitted the proposal to the government in March 2007 for permitting, the completion of which was finally announced in May 2008. In the meantime, the National Rail Administration project management team of planners and designers worked on the detailed railway plan for the selected route. The project is projected to cost SEK 1.2 billion.
3. The name of the community is fictitious.
4. BRVT 2006:01, 2006-01-25, Norge Vänerbanan. Dubbelspår Velanada-Prässebo, p. 6.
5. BRVT 2006:01, 2006-01-25, Norge Vänerbanan. Dubbelspår Velanada-Prässebo, pp. 28–30.
6. BRTV 2006:01, 2006-01-25, Norge Vänerbanan. Dubbeslspår Velanada-Prässebo, p. 29
7. BRVT 2006:01, 2006-01-25, Norge Vänerbanan. Dubbeslspår Velanada-Prässebo, pp. 22–23, 30.
8. BRVT 2006:01, 2006-01-25, Norge Vänerbanan. Dubbeslspår Velanada-Prässebo, p. 93.
9. The county board is a regional-level public administration with a mandate to coordinate various interests from an overall national perspective. It also has supervisory powers to ensure observance of laws and regulations, and acts as an environmental licensing authority issuing permits and setting conditions for permits for activities that could harm the environment, in accordance with the Environmental Code.
10. A community along the Norway–Väner line where West Traffic decided to build a train station. The name of this community is fictitious.

References

Beaumont, M. and M. Freeman (eds). 2007. *The Railway and Modernity: Time, Space and the Machine Ensemble.* Oxford: Peter Lang.

Binde, P. and Å. Boholm. 2004. 'The Discursive Amplification of Risk in a Swedish Case of Rail Track Planning', in Boholm, Å. and R. Löfstedt (eds), *Facility Siting: Risk, Power and Identity in Land-Use Planning.* London: Earthscan, pp. 160–176.

Boholm, Å. 2008. 'The Public Meeting as a Theatre of Dissent: Risk and Hazard in Land Use Planning', *Journal of Risk Research* 11(1–2): 119–140.

———. (ed.). 2000. *National Objectives – Local Objections: Railway Modernization in Sweden.* Göteborg: CEFOS.

————. and Löfstedt, R. (eds). 2004. *Facility Siting: Risk, Power and Identity in Land Use Planning*. Earthscan: London.

Bratman, M.E. 1992. 'Shared Cooperative Activity', *The Philosophical Review* 101(2): 327–341.

————. 1999. *Intentions, Plans, and Practical Reason*. Stanford, CA: CSLI Publications.

Carter, I. 2001. *Railways and Culture in Britain: The Epitome of Modernity*. Manchester: Manchester University Press.

Corvellec, H. 2001. 'Talks on Tracks: Debating Urban Infrastructure Projects', *Studies in Cultures, Organizations and Societies* 7(1): 25–53.

Falkemark, G. 2006. *Politik, mobilitet och miljö. Om den historiska framväxten av ett ohållbart transportsystem*. Hedemora: Gidlunds förlag.

Flyvbjerg, B. 1998. *Rationality and Power: Democracy in Practice*. Chicago: University of Chicago Press.

Gilbert, M. 2006. *A Theory of Political Obligation*. Oxford: Oxford University Press.

Harrington, R. 2000. 'The Railway Journey and the Neurosis of Modernity', in R. Wrigley and G. Revill (eds.), *Pathologies of Travel*. Amsterdam and Atlanta: Editions Rodopi B.V., pp. 229–260.

Hobart, M. 1993. 'Introduction: The Growth of Ignorance?' in M. Hobart (ed.), *An Anthropological Critique of Development*. London: Routledge, pp. 1–30.

Ingold, T. 2000. *The Perception of the Environment: Essays in Livelihood, Dwelling and Skill*. London: Routledge.

Karlsson, M. 2010. 'Göta Älv River Risk Governance: A Case Study of Consensus-style Regulation', in *CEFOS rapport 2010:1*. Göteborg: Centrum för forskning om offentlig sektor (CEFOS).

Kelman, S. 1981. *Regulating America, Regulating Sweden*. Cambridge, Mass.: MIT Press.

Konopasek, Z., T. Stöckelova and L. Zamykalov. 2008. 'Making Pure Science and Pure Politics: On the Expertise of Bypass and the Bypass of Expertise', *Science, Technology and Human Values* 33(4): 529–553.

Laclau, E. and C. Mouffe. 1985. *Hegemony and Socialist Strategy: Towards a Radical Democratic Politics*. London: Verso.

Lave, J. 1988. *Cognition in Practice*. Cambridge: Cambridge University Press.

————. 1997. 'The Culture of Acquisition and the Practice of Understanding', in D. Kirschner and J. Whitson (eds) *Situated Cognition: Social, Semiotic, And Psychological Perspectives*. Mahwah, NJ: Lawrence Erlbaum Associates, pp. 17–35.

————, and Wenger, E. 1991. *Situated Learning*. New York: Cambridge University Press.

Löfstedt, R.E. 2005. *Risk Management in Post Trust Societies*. Basingstoke: Palgrave.

Luhmann, N. 1995. *Social Systems*. Stanford, CA: Stanford University Press.

Lundqvist, L. 1980. *The Hare and the Tortoise: Clean Air Policy in the United States and Sweden*. Ann Arbor: University of Michigan Press.

Marcus, G. 1995. 'Ethnography in/of the World System: The Emergence of Multi-sited Ethnography', *Annual Review of Anthropology* 24: 95–117.

O'Toole Jr., L.J. 2003. 'Interorganizational Relations in Implementation', in B.G. Peters and J. Pierre (eds), *The Handbook of Public Administration*. Los Angeles and London: Sage, pp. 142–152.

Parsons, T. 1968. 'Social Interaction', in D.L. Sills (ed.), *International Encyclopedia of the Social Sciences*, vol. 12. New York: MacMillan.

————. and E. Shils. 1951. 'Categories of the Orientation and Organization of Action', in T. Parsons and E. Shils (eds), *Toward a General Theory of Social Action*. Cambridge, MA: Harvard University Press.

Pierson, P. 2000. 'Increasing Returns, Path Dependency, and the Study of Politics', *The American Political Science Review* 94(2): 251–267.

Pressman, J.L. and A. Wildavsky. 1973. *Implementation: How Great Expectations in Washington Are Dashed in Oakland*. Berkeley: University of California Press.

Räisenen, C. and A. Linde. 2004. 'Technologizing Discourse to Standardise Projects in Multi-project Organizations: Hegemony by Consensus?' *Organization* 11(1): 101–121.

Saint, M., R.J. Flavell and P.F. Fox. 2009. *NIMBY Wars: The Politics of Land Use*. Hingham, MA: Saint University Press.

Stoffle, R., M.N. Zedeno, A. Eisenberg, R. Toupal and A. Carroll. 2004. 'Shifting Risks: Hoover Dam Bridge Impacts on American Indian Sacred Landscape', in Å. Boholm and R. Löfstedt (eds.), *Facility Siting: Risk, Power and Identity in Land Use Planning*. London: Earthscan, pp. 127–143.

Statens Offentliga Utredningar [SOU] 2009. Höghastighetsbanor – ett samhällsbygge för stärkt utveckling och konkurrenskraft. SOU 2009: 74, URL: http://www.regeringen.se/content/1/c6/13/14/95/7db8099f.pdf (retrieved 2013-01-21).

Strathern, M. 2000. 'Afterword: Accountability', in M. Strathern (ed.), *Audit Cultures: Anthropological Studies in Accountability, Ethics and the Academy*. London and New York: Routledge.

Suchman, L. 2003. 'Organizing Alignment: The Case of Bridge-building', in D. Nicolini, S. Gherardi and D. Yanow (eds), *Knowing in Organizations: A Practice-based Approach*. Armonk, NY, and London: M.E. Sharp, pp. 187–203.

Svensk Författningssamling [SFS]. 1987. Plan- och bygglag [Planning and building act]. SFS 1987:10, URL: http://www.riksdagen.se/sv/Dokument-Lagar/Lagar/Svenskforfattningssamling/Plan--och-bygglag-198710_sfs-1987-10/ (retrieved 2013-01-21)

———. 1998. Miljöbalk [Environmental code]. SFS 1998: 808, URL: http://www.riksdagen.se/sv/Dokument-Lagar/Lagar/Svenskforfattningssamling/_sfs-1998-808/ (retrieved 2013-01-21)

———. 1995. Lag om byggande av järnväg [Railway building act]. SFS 1995: 1649, URL: http://www.riksdagen.se/sv/Dokument-Lagar/Lagar/Svenskforfattningssamling/sfs_sfs-1995-1649/ (retrieved 2013-01-21)

van den Hove, S. 2006. 'Between Consensus and Compromise: Acknowledging the Negotiation Dimension in Participatory Approaches', *Land Use Policy* 23: 10–17.

Vanderstraeten, R. 2002. 'Parsons, Luhmann and the Theorem of Double Contingency', *Journal of Classical Sociology* 2: 77–92.

Vogel, D. 1986. *National Styles of Regulation: Environmental Policy in Great Britain and the United States*. Ithaca, NY: Cornell University Press.

Winter, S. 2003. 'Implementation Perspectives: Status and Reconsideration', in B.G. Peters and J. Pierre (eds), *The Handbook of Public Administration*. Los Angeles and London: Sage.

City of Cuzco. Source: Philip Baird, www.anthroarcheart.org

Chapter 3

INVADED CITY

Structuring Urban Landscapes on the Margins of the Possible (Peru's Southern Highlands)

Sarah Lund

Introduction

Recent discussions about the ambiguities of bureaucracies and regulatory practices focus on contexts described as marginal to the state – borderlands or 'third spaces' (Das and Poole 2004). Such marginal placement is neither fully within accepted practice nor outside existing bureaucratic parameters. The in-between quality of these situations sheds light on many conflicting assumptions concerning citizenship and other kinds of belonging the nature of property and its evolving often contradictory valuations within the nation state; and understandings of the nation state that go beyond concrete territory within fixed political-economic boundaries to encompass third-space encounters of subjugation and resistance. From the borderland vantage, it becomes clear that the state, often in contradictory ways, projects spatial images by the ways it lays claim to territory. Such tropes can play out as conflicting and unintelligible in the personal lived experience of marginally placed people, especially when relating to bureaucratic practices.

This chapter sees the borderland face of planning and regulatory practice as endemic to bureaucracies, especially during times of mass movement, when state intervention and regulation is required and legitimated as a means to gain control over rapid change and informal initiatives. Here such issues will be examined through the prism of land invasions in Peru's southern highlands. During the 1970s a time when land reform legislation was being implemented, the peasantry invaded hacienda lands through-out the countryside as an informal means of accelerating expropriation. The political consequences and lessons learned from these actions are cur-rently debated (cf. Mallon 1998; Stern 1998). From various field observa-tions and experiences beginning in 1977 in the agricultural cooperative at Pincos (Andahuaylas), to the immediate aftermath of invasions in Lima in 1981, through stories of invasions on 'abandoned' lands in Chanchamayo in 1984, and finally to the changing urban landscape of Cuzco from 1977 to 2004, invasions emerge as a strategy with a recognizable logic and pro-gression, even as they are found to be difficult to control and rife with haphazard developments.

The historical context of confrontation and the disparate cultural en-counters land invasions generate reveal slippage between official and in-formal understandings. In such situations, powerfully projected images and categories of national territory become objects of political negotiation and repositioning.

History of a Dichotomy

In Peru, national spaces are described in terms of the discrete regions of local and national life. Indigenous peasant communities in particular are localized at a cultural and social 'remove' from national life, imagined as existing on a geographically distant margin designated as essentially ru-ral and uncivilized (Poole 2004). Furthermore, Peru's geography is clas-sified into three contrasting zones that dominate the national landscape: the narrow Pacific coast with its large population centres, centralized state administration, and economic wherewithal; the rugged Andean region that stretches down the middle of the country, imposing a physical bar-rier seen as inhibiting modernization as well as physical movement; and the eastern lowlands of Amazonas with their rich natural resources, envi-sioned as awaiting national expansion and settlement. Centralized Peru-vian bureaucracies and styles of governance project the spatial imagery of national territory in terms of centre and periphery – the central coast and the periphery east of the Andes – that is, from the urban out to its sur-rounding hinterlands.

Peru's territorial imagery was forged by the country's historically central role in Spain's colonial empire, which was envisioned as part of a wider Christian evangelization campaign and associated with ideas of a truly global order (Muldoon 1991). Throughout all of Spanish America, indig-enous populations were ruled under a specific administration and laws, *á repúblico de los indios,* quite separate from what applied for the Spanish and Creole populations (cf. Thurner 1999). Especially in Peru, many indigenous Andean peoples were forcibly resettled into nucleated towns (*reducciones*) where Spanish order and values of governance were imposed. From 1570 on, these nucleated town settlements facilitated evangelization and made bureaucratic ordering more effective (Gose 2008). As Christian places, nucleated towns were spaces envisioned as interspersed within an otherwise evil landscape of demons and idolatrous practice (Gose 2008). Today these towns remain centres of bureaucratic administration, jurisprudence, religious institutional life and economic activity.

After independence in 1825, the 'Two Republic' administrative model in Peru was abolished, yet many structural aspects of the model remained in place into modern times (cf. Walker 1999). In particular, indigenous tribute or 'labour tax', though abolished in 1854, was periodically reinstated throughout much of the nineteenth and early portions of the twentieth centuries (Larson 2004). The 'discursive flux' characteristic of the Republican period (Thurner 1999: 35) is also discernible in the vacillating government policies of the twentieth century. While positing a cohesive nation, shifting government policies today continue to project Peru as made up of contradictory populations of indigenous tributary subjects and individual propertied citizens. For example, mandatory communal work projects quite similar to aspects of the old tribute system have been required of indigenous populations living in the dispersed 'annexes' of uplands surrounding nucleated towns. Administrators in the nucleated district capitals demand labour contributions from inhabitants of outlying settlements on the grounds of their rural residency outside of the towns, a much resented practice.

During the nineteenth century and into the twentieth, landholding estates or haciendas in the highlands expanded their boundaries onto the communal territories of dispersed peasant communities on their periphery. Many landless people became bonded labourers (*feudetarios*) living out their lives in a world unto itself, where all authority rested with the hacienda owner or *hacendado*. Within the hacienda, the hacendado wielded a form of privatized public power, a function of his historical status as representative of both the state and the principal forms of private and extrajudicial power (Poole 2004).

Hacienda exploitation and territorial expansion were partially functions of the ambiguous status of the independent peasant communities known as Comunidades Campesinas, which were internally administered as corporate entities with land held jointly within the group. In the southern Andes, territorial conflicts with other communities, and between the community and local hacienda encroachment, were endemic (cf. Mallon 1998). These regional pressures further fostered closed corporate organizational forms in which internal legal matters were dealt with by customary law, for example in land use issues and border conflicts. Simultaneously and to varying degrees, community members were individual citizens with rights and obligations as Peruvian citizens, which was particularly apparent when they travelled beyond their own localities or relocated to other regions. In such circumstances the corporate status of belonging to one of the Comunidades Campesinas held little relevance. As private persons, each was subject to the individual contractual requirements of Peruvian citizens (Lund 2001).

Twentieth-century policymakers in Peru proposed a number of contradictory citizenship regimes whereby spatial and political identities were fused to varying degrees and state policy activated communities' efforts to register and gain legal recognition. First, the 1920 constitution reinstated corporatist principles of communal landholdings and gave peasant communities incentive to gain legal recognition and juridical status over communal territories. This marked the state's emergence as a powerful regulator in the countryside that would insure indigenous communities' strong precedence in subsequent years. Agrarian reform was the single most noteworthy attempt to create a 'corporatist citizenship regime' (Yashar 2005) at a time of huge land inequalities and pervasive peasant mobilizations (cf. de la Cadena 2000). The landowning classes were dismantled via expropriation, and by 1977 the haciendas were virtually eradicated (McClintock 1981). President Velasco complemented his agrarian reform legislation with a statute on Comunidades Campesinas, reorganizing them along cooperative lines to fit standardized forms of political organization. This undercut traditional forms of leadership and participation, but by reorganizing in the newly prescribed way, peasant communities were able to legally reclaim lands previously lost to the haciendas.

In addition to reorganizing the Andean countryside, Velasco promoted colonization projects east of the Andes that channelled migrants onto lands officially designated 'abandoned' and thereby state-owned. Acquiring use rights over such sites involved petitioning and eventually, in some cases, titling. Such experiences in lowland colonization projects fostered appreciation for the sites that had potential for settlement. Pinpointing 'abandoned' state-owned sites became part of the strategy for land occupancy, and regulating abandoned status would remain a contentious issue.

By the early 1980s, much of what Velasco's socialist-inspired reforms had set in motion was already under revision. President Morales Bermudez gradually replaced the corporatist model of citizenship suggested by Velasco's peasant community organizations with ideas privileging the role of the individual in both the political and economic arenas. Protected land regimes in the indigenous Comunidades Campesinas were challenged, and the loans and various improvement programmes that had supported agriculture within the land reform cooperatives were withdrawn. Vacillation of national rural/agricultural policy resulted in redistributing parcels of land, which eventually could become titled as privately owned, to individual workers. Passage of the Ley de Tierras (Law 26505) lifted protections for community-held lands, and the size of private land holdings was no longer capped.

Urbanization in the southern highlands over the last forty years must be understood in terms of the shared historical experience of people being both corporate and private persons (Lund 2001; cf. Ødegaard 2010). Because this ambiguousness has spatial implications in the complex imagery of Peruvian landscape, the experience of this dual status is highlighted by movement over boundaries between rural and urban areas. Large-scale migration from the Andean hinterlands, particularly massive during the insurgency of the 1980s and 1990s, must be understood in this light. And seen through the lens of the planning and administration of the new urban communities that arose during the civil upheavals, the contrasting regimes – formal organizational administration versus cultural understandings and misunderstandings of autonomous collective identities – become apparent in a particularly forceful way.

Land Invasions as National 'Third Spaces'

Exploration of Peruvian 'young towns' (Lloyd, 1980) or *pueblos jovenes* and their establishment provides a prism through which to discuss planning as a response to social movements and historical change. Many urban settlements in Peru were initiated by land invasions similar in planning and application to those occurring in the countryside in response to hacienda expropriations and rural popular mobilizations. As the cases presented below will show, the contrast between urban and agricultural land invasions lay in official codifications rather than physical distance. Rural expropriated property often abutted urban settlements and was easily targeted for invasion. Urban invasions and settlements often started as not-very-rural affairs.

It has been suggested that these dramatic developments in Peru's cities were officially regarded as a convenient means to solve Peru's notoriously large, ever-growing housing shortage (cf. Driant 1991). Although building societies were sometimes organized to control the development of new neighbourhoods, urban squatters were largely left to arrange their own water, sewage, public transport, educational facilities and the like. Residents appointed councils to request services from the government and mobilized themselves to pool resources in ways similar to the corporate governance forms fostered in the recognized Comunidades Campesinas. Nevertheless, residents of the *pueblos jovenes* had the long-term goal of acquiring private title to their homes, despite the long process of 'corporate' acquisition that was prelude to such titling.

The contradictions of planning practice in response to land invasion have been described as 'urban inversion' (de Soto 1990), whereby first an individual occupies a residential lot as part of group occupancy, then a house is constructed through incremental stages and ultimately, many years later, individual title to the property is attained. Government planners and settlers both must renegotiate the status of ownership and the nature of emergent private property during this process. The ambiguity of such situations is obvious. Illegal practices involving property rights gradually become encapsulated within the formal prescriptions of urban planning and organization. The state local bureaucracy is participatory in this process, both in its permissiveness in overlooking illegal activity and in the degree to which urban neighbourhoods are allowed to evolve along the lines of their own plans for the future. I would not suggest that the permissive response to land invasions is uniform, or that it is purely an attempt to incorporate excluded portions of the population into the fabric of the nation. Yet the long-term consequences of urban administrative organization suggest (Lund 2001) that the urban processes observed here denote profound ramifications for the nature of the state. Indigenous urbanization on the national map is a dawning transformation facilitated by the long-standing intimate spaces between the formal and vernacular styles of governance.

How, then, might we view these urban transformations from planned chaos to ordered surroundings as intimately related to the dynamic interrelationships of a social movement, of bureaucratic expectations and responses, and of chance encounters? First I would address this question in terms of value constructions of national space as ethnically marked.

Confounding Urban Cuzco

In Peruvian national imagery, the concept of the urban is problematic and often misleading. As has been discussed above, urban spaces have long been privileged in Peru, and grasping the diversity of urban realities is confounded by the variety of strategies that categorize citizens in terms of a value hierarchy of place. Class, ethnicity and race have historically been glossed in terms of the dichotomous contrast between the urban and the rural (cf. Orlove 1993). After discussing the valuation of urban space in Cuzco from an upper-class perspective, I will consider relocation to urban settings through the prism of rural land invasions and their subsequent 'domestication' in the city landscapes of Cuzco. Urbanization is increasingly perceived as a gateway to the making of a middle-class life in Peru, implying that upward social mobility becomes a specifically urban spatial phenomenon. Old hierarchies are challenged in this displacement.

Drinking late afternoon tea in an upper-class home overlooking Cuzco in the early 1990s, I was taken aback by a conversation about the panoramic view of the city. The hostess and several of her guests, who had grown up in Cuzco City in the early 1940s, were lamenting the dramatic changes evident in the contemporary view spread before us. Beyond the demarcated colonial city centre, encircling mountains were illuminated by the electric street lights of recent settlements. According to the emotional conversation around the table, the mountains had been taken over by rural squatters and no one was doing anything to control the situation. In the women's childhood, no settlements had disturbed the view because the uplands encircling the city had been privately owned, either as marginal hacienda lands or as part of the extensive territories held even then by the church (cf. Jacobsen 1997; Mejia Navariete 1990). Now, however, Indian *campesinos* (*Indios campesinos*) were being allowed to invade Cuzco's uplands as a direct result of the expropriation of their families' haciendas after the land reform of 1969. By invading marginal land, peasants from the countryside had found a way to relocate their families in Cuzco, and the beautiful view of the city was ruined forever.

The rural/urban perceptions suggested by the social conversation were surprising because land reform had always been seen as a tool for social change in rural Peru. David Collier (1976) even suggested that the legislation was consciously promoted as a policy to discourage urbanization. The Velasco government clearly intended to break the economic and political stranglehold of the old hacendado families in the hinterlands, give agricultural lands to local peasants either through cooperative organization or as private parcels, and thereby invigorate rural corporate traditions. For these women of Cuzco, however, land reform had ruined Peru's southern highland cities by opening them to an unprecedented degree of rural urban migration. According to my hostess and her friends, the result was geographic chaos where earlier there had been order and harmony.

Official contrasts, for example, in the national census, also insist upon imageries of separation and contrast between rural and urban rather than seeing them as inter-dynamic sites with shared overlapping histories. Two instances of land invasions on the margins of the city of Cuzco, discussed below, will reveal such places to be converging upon and shaping the standardized categorizations of urban and rural regulated land tenure systems, whose boundaries obscure much of what the city of Cuzco is (cf. Mendoza 2004).

Land Invasions: A Rural Precedence Brought to Town

As a strategy, land invasions appear to be systematically applied in rural areas in conjunction with land reform legislation. Reviewing the situation of 1973 in Andahuaylas, some authors (Mallon 1998) discuss how particular haciendas in the region were specifically targeted by leftist leaders within the peasant mobilization leagues originally organized as part of the land reform initiative in the first place. In one case, two competing communities invaded the hacienda at Pincos: one group of workers led by local leaders were encouraged to invade Pincos by the departing hacendado, who wanted his own workers to take over the estate, and a second group from a neighbouring community whom outside agitators mobilized to take over Pincos, the last hacienda invaded in the province. When local villagers blockaded the road, there was a violent confrontation and someone was killed. The peasant invasions reflected local conflicts and, in more positive terms, demonstrated unusual leadership skills, political strategy and unexpected alliances (Skar 1984). In the case at Pincos, both local peasant communities and more distant villages led by a politically radicalized leadership sought to expedite the stalled expropriation process. Rural land invasions became part of a national drama in which occupancy implemented expropriation and agrarian reform legislation was accomplished. Haciendas finally were expropriated after the fact of their being physically occupied.

In subsequent years, land invasion also became the paradigm for urban expansion in the sierra. The hacienda and urban invasions I have known, some of land abutting city limits in places such as Cuzco, can be seen as related phenomena. With the expropriation of Cuzco's haciendas, marginal lands on the slopes above the city were purposefully targeted for invasion. An ongoing concern aired frequently amongst the urban invaders echoed discussions I had heard many times on the agrarian cooperative at Pincos: would former landowners be allowed to reclaim land left fallow?

Were the hacendados coming back? Indeed, if agrarian cooperatives were unable to keep the expropriated lands productive, reclamation became a possibility.

While agricultural cooperative members expressed concern that the hacendados would be allowed to return to take over uncultivated lands, fallow marginal lands on the fringes of cities like Cuzco were rather seen as opportunities. Open terrain expropriated as agricultural in the 1970s that was still unutilized by the early 1980s invited invasions as a means of solving an ever growing housing crisis faced by migrants and young city dwellers alike. Unutilized agricultural land administered by cooperatives invited the return of hacendados, while similar lands bordering the city came to be viewed as inviting migrant occupancy. A conversion of rationalities occurred between agricultural land and urbanization, and a new kind of competition arose between individual farmers, referred to as 'hacendados', and groups of migrants from the countryside with their counterclaim that the land reform was intended for them.

Once land reform had opened up Cuzco to new kinds of settlement, the process was dramatically accelerated when Sendero Luminoso's armed struggle in the rural areas largely west of Cuzco in the 1980s and 1990s (Contreras 1991) forced many people from the beleaguered department of Apurimac to flee their communities, arriving in Cuzco virtually destitute. This population pressure at the margins of the city occurred at a time when land tenure issues related to the land reform had played out to a certain extent. Indeed, Mallon (1998) has argued that both discontent with the agrarian reform outcome and the reform's peasant mobilization programmes were significant factors in the emergence of Sendero Luminoso in the first place.

The two urban invasions discussed below occurred at a time when other interested individuals from influential Cuzco families had already attempted to acquire fallow lands of ex-haciendas on the grounds that the cooperatives were not keeping them under cultivation – that they were 'abandoned'. Their claims couched in terms of agricultural goals and national needs, held hidden motivations, in particular the prospect of acquiring lucrative areas for development. At first the claimant farmed the expropriated lands in order to occupy them and meet the requirements laid down by the Ministry of Agriculture. However, throughout the 1980s and 1990s, much of the legal activity concerning claims and counterclaims to these fields was driven by an underlying appreciation that in the future, such areas would become urban developments. Well-informed Cuzcenos therefore vied for rights to cultivate 'fallow' agricultural lands in hopes of being able to realize their potential as real estate in the future.

Meanwhile, distressed migrants from politically volatile areas of Apurimac were arriving in large numbers. They viewed expropriated lands as ideally theirs by the intention of the law, arguing that the upland acreage should be turned over to rural agricultural workers and peasant community members such as themselves. In many instances they articulated their claims further, citing the fact that they had been forced from their own communities by the violence. Their acute need gave a sense of social justice to their actions and demands, especially because the state had been unable to protect them in their home provinces. Though the invasions were illegal, the government's attitude was a permissive one aimed at diffusing political demands and meeting the dramatic needs of displacement.

Intimate Occupancy: A Way Forward

In Cuzco two urban development sites, which I refer here to as Federacìon Rosapata, invaded in the early 1980s, and Federacìon Limatambo, invaded in the early 1990s, illustrate the ongoing realization of the conversion from propertied hacienda to urban dwelling site. The two circumstances exhibit similarities as well as significant differences, and their comparison enables a consideration of various planning solutions over time. Discussing these associations can lead to appreciation of how spontaneous takeovers came to be incorporated into the urban fabric of the city of Cuzco. Planning was a necessary component of the process, as were litigation and a series of resettlements/realignments. Nevertheless, much was also accomplished in anticipation of planning, in expectation of litigation and in appreciation of the need to realign boundaries over the course of several years. With reference to the organized initiative of the residents as informal and outside the law (de Soto 1990), I will explore how such settlements gradually become institutionalized through the participation of many interest groups composed of people with overlapping identities, all with a particular appreciation of a shared historical experience in the recent past.

On the steep mountainsides above Cuzco's airport, land invasions at Rosapata in the early 1980s took place by gradual accretion rather than sudden takeover. First, mat huts were put up on uncultivated margins along the roadside and in between cultivated fields in a checkerboard of urban/agricultural settlement, initially in the lower section of 3 hectares but gradually expanding to the upper area of 2.2 hectares. Earlier, in the late 1970s, the Agricultural Ministry had given title to an individual farmer from Cuzco with no prior connection to the property. Referred to as the *hacendado*, the man planted maize in the fields to make his claim tangible. When people began to build houses amongst his fields he went to court, arguing that the land was zoned for agricultural use and not for dwellings. However, the eighty-two households persisted in building and in 1984 established the formal organization of Federacìon Rosapata.

Confrontations with the farmer continued for years. One household kept pigs in an enclosed garden, pegging them out to graze along the verges of the fields. Complaining that pigs were getting loose in his maize and causing damage, the farmer demanded compensation. The pig owner refused: the farmer had no proof and could have been making up the story to harass them. Subsequently the pigs began to die, and the hacendado was suspected of poisoning them, again an accusation without evidence. Accusation, intimidation and suspicion were ongoing aspects of the personal relationships between squatters and farmer as they competed for the rights to land at Rosapata.

Besides keeping domestic animals, most families planted their own plots with maize and vegetables in the first decade of settling Rosapata. They often teased each other about their peasant ways, such as when the women crooned over the corn as it tasselled or a favourite guinea pig was found with a new litter. Official requirements for agricultural land use meshed with household habits and preferences. Eventually the federation petitioned the ministry, and by 1989 it had received permission to settle the area and the farmer's title was retracted.

Land at Rosapata was steep and difficult to cultivate, and because the organization was willing to take on lawsuits, Rosapata was eventually rezoned as an urban area. To carry on with the legal work of full recognition, all federation members paid monthly dues and participated in bimonthly improvement projects. In the early stages of land invasions, occupancy was an overriding principle. One settler family from the upper area originally was assigned a well-placed lot in the lower section on which to build. Someone else occupied it before they managed to move to the site, and they were reassigned an inferior lot in the upper section. The family immediately moved onto the land, fearful of being displaced again, even though this initial occupancy was like camping out. Eventually they began making adobes in the creek bottom far below, slowly raising their house by hauling each adobe up the cliff side on their backs. In time a high wall enclosed even their sloping garden as they attempted to deal with washouts and erosion.

One homeless woman, Vicentine, acquired her own lot much later and built herself a tiny house of mats and adobe on the edge of the canyon.

Together with her husband, who worked in Puerto Maldonado, Vicentine purchased the lot from the federation for $1,000, she told me. Feeling compassion for the woman, her neighbours helped her acquire the lot by requesting permission for her to build on the inappropriate site so precariously perched. With their recommendation Vicentine was accepted as a member and finally was able to provide a home for her many children. She too began to work on the required Sundays.

Prior to these improved circumstances, Vicentine had squatted in one of the houses under construction belonging to a local teacher who lived and worked outside Cuzco. Vicentine's job was to guard the partial construction with a single roofed room and to keep thieves and suspect neighbours from stealing the construction materials piled up in the courtyard. Occasionally the teacher returned to Cuzco and the two women lived on the site together. Vicentine's presence on the construction site allowed the teacher to retain the occupancy required to demonstrate need and to avoid land speculation. However, the requirement posed dilemmas as well. Frequently I encountered arrangements such as this one in which the owner/occupant was virtually never in residence but found family members or hired others to stay on the site. Participants engage in land invasions to solve housing needs, but usually they are also highly mobile and dependent on finding work wherever they can. The rules of the federations insist on permanent occupancy, but the occupants' lives are anything but stationary.

In the early phases of occupation, an obviously destitute woman living on the house site strengthens an individual's claim indirectly as well. Ideally lots are distributed on the principle of need, indigenous peasants having special rights as beneficiaries of the land reform. Urban middle-class mestizos also face housing shortages and frequently have special relationships with leaders of invasions. When participating with others in invasions, they have been seen to piggyback their way to acquiring a building site; at times complaints about this were made in private. Once Vicentine was present, the teacher kept a low profile and avoided occasion for awkward questions. After settlement at Rosapata had coalesced, questions of the relative rights to a lot largely were put aside. By then house construction was well under way and much of the neighbourhood had been settled by the needy and others hardy enough to live through the first arduous years of establishment.

To meet some of the requirements for attaining full recognition as a legitimate *pueblo joven* (cf. Calderon and Olivera 1979), the federation launched a number of improvement projects with occasional financial assistance and technical advice from the Ministry of Housing and Construction. Rosapata's steep upper neighbourhood benefited only partially. It was difficult to lay out proper roads on the steep incline, and during the rainy season, paths between the houses became nearly impassable. Residents on their way to town negotiated the slippery mud in bare feet while carrying their shoes. During work projects every household sent representatives to dig ditches for the water main, but once the pipes were connected to the network, pressure proved insufficient to bring water into the upper houses. By the early 1990s many were complaining that their money and labour had been to no purpose. The resentment was especially tangible during work sessions when upper area residents worked beside their neighbours from lower down, fully aware that their efforts would benefit the others but not themselves.

One woman, upon returning from a Sunday work project on the water main, announced she had been fined 240 soles for not attending earlier and expressed anger at the meaningless expense. The federation council had insisted she pay the arrears, emphasizing that everyone benefited from the projects because they were part of the improvements required to advance Rosapata's claims for full recognition. Over the years it was difficult to keep residents focused on shared 'corporate' goals with ephemeral benefits that did not bring concrete improvements to their own homes. All infrastructural improvements at Rosapata were made by way of the self-help approach, and the properties did improve, gradually re-creating urban spaces to meet requirements for full recognition and eventual individual titles.

The risk taken by the residents at Rosapata seemed worthwhile. By the time the area was rezoned as residential, it boasted houses at various stages of construction. Rough streets were laid out, some even surfaced. Municipal spaces such as a soccer field were built, and water lines and bus routes connected the residential areas with the city. Meanwhile, although the farmer's land title had been revoked, he continued to legally contest the decision despite all available land now being built on.

Though the occupancy was generally orderly and relatively conflict-free as it gathered momentum over time, of course some people at Rosapata were cheated. Its diverse membership comprised not only peasants arriving in the city but also opportunists amongst them, as people knew well. The federation president in one nearby neighbourhood had been jailed for trafficking in land titles. Rosapata's membership, the federation board and the various bureaucratic advisers all completely rejected profiting on land invasions. Such speculation jeopardized their claims of just occupancy by invasion. Nor was the compromise of ancient monuments by invaders tolerated. In one instance at the crest of the hill just above

Rosapata, new squatters who had built on Incan ruins were charged with damages by the National Institute for Cultural Patrimony.

The ongoing awareness as to how best to occupy, legally lay claim to and thereby consolidate rights over an area through time seemed to resonate with earlier land reform concerns and rhetoric voiced by peasant leaders in the agrarian cooperatives at Pincos. Only state-held lands were invaded, especially places seen to be taken over by interested parties hoping to profit through land titling. The invasion at Rosapata advanced the invaders' interests strategically by aiming to inspire a response of tolerance and permissiveness on the part of the state rather than forcible eviction, precedence being observed in cases of invasions of haciendas both in the countryside and at the edge of the city.

On the other side of Cuzco, more recent land invasions in the 1990s resulted in quite a different type of emerging neighbourhood at Limatambo. In this instance, violent takeovers and subsequent expulsions followed one another in a series of confrontations between invaders and police. The 72-hectare expropriated site, one of many areas remaining in legal limbo after land reform, had been the object of a series of court decisions defining its legal status. The inactivity exacerbated competing expectations among different sectors of the population, and after nearly a decade in the courts, the site, described as rustic hacienda land (*predio rústico*), finally was awarded to an individual prominent Cuzceno. However, the level field was particularly attractive for housing development because buses on their way to the city centre frequently stopped on a major asphalted road intersecting the site. Furthermore, Limatambo had relatively easy access to water, another crucial factor for housing settlement. As in Rosapata, the land at Limatambo was state-owned property finally expropriated in 1976, and here too, a man from a well-known Cuzco family had been granted free title to the property for 'agricultural purposes' (*título de adjudicación*).

Invasion at Limatambo was planned to block what was perceived as usurpation of the site. The invaders, led by an educated unmarried man whom members referred to as 'the Engineer', largely came from amongst the displaced people flooding into Cuzco in the early 1990s. The membership roll lists the vast majority of the 216 households as originating from Apurimac, and many of these residents told me of their traumatic flight to relative safety in the city. This large pool of needy people quickly filled the two-tiered field, first laying out the section closest to the road and shortly thereafter occupying the larger swath of land beyond. Though there had been earlier evictions at Limatambo, these families were convinced of the likelihood of ultimately winning rights to settle on the land because they were displaced people who, as victims of the insurgency, ultimately represented tangible evidence of the government's inability to protect them and control the countryside. These families were quite aware of the rhetorical potential of their situation as well as its harsh reality. Unlike the man who held title, their motive rested not in agricultural production but in need. Attempts in the courts to revoke earlier titling followed, and though these were unsuccessful, their petition to gain legal acceptance nevertheless accomplished its aim in 1994 and Limatambo became a recognized *pueblo jovèn* aspiring to full recognition. The ambiguity of titling remained unresolved, however, and the process of legal entitlement promised to be difficult.

Despite legal uncertainty, individual members continued to build houses on their assigned lots. Street committees were established, as were a number of secretariats overseeing the economy, the coordination of activities and social assistance, all coordinated by the federation board in the prescribed way (cf. Calderon and Olivera 1979). The centralizing organizational form was a requirement for participating in the formalization processes overseen by the Ministry of Housing. During the 1990s, President Fujimori's programmes aimed at greater efficiency and simplification in the titling process. As such they have been seen as a move away from the greater emphasis on the 'corporate' organizations of *pueblos jovenes* promoted by Presidents Velasco and Morales (Ødegaard 2010). But while emphasis and form have differed over time, laws governing the establishment of *pueblos jovenes* have rested upon a collective approach to forming neighbourhoods similar to the cooperative principles established by land reform. These organizational requirements had been anticipated at Limatambo before the fact of invasion. The original families had secretly appointed their representative board before the occupation took place, and during the initial period these representatives decided the strategies necessary to quickly settle as much of the land as possible. Collectively acquiring basic services as means of eventually acquiring individual property titles would follow, and the participants were well aware of this requirement.

Unlike Rosapata, which attained recognition through accretion of housing lots amidst the fields throughout the 1980s, the association at Limatambo relied upon more formal aspects of planning through the 1990s. First the members built a small chapel, and their parish priest was invited to perform a mass and bless the opening of the new neighbourhood. Through him, the federation was put into contact with a Dutch NGO that helped fund resettlement of displaced people, and a successful application was made for the construction of a community centre. Each household provided a specified number of adobes for the walls, and the NGO provided cement for the foundation and paid for the building's windows and roofing. It took a number of weeks to raise the building. The labour was provided by members, many of them women who received rice, pasta and oil in payment for their work. The food was taken home to their families rather than prepared or eaten in a communal kitchen. Eventually the community centre housed local educational activities.

Limatambo's location beside the main thoroughfare facilitated provision of other infrastructure, such as rudimentary roads, but raising individual houses proved difficult for many families who continued to live in provisional huts and struggled to finance construction of proper dwellings over a long period. Again the federation board sought NGO funding from various sources earmarked for resettling the many displaced families at Limatambo and thus was able to help some acquire construction materials. Establishing need was one of the requirements, and the fact that a significant number of displaced families lacked identity documents made promoting them as candidates for aid even more difficult.

The sites at Rosapata and Limatambo were both carefully selected for invasion. The similarities in these strategic choices suggest a conscious sensibility of the kinds of situations likely to elicit more or less leniency. As state lands expropriated under the land reform, both sites had been intended to benefit a particular part of the population formerly exploited by the hacienda system over generations. But because the sites were designated as agricultural land and had been left fallow, seemingly abandoned, individual entrepreneurs attained free title to take up cultivation. The title awards were commonly perceived as an unjust evasion of the original intent of the law. Especially in the case of Limatambo, the conflict over titling rights on what was a very attractive piece of real estate played out over years and remains unsettled. Many inconsistencies in legal positions and rulings must be resolved before individual titles are possible, but for the time being the federation there has partially vindicated its claims by winning legal recognition as an aspiring *pueblo jovèn*.

Conclusion

Peru, a place with a complex past, has a centralized state administration removed from the regional lives of its inhabitants in a uniform way. Given its large indigenous population's history of ethnic/racial spatial segregation in marginal areas, the experience of being Peruvian, for many, has not included equal treatment as citizens. While ethnic and racial identities are notoriously fluid in such marginal settings, there is a shared consciousness of positioning vis-à-vis state bureaucracies, which is part of the disglossia that occurs between a kind of public presentation and what goes on in the privacy of land invasion planning and implementation. Official regulations are respected, as when people are fined for building on ruins or invaders expelled. Nevertheless, a fine-tuned appreciation of political vulnerabilities is crucial in dealings between invaders and state representatives. Furthermore in such dealings, differences between individual bureaucrats are appreciated, and many rules will necessarily be bent simply through attrition. People without housing must make homes for themselves as best they can, and their presence, vulnerability, and unmet needs cannot be denied. Their simple persistence re-creates invaded lands into recognized urban spaces and feeds hopes of acquiring private title in future. As the two cases summarized above show, planning evolved from informal to greater formalized control as the federations sought to come into line and attain formal recognition by following organizational specifications and activities. What seems remarkable in the process is the many years that elapse before all such qualifications are met, during which time much uncertainty remains and degrees of non-fulfilment are forgiven.

The case from Cuzco presents theories of planning with particular considerations. First, the historically specific and deeply politicized nature of planning administration cannot be overlooked in such an instance. Post colonialism with its contemporary sensibilities is one aspect of the evolving politics of the agrarian reform that was assumed complete upon the legislation of 1968. Furthermore, planning in Peru is far from comprehensive and rather illustrates the patchwork nature of state intervention. In such fragmentary terrain, we come to appreciate that spatial categories such as urban and rural, so important to state run programmes like land reform, are also performed realities that new urbanizing areas manipulate to their advantage. This goes beyond rational strategy and rather should be considered inherently part of everyday life in the Andes, an experience that is simultaneously urban and rural. Finally, having considered these examples, we can reflect on how the state actually tolerates and to an extent condones illegal activity that unfolds within prescribed limits. Private dreams become realities through a series of slippages in which planning responds to unfolding developments that transform public lands into the private property of homeownership.

References

Calderon, C. J. and L. Olivera. 1979. *Manual de Poblador de Pueblos Jovenes*. Lima: DESCO.

Collier, D. 1976. *Squatter and Oligarchs: Authoritarian Rule and Policy Change in Peru*. Baltimore: Johns Hopkins University Press.

Contreras, I. E. 1991. *La violencia politica en Apurimac; su impacto social y economico*. Cuzco: Centro de Estudios Regionales Andinos, 'Bartolome de las Casas'.

Das, V. and D. Poole (eds). 2004. *Anthropology in the Margins of the State*. Santa Fe, NM: SAR Press.

De la Cadena, M. 2000. *Indigenous Mestizos: The Politics of Race and Culture in Cuzco, Peru, 1919-1991*. Durham, NC, and London: Duke University Press.

de Soto, H. 1990. *El otro sendero*. Lima: Instituto Libertad y Democracia.

Driant, J.-C. 1991. *Las barriadas de Lima: historia e interpretacion*. Lima: IFEA/DESCO.

Gose, P. 2008. *Invaders as Ancestors: On the Intercultural Making and Unmaking of Spanish Colonialism in the Andes*. Toronto: University of Toronto Press.

Jacobsen, N. 1997. 'Liberalism and Indian Communities in Peru 1821–1920', in R. Jackson (ed.), *Liberals, the Church and Indian Peasants: Corporate Lands and the Challenge of Reform in 19th Century Spanish America*. Albuquerque: University of New Mexico, pp. 123–170.

Larson, B. 2004. *Trials of Nation Making; Liberalism, Race, and Ethnicity in the Andes, 1810-1910*. Cambridge: Cambridge University Press.

Lloyd, P. 1980. *The 'Young Towns' of Lima: Aspects of Urbanization in Peru*. Cambridge: Cambridge University Press.

Lund, S. 2001. 'Bequeathing and Quest: Processing Personal Identity Papers in Bureaucratic Spaces (Cuzco, Peru)', *Social Anthropology* 9(1): 3–24.

Mallon, F. 1998. 'Chronicle of a Path Foretold? Velasco's Revolution, Vanguardia Revolucionaria, and "Shining Omens" in the Indigenous Communities of Andahuaylas', in S. Stern (ed.), *Shining and Other Paths; War and Society in Peru, 1980–1995*. Durham, NC: Duke University Press, pp. 84–117.

McClintock, C. 1981. *Peasant Cooperatives and Political Change in Peru*. Princeton, NJ: Princeton University Press.

Mejia Navariete, J. 1990. *Estado y municipio en el Peru*. Lima: Consejo Nacional de Ciencia y Tecnologia.

Mendoza, Z. 2004. *Shaping Society through Dance: Mestizo Ritual Performance in the Peruvian Andes*. Chicago: Chicago University Press.

Muldoon, J. 1991. 'The Conquest of the Americas: The Spanish Search for Global Order', in R. Robertson and W. Garrett (eds), *Religion and Global Order*. New York: Paragon, pp. 65–85.

Ødegaard, C. 2010. 'Land and Labour in Processes of Urbanization: The Dialectics between Popular Practices and State Policies in Peru', *Forum for Development Studies* 37(1): 113–135.

Orlove, B. 1993. 'Putting Race in Its Place: Colonial and Postcolonial Peruvian Geography', *Social Research* 60(2): 301–336.

Poole, D. 2004. 'Between Threat and Guarantee: Justice and Community in the Margins of the Peruvian State', in V. Das and D. Poole (eds), *Anthropology in the Margins of the State*. Santa Fe, NM: School of American Research Press, pp. 35–65.

Skar, H. 1984. *Warm Valley People: Duality and Land Reform among the Quechua of Highland Peru*. Oslo: Universitetsforlaget.

Skar, S. 1995. 'Appropriating Pawns: Andean Dominance and the Manipulation of Things', *Journal of the Royal Anthropological Institute* 1(4): 787–803.

Stern, S. (ed.). 1998. *Shining and Other Paths: War and Society in Peru, 1980–1995*. Durham, NC: Duke University Press.

Thurner, M. 1999. *From Two Republics to One Divided: Contradictions of Postcolonial Nationmaking in Andean Peru.* Durham, NC: Duke University Press.

Walker, C. 1999. *Smoldering Ashes: Cuzco and the Creation of Republican Peru, 1780–1840.* Durham, NC: Duke University Press.

Yashar, D. 2005. *Contesting Citizenship in Latin America: The Rise of Indigenous Movements and the Postliberal Challenge.* Cambridge: Cambridge University Press.

BOTHO
SECHABENG
A feeling of
community

A description of forms of tenure in
Transvaal rural communities by the
Transvaal Rural Action Committee (TRAC)

RESEARCH COMPILED IN 1992 BY NLC AFFILIATES & CONTRACT RESEARCHERS FUNDED BY KAGISO TRUST

Botho Sechabeng.

– Chapter 4 –

TENURE REFORMED
Planning for Redress or Progress in South Africa

Deborah James

Introduction

Planning 'seeks to make the will of the people in some way compatible with efficient control' (Robertson 1984). Whereas such planning was a paradigmatic undertaking of states in the post-war era, the outsourcing of many state functions and the establishment of parallel bureaucracies – often by NGOs – have been seen as both cause and effect of the progressive weakening of states and their functions (Abram and Weszkalnys, this volume). NGOs have become involved in 'planned interventions' (Long 2001), drafting policies and laying out designs to shape the future. Rather than replacing the state, however, they interact with it in the enterprise of planning 'to turn an unreliable citizenry into a structured, readily accessible public' (Selznick 1949).

Such outsourcing of state functions has been associated with neo-liberalism and seen as a sign of 'neoliberal governmentality' (Ferguson and Gupta 2002). The programme of planned intervention described below sounds like an enclosed and self-referential system, and hence is evidence of 'South African exceptionalism' (Bernstein 1996), but the country's economy is of course implicated in global trends. It was incorporated into the sphere of global trade and industry during the 1990s on terms that hindered competition in the world market. This resulted in a loss of jobs in industry, the government's adoption of strict restrictions on state spending and its pursuit of an economic restructuring similar to that implemented in many other countries. Some have claimed that South Africa's new political leaders showed unwarranted enthusiasm in choosing the path of privatization rather than delivering welfare and safeguarding the interests of the poor and marginalized, attributing the failure of all of these to strategies followed by the new elite within the context of the neo-liberal global economy rather than to the complex and particular history of South Africa or to its specific social and legal culture (Bond 2000; Marais 2001).

From this point of view, it seemed clear that poor people in post-1994 South Africa were destined to enjoy little improvement in their well-being. It seemed extremely difficult to implement ambitious plans for restructuring the ownership of property and redistributing it under conditions of austerity and without backup from state welfarist programmes or the state subsidies that had supported white-owned farming enterprises during the apartheid era. The World Bank's 'small family farm' model of ownership and production had a formidable influence on the design of South Africa's land reform programme (Hall and Williams 2003; van Zyl, Kirsten and Binswanger 1996), but critics pointed to its inappropriateness as a means of addressing poverty, claiming that the World Bank approach would bolster the fortunes of only a small, nascent middle class (Sender and Johnston 2004). And even when better-off people became beneficiaries, as was increasingly the trend towards the end of the 1990s, their chances of making a good living seemed remote, given that the supportive framework provided by the state marketing boards and state-planned economy of the apartheid era had long been abandoned (Bernstein 2003: 206; Hart 2002: 227–228).

Describing the country as quintessentially 'neo-liberal', however, risks oversimplification by giving the impression of an apparently seamless web of intention. Differentiations and disputes between state and non-state actors should be recognized, even while acknowledging that they perform roles with a seemingly unified governmental effect. The movement of personnel (and ideas) from the 'third sector' to the state and back again (Lewis 2008a, 2008b), particularly in a post-transitional society such as the new South Africa (James 2002), similarly creates unevenness in the smooth fabric of planned intervention but does not tear it asunder. South Africa, despite its much-criticized shift from an initially redistributive policy to a more growth-oriented one in the wake of its second democratic elections, has been characterized as having a 'distributional regime', given the importance of state spending and the extent of citizen dependence on it (Seekings and Nattrass 2006). Alternatively, it is a regime that achieves 'distributional' ends in a quintessentially 'neo-liberal' manner (James 2012). Market ideologies and self-enrichment combine with government intervention in often unexpected ways, making the blanket term 'neo-liberal' overly homogenizing (Sanders 2008).

During the South African transition, state–NGO relations changed considerably. Starting out with a welfarist role during apartheid, NGOs were raided for their staff by the transitional government, but in-house disputes often erupted into overt confrontations that paralleled ideological disputes within the ruling African National Congress (ANC), whereupon many NGO and other activists resigned from their government positions. Seismic changes that saw top ranks of government personnel changed but lower-level bureaucrats retained also played their part in complicating any simple story counterposing the state against the third sector. Despite such changes and disputes, both sides played their part in planning for the new dispensation. Contestations have both blurred boundaries between the state and the NGO sector[1] and sharpened lines of definition within that sector. New kinds of conflict are continually generated as certain actors align themselves with national policy while others contest it from the local level. At issue have been key questions about the nature of public morality, the division between the public and the private, the entitlements and obligations of citizenship, and responsibility for the welfare of the poor.

'An Extraordinary Degree of Planning'

South African blacks were subjected to a 'quite extraordinary degree of planning' and legislation during apartheid (Crush and Jeeves 1993), and it was recognized that equivalent efforts would be required to undo apartheid's schemes. Mindful of earlier racial divisions and inequalities, the new South African government, determined to structure the transfer of farm land across the racial frontier as an organized process rather than allowing Zimbabwe-style 'land grabs', proposed a 'market'-based acquisition of land to be purchased from 'willing sellers' by 'willing buyers', mediated by state officials from the Department of Land Affairs (DLA).

The recognition of a need for different categories of policy – *restitution, redistribution* and *tenure reform* – is based on an understanding of both differing needs in the future and different communities' divergent past experiences on the land. Members of the human rights law fraternity and the well-developed NGO sector as well as a range of outside experts were consulted to research previous systems of landholding and help envision how future economic well-being might also be assured.

The succession of iniquitous laws that established separate territories for blacks and robbed them of their existing land rights are well known. They ranged from the 1913 Natives Land Act, which legislated a distinction between the white-owned areas that made up over 80 per cent of the land area and the 'reserves' (later 'homelands') that occupied the remaining 13 per cent of the land, to the 1936 Native Trust and Land Act, which augmented the area of these homelands to accommodate their existing populations as well as the thousands of people displaced by the infamous 'population removals' of the 1950s to 1970s. Accompanying the removals were strategies of control necessitating other laws.[2] But although the picture of starkly racialized dispossession – black displacement by white settlers, followed by state-endorsed separation of territory – is accurate in its broad outlines, the regional processes were more complex, leaving as many differentiations within the ranks of black landholders as there were factors uniting them. Through much consulting of experts, designers of policy attempted to take cognizance of these variegated experiences when they passed a series of acts after 1994.

The most obvious 'beneficiaries' of reform were to be former title-holding landowners relocated to the homelands during apartheid's 'black spot' removals. Their property rights have been clearer-cut and easier to assert and retrieve – through *restitution* – than those of other claimants. As members of the nascent African middle class (Murray 1992), they also have a greater sense of entitlement; some simultaneously owned property in cities like Johannesburg. Displacement from both later allowed double compensation in some cases. The initial growth of South Africa's human rights NGOs, especially those concerned with land issues, is partly attributable to these communities' highly motivated efforts to reclaim land well before the demise of apartheid (Levin 1996; Palmer 2001; Wotshela 2001).

A second initiative, *redistribution,* aimed at people who never previously had secure claims on landed property, was designed to enable them to purchase farms with the aid of government grants. Its intended beneficiaries – mostly residents of the homelands and of white farms – are likely to belong among the poor and 'historically oppressed' (Lahiff 2000). They overlap somewhat with the beneficiaries of the third subdivision, *tenure reform,* designed to encompass the land needs of both homeland residents and farm dwellers. While the former have resided under chiefly control and held land under 'customary' tenure, the latter defy easy classification: they include both those who long ago left their homes on South Africa's white farms and, most important for the present essay, those who still reside on them, to whom *tenure reform* is intended to give greater residential security. Between these two poles is a range of farm-dwellers expelled from – or voluntarily quitting – the white farms at various moments over the past half-century. Those remaining on the farms, often derogatorily seen as 'squatters', still view themselves as entitled to claim what was theirs by right, or at least to demand greater security where they are.

In sum, state planners and their collaborators in the NGO sector have been cognizant of a range of contextual and historical divergences in the history of land dispossession, and have designed policy categories to accommodate them. Inevitably, however, like many other categories imposed by policymakers on a local populace, the separate kinds of beneficiaries for whom these three subdivisions were originally designed have often been intertwined in practice (Lahiff 2000; Murray 1996). Restitution, aimed at former title-holders who mostly lived outside the homelands, has been invoked to reinstate apartheid's homeland-dwelling victims. Redistribution, aimed at Africans who never held title to landed property, has served as a means for former title-holders to claim restitution if they were ineligible for this programme because their dispossession occurred before the official 1913 'cut-off date'.[3]

South African Land Reform Legislation

Category	Date	Act	Intention
Restitution	1994	Restitution of Land Rights Act	To provide for the restitution of rights in land to persons or communities dispossessed of such rights after 19 June 1913 as a result of past racially discriminatory laws or practices. To establish a Commission on Restitution of Land Rights (CRLR) and a Land Claims Court.
Restitution/ Redistribution/ Tenure Reform	1996	Communal Property Associations Act (CPA)	To enable groups to acquire, hold and manage property as agreed by members and according to a written constitution
Tenure Reform	1996	Land Reform (Labour Tenants) Act	To safeguard the rights of labour tenants who had been remunerated for labour primarily by the right to occupy and use land
Tenure Reform	1996	Interim Protection of Informal Land Rights Act (IPILRA)	To protect people with informal rights and interests from eviction in the short term, pending more permanent legislation (i.e. CLRA)
Tenure Reform	1997	Extension of Security of Tenure Act (ESTA)	To give farm occupants rights of occupation on private land. Establishes steps to be taken before eviction of such people can occur
Tenure Reform	2004	Communal Land Rights Act (CLRA)	To provide for legal security of tenure by transferring communal land to communities and provide for its democratic administration by them

Source: Data from www.info.gov.za/acts/ Adams 2000

The general ideological thrust of the land reform programme, then, has encompassed a broad vision of restored rights, sovereignty and citizenship for the African population, informed by the prevalence of human rights lawyers and NGO activists in drafting the constitution and in setting up the programme itself. At the same time, its detail embodies a series of subdivisions that separate those with more visible and obvious (former) rural land rights from those rural dwellers with few apparent rights of any kind.

Law, Property and Citizenship

The restructuring of land ownership was a far-reaching and ambitious exercise. For every scheme devised after 1994 that failed to deliver the expected benefits, there were planners, lawyers and NGO who developed even more sophisticated designs to remedy past mistakes. They brought considerable energies to bear upon this project, drafting and redrafting legislation, planning and replanning legal systems of ownership and subjecting existing plans to considered critique. The plans were thus both utopian and carefully drawn, informed by an awareness that African land rights are often overlapping and multiple rather than exclusive and proprietary, that flexible legislation would hence be needed to adjudicate conflicting claims and ensure that decisions taken would be adhered to, and that legislation alone would not suffice but that institutions enabling mediation and conflict resolution would be required (Claassens 2000; Cousins 2002).

The connection between land and citizenship was fashioned at the point where law and society intersect. South Africa – ironically, given its 'racist and oppressive state' – was home to a liberal social and legal culture that embodied principles contradictory to those enshrined by the state (Chanock 2001: 20). While an increasingly coercive regime was enforcing a racial order in which African customary law, territorial segregation and denial of property ownership were tools of subjugation, human rights lawyers working hand in glove with NGOs were subverting this order, using liberal visions of the law intersecting with ideas on African customary rights. It was through the interactions between such lawyers and their dispossessed African clients that connections between land ownership and citizenship were partly forged in the years leading to South Africa's transition.

Liberal ideals thus coexisted with a 'racial modernist' regime (Bozzoli 2004), the stony immovability of the latter accounting, in part, for the headily utopian character of the former. There were contradictory aspects to the conceptualization of property rights as developed in the course of dialogue between African communities – especially former title-holders – and the mostly white English-speaking middle-class activists devoted to restoring these rights who, in their bid to challenge the state in its removals policy, had researched the nature of these communities' concepts of land tenure. Their outrage at the apartheid state's infringement of African ownership rights was fed by a Euro-American model of inviolable 'private property'. Members of this constituency also emphasized egalitarianism. They saw this as deriving from African custom, but the emphasis also drew on a tradition in European thought that sees land as a common good for the benefit of all (Hann 1998: 321). The resulting model of ownership was a hybrid based on African ideas of landholding filtered through two contesting counter-discourses in European thought, one privileging the private dimension of property and the other stressing the need to secure it for the public good (Hann 1998). This dialogical model of property ownership combined private and communal, modern and traditional ideals of landholding and landownership, in sometimes contradictory ways.[4]

Given this legacy, the undoing of apartheid required creation of a unity of territory and government where previously there had been division. Land and rights became indissolubly connected in the public mind, partly because of clashes during the 1980s between the state and the people whose property, land and citizenship rights it was undermining. Restoring land to its former occupiers was seen, by those in the human rights activist and NGO community, as both reinstating civil liberties formerly denied and also assuring the rights of people – especially the most poor and vulnerable – to secure residence in the future. Initially, then, a language of 'rights' and especially 'land rights', rather than one about 'property/ownership', was enshrined at the heart of debates about reform. But a second line of argument, increasingly important in the late 1990s and early 2000s, foregrounded the economic benefits to be gained from secure ownership of property. The two approaches were linked in the early years of the land reform programme, drawing many former NGO officials into state employment. But the government's subsequent shift towards more explicitly neo-liberal economic policies has resulted in the rights-based approach's decoupling from the property-oriented/economic one, with the latter tending to be favoured, especially after the second democratic elections in 1999, when Mbeki replaced Mandela as premier and restaffed the DLA. With this altered direction and the accompanying substitution of personnel, numerous former NGO activists and human rights lawyers, having briefly worked for the state, rejoined the NGO sector, using legal means to challenge the government and enforce the more egalitarian vision of the land reform programme's priorities. Ironically, having first helped to design the programme, they became its sharpest critics.

The State, NGOs and the Land Question

People from these divergent backgrounds became almost indistinguishable in the heady and utopian period just after the 1994 election. They have since discovered ever more divisive ideological justifications for their divergent positions. At the same time, however, they often find themselves having to work together in a series of uneasy coalitions.

NGOs in South Africa have typically combined loftier concerns with the more humdrum provision of practical assistance. In the last two decades of the apartheid regime, these organizations began to proliferate, encouraged by evidence of social problems and the need for essential services as well as by the availability of foreign donor funds. Among the most active of these were a series of land NGOs and a legal NGO, the Legal Resources Centre (LRC), which played a key role in defending communities threatened with displacement. The expertise of personnel in this sector made them obvious targets of recruitment after 1994, when the newly oriented DLA was charged with implementing the land reform programme. It was the high profile of these former NGO officers that gave this programme its initially strongly 'rights-oriented' character, a reaction to, but also a result of, the fact that apartheid South Africa had in turn been 'quite self-consciously a legal order' in which 'nothing was done without legal authorisation, from removals to detentions' (Martin Chanock, quoted in Palmer 2001:4). Despite the novelty of the brief this department had now undertaken, there were some strong continuities with earlier practice: the dispossessors' preoccupation with law was matched by a similar preoccupation among those now championing, and restoring, the rights of the dispossessed.

A key figure in the transitional moment that brought NGO personnel into the government was human rights lawyer Geoff Budlender, who was recruited from the third sector to serve as director-general[5] of land affairs under Mandela's government. Defending the 'rights-orientation' and the careful, almost legalistic character of land reform planning, he maintained that 'people need rights to be able to hold government to'.[6] Conceding that there had been criticisms of the excessively complex new laws and their endless sub-clauses inserted 'to cope with various eventualities', he nonetheless pointed out that the real vindication of the 'legal' approach came with the rapid change of direction after the 1999 elections, when he and most of his colleagues were replaced by a new battery of officials handpicked by Mbeki's new Minister of Land Affairs Thoko Didiza:

> It's true that we over-legislated, but ... people do need firm rights. For example, under the Tenure Security Act, there was a provision which said 'The Minister

may make part of the farm available for worker ownership'. There was a dispute over whether the 'may' ought to have been 'shall'. The legal adviser said we ought to make it 'may', then there was a big fight about it. The 'shall' won. And now the new Minister has closed down the programme. We were right to stick with 'shall' – the 'shall' will make a big difference now that the policy has shifted. One needs a hook, a definite point of reference, and the law can provide this.[7]

Moving back into the NGO sector after their brief five years in office, Budlender and many of his colleagues found themselves in an anomalous position. Until 1994, the LRC had used its legal muscle to challenge the apartheid state's intent to shift the African population around the countryside. Now, after 1999, it would be using that muscle to hold the post-apartheid state to the laws its activists had passed whilst briefly occupying state positions and holding state portfolios. Of these laws, the ones now seen as most significant were intended to secure especially the most vulnerable parts of the African population within those country areas to which they had been scattered. At this point, after 1999, activists started directing their energies to safeguarding the informal rights of the landless via 'tenure reform'.

Obstacles to achieving the new programme's goals had existed before this change of ministers and their henchmen, however. Since 1994, the DLA had still been staffed and run, at lower levels, by administrators inherited from the apartheid regime. It was they who were said to be unwilling to share the egalitarian vision of their new masters:

> They had inherited attitudes to these communities and could not conceptualise a different framework, or think that people might behave differently. They believed that our policy was one which was designed to facilitate 'squatting', as they called it. They were only interested in dealing with people who *owned* the land. They had a bias towards title and private property, so they easily understood claims in which people had actually owned property beforehand, but not the ones ... involving former labour tenants and rental tenants who had been removed from the land.[8]

Harding regards these officials' reluctance to attend to the more informal rights of 'squatters' as an important factor in the programme's much-decried failure to deliver on its initial promises in the first five years of its existence. Other factors cited include the DLA's minuscule budget and the fact that its minister from 1994 to 1999, Derek Hanekom, was a white Afrikaner who was relatively junior in the ANC. The apartheid-era administrators' disdain for 'squatters' and non-landowners points towards a further continuity of ideology, which was to become consolidated after Mbeki's new minister, Thoko Didiza, took office. Here, several commentators have remarked on a key irony. It was Mandela's (white) minister, Derek Hanekom, who felt at ease when travelling to the countryside to visit landless communities, while his (black) successor Didiza – who sympathized less with 'the landless' than with those who, like her own family, had been title-holders – felt more at home among the African middle class or in the company of chiefs, and rarely spent time visiting the rural poor. Referring to the change in leadership and in personnel, some analyzed the post-1999 change in the DLA as the result of a 'race' conflict. But other commentators, instead of looking at the shift in departmental personnel, referred instead to the changing constituency that the department, in its earlier and later incarnations, had seen itself as serving, thus analysing it as a conflict of 'class'.[9] Whichever of these is most accurate, many people noted the parallel between the disregard for the rights and well-being of 'squatters' manifest among apartheid-era bureaucrats in the DLA, and a similar indifference to their plight by those working under the new minister.[10]

Landlessness Revisited: The Case of 'Tenure Reform'

Despite the fierce disagreements between the state and NGOs through all these processes, and the intensifying ideological battle over whether 'property' or 'rights' should prevail, the two found unity of purpose in attempting to ameliorate the plight of farm workers – the intended targets of 'tenure reform'. Although they are increasingly at odds over the newly implanted concerns of *national* policy, NGOs and state alike have focused much *regional* effort on planning for such people. But personnel in the two sectors, although collaborating closely on various cases of tenure reform in the countryside, nonetheless are driven by divergent motivations.

Broadly speaking, those in the NGOs consider inalienable rights to be more important than the realizable property that state employees prioritize. Recurrent themes are discernible here. The discourse on rights as protected and enforced by legal frameworks and as containing the full entitlements of the citizen echoes the 'rights talk' of 1980s social movements against apartheid and the influence of the lawyers who designed the land reform programme. In contrast, the emphasis on property – a more material and concrete acquisition – holds associations with forward-looking state pragmatism. Those favouring property see the implementation of rights as excessively legalistic and cumbersome, and instead favour the achievement of realistic short-term goals.

The interplay between these contesting positions can be illustrated by the case of a tenure reform workshop held in November 2003.[11] The purpose of the workshop was to establish some common ground, and a common *modus operandi*, between NGO and state employees operating within eastern Mpumalanga. Workshop participants from both sectors had frequently been called upon to defend the fragile entitlements of African farm-dwellers against the whites on whose properties they live and by whom they are in constant danger of being evicted under the terms established by ESTA (see diagram).

The participants in the workshop, employees of both the provincial NGO The Rural Action Committee – Mpumalanga (TRAC-MP) and the regional wing of the DLA, had expended much effort giving force to the law by protecting farm-dwellers from summary evictions. This usually involved difficult, highly personalized negotiations between individuals – specific farmers and their workers or tenants – whose interests increasingly appeared to be utterly divergent. Although NGO officers and state officials had a common interest in facilitating negotiations like these, they also disagreed on some key principles.

The arguments were played out via a simulation game, in which participants imagined a typical eviction scenario and listed the mediation strategies they would use. The imaginary scenario was as follows. A white farm owner dies. His children, no longer resident there, resolve to sell the farm. The new owner decides to switch to a new farming strategy. Two groups of workers are living on the farm. One has lived there for five years while providing labour under contract. The other has resided on the farm as tenants for almost a century; its members work elsewhere or are unemployed, but they do not provide labour on the farm. The farmer wants to evict the latter group, whose members, in the simulation game, are asking for assistance.

The rhetoric used to discuss solutions to this made-up problem pointed to the source of disagreement. Fieldworkers from TRAC-MP insisted that no action be taken that would jeopardize these workers' rights to live on the farm or graze their cattle there. However impractical this seemed in the light of the imaginary farm owner's determination to pursue eviction, their focus was on maintaining existing rights based on past practice, and on the need to ensure that these not be 'downgraded'.

State functionaries from the regional DLA, in contrast, had a more pragmatic approach. They seemed to shrug off the importance of past precedent, insisting that future-oriented development was of greater importance. Instead of nostalgically adhering to an unviable way of life, they suggested, it was better to look forward to a new one. 'It is not right to say, just because people have been staying like this for 40 years, that this is fine,' said Star Motswege of the DLA, pointing to the environmental degradation that would result from allowing overgrazing by workers' cattle. 'Our aim is to improve the situation, to make lives better.'

These debates were fierce, but there was agreement, at least, over the separate but related question of payment. If these imaginary farm-dwellers had no option but to accept resettlement elsewhere, all present agreed that paying for this was not the state's responsibility but rather the farmer's moral obligation. 'This will be on the shoulders of the farmer completely, not on the shoulders of the government', said Thomas Ngwe-nya of TRAC-MP. His government counterparts assented vigorously. All present agreed that using 'public funds' for the purpose of buying land to settle evicted labourers – as members of the right-wing white farmer organization Transvaal Agricultural Union had recently suggested, to the outrage of all – would be to misuse them. Instead, it should be a white farmer's obligation to buy land for his evicted workers.

It turned out that the workshop, the debate, and the concurrence over farmers' moral/financial obligation had been sparked by an actual case. A group of cattle-owning farm-dwellers, threatened with eviction, had indeed visited the regional offices of the DLA to seek advice. The DLA had responded by helping tenants use their pooled government grants to buy alternative land, where they then resettled with their cattle. Some months later these relocated tenants visited the land NGO, voicing their dissatisfaction with the new living arrangements, particularly the lack of grazing for their cattle. The NGO officers were critical of their government counterparts for having failed to clarify the farm-dwellers' existing rights at the outset, and for having moved so swiftly to resolve the case through recourse to mere property ownership. The case, they insisted, ought to have been taken to court, if necessary, to establish the legitimacy of these rights, since only the setting of legal precedents could enable progress in land reform. The government functionaries retorted that a speedy reso-lution of the problem had required decisive action rather than allowing the building up of further conflict, and that there would have been little purpose in establishing 'rights' in a situation where personal relationships were so fraught. Implicit but not fully explored in these discussions were assumptions about the obligations of white farmers. When participants in-sisted that farmers bear the costs of buying land to resettle workers off their farms, they were motivated jointly by a wish to save government money and a conviction that white farmers not be excused from their moral duty.

An earlier set of discussions, held some two years previously with em-ployees in Limpopo Province's land NGO, Nkuzi, illuminates how land disputes continue to centre on expectations about white farmer obliga-tions. Nkuzi's successes in settling eviction cases had been few, mostly because conflicts often progressed too far before the NGO was informed. Where success had been achieved, the cause of the eviction was contingent

– such as the death of the owner, or the advanced age of the farm worker – rather than based on intractable structural disputes.[12]

Whatever the cause, NGO negotiations often required recourse to warnings of legal action. The Venter family had threatened to evict a farm labourer called Toki Maphosa from their farm at Rooipoort on the grounds, oft-rehearsed in such cases, that 'there cannot be two farmers on the one farm'.[13] The Venters offered to pay Maphosa ZAR 15,000 (£1,500) to cede his rights to remain resident on their property and enable him to buy property elsewhere, a proposal reminiscent of the DLA officers' approach at the workshop. The offer of money was tempting, as it would have provided partial payment for a house in a planned peri-urban township with services and amenities, but Nkuzi warned him not to accept this financial settlement, primarily because he would have had to sell his cattle, had he moved to a township or 'agri-village'. With Nkuzi's advice, Maphosa managed instead to establish his informal rights of occupancy and grazing on the land where he had been living.[14] In the resulting agreement, a tenant, regarded by the farm owner as having no more entitlements than a mere 'squatter', emerged as having rights by virtue of his long-standing occupancy. The farm owners fenced off a section of the farm for Maphosa's use, and he was given legal title to the piece of land that would be enforceable in any future dispute.

This resolution to the dispute precisely mirrored the outcome of the discussion, described to me by Geoff Budlender, over the clause stating that 'The Minister may make part of the farm available for worker ownership', in which the 'may' eventually became 'shall'. In such cases, even when farmers proved less than amenable to recognizing the tenure rights of their workers, NGO action, backed by legislation passed during the early phase of land reform, forced the acknowledgement of informal land rights. The NGO workers were harnessing the legislative power of the state, apparently to good effect. Such protection of the rights of the landless, operationalized through the combined efforts of state and society, appears to fulfil the utopian promise inherent in the early years of land reform. But the success of these cases relied on a form of outsourcing to achieve state effects: on private white landowners playing a role in recognizing farm workers' rights to continue living on their farms.

Such actions by NGOs amount to acknowledgement that welfare provision for the landless and dispossessed ought properly to be secured with the compliance of those private property owners willing – or forced through legal means – to bear this burden. Here, an irony is in evidence. Paternalist dependency, often bitterly resented, had lain at the heart of farmer/labourer relationships in an earlier period (van Onselen 1996). The end of the apartheid regime was meant to bring equity, a basis for independent citizenship, and hence an escape from such relationships. But for a farm-dweller such as Maphosa, gaining complete freedom from land-based dependence would have meant losing his rights as a rural cattle owner and becoming an urban or peri-urban resident fully responsible for the payment of services. His rights as a citizen, although in one sense secured, would have been severely circumscribed.

Moving forward again to the 2003 tenure reform workshop: the disagreements between state and NGO personnel during the simulation game echo a long-standing debate over land and its significance. The perspective focused on broadly defined 'rights' involves a principled stand based on past practice, however impractical. Yet short of taking cases to court, itself perceived as a lengthy and often unpredictable procedure, there are few means to implement these rights, other than appealing to – or attempting coerced recognition of – the obligations of white farmers. The 'property' perspective, arising more out of pragmatic considerations, uses the rhetoric of future-oriented development and planning. Whereas the 'rights' orientation seems to be motivated by a backward-looking traditionalism in its assertion of tenants' needs to sustain their cattle herds, the 'property' orientation looks forward to modernity and progress in its preference for relocating country-dwellers in towns or urban-style agri-villages. In so doing, however, it proposes to remove such people from the frameworks in which they have been able to rely on others, better off than themselves, to provide resources. The state's model of the modern citizen is one who receives and pays for services, not one reliant on the paternalism of power-holders for goodwill.

These attempted solutions to farm worker landlessness evoke the dichotomous alternatives of herders freely grazing their cattle as they did in the past or proletarians displaced from the land into quasi-urban settlements. They indicate major discrepancies in how the two sectors visualize their respective roles in satisfying the demands of 'the landless'. Contrasting the imprecisely defined rural rights based on a customary lifestyle, on the one hand, with definite ownership of circumscribed property, on the other, these cases illuminate the conflict between a populace defending customary forms of livelihood and a modernizing state.

Discussion

Is it the case, then, that the South African state has paradoxically assumed a more central and visible role in governance by having many of its responsibilities towards the landless performed – and many of its policy directions contested, or even partly determined – by non-state actors, such as the land and legal NGOs? At a local/provincial level, or when concerning themselves with the practicalities of land access, these NGOs serve as a sort of extended civil service, carrying out functions that the DLA has neither the capacity nor the resources to perform on its own. Here, the need to plan for land reform, and the actions considered necessary to implement such planning, provide a basis for cooperation and convergence between the two sectors. It is here that the NGOs are most state-like in the purely administrative sense. At the national level, in contrast, a split developed between these two sectors, not only because of state 'outsourcing' but also because of swift political changes and the accompanying rapid shifts in personnel at the ministerial level. The contest over the nature and extent of landlessness progressively deepened this split. The original, inclusive vision of land rights – as symbolizing and encompassing both economic well-being and the political entitlements of citizens – provided the means for state and NGOs, ideologically and practically, to merge.

But as the difficulties in transforming the status of the landless became increasingly clear, the state began to restrict its focus. Influenced in part by experts at the World Bank, with its emphasis on the economic role of small farmers, the state focused its efforts (inasmuch as it made any efforts at all – the programme was increasingly poorly funded) on three areas. It restored the property of those who originally were landed, or paid them compensation for its loss; it provided land anew through redistribution to those who might in future find gainful employment through its use; and it resettled farm workers in quasi-urban agri-villages. The narrowing of this focus was simultaneously guaranteed by the re-staffing of the department and especially by the change in its ministerial and directorial personnel. At this moment, from the perspective of those in the human rights legal fraternity who had moved out of state employ, the government, by ignoring the rights and hence neglecting the welfare of its poorest citizens, was failing to achieve one of its crucial functions. The NGOs, de-staffed and re-staffed in their turn, began to elaborate their moral task as one of ensuring the well-being of the truly landless and dispossessed. In reverting to a recognition that such welfare was best assured by holding individual landowners to account for their farm workers' well-being, they were contributing to the outsourcing of state functions. But when they successfully pressed their government counterparts to acknowledge their responsibilities in respect of welfare provision, they were fulfilling citizen expectations by performing a role thought to be properly that of the state: acting in the interests of the public good and ensuring – in however distorted a manner – the provision of welfare.

Conclusion

Can it be claimed that land reform planning in South Africa represents an attempt 'to turn an unreliable citizenry into a structured, readily accessible public', as Selznick claimed for the era of state planning (see also Robertson 1984)? Ferguson and Gupta (2002) indicate that states in relation with NGOs/civil society operate in a manner very different from 'the nation-building logic of the old developmentalist state, which sought to link its citizens into a universalistic national grid'. Instead, the 'new political forms that challenge the hegemony of African nation-states', whether NGOs or social movements, may appear to be 'local' or 'grassroots' but in fact have strongly transnational dimensions. Such political forms, they suggest, should be thought of as 'integral parts of a transnational apparatus of governmentality' (2002: 994). Having made this point, however, the authors fail to flesh out a central question raised by their analysis: are we to see such an 'apparatus' as following the logic whereby state functions, although outsourced to non-state agents (including individual subjects), nonetheless produce 'governmental results' (2002: 989)? We are still left with the impression that 'neo-liberalism' serves as a single explanatory and analytic umbrella under which vastly discrepant phenomena can nonetheless be brought together (Kipnis 2007; Sanders 2008).

It was mentioned earlier that, despite the much-criticized shift from an initially redistributive policy to a more growth-oriented one in the wake of the second democratic elections, South Africa's regime has been characterized as 'distributional', given the mediating effects of state spending (Seekings and Nattrass 2006). Both during and since apartheid there has been a strong sense of citizen dependency – and insistence – upon pensions, child benefits and the like. The socio-economic setting is thus one where classically 'neo-liberal' ideas and practices (here focused on modern property ownership) coexist with expectations of state welfarism, even paternalism (here centred on notions of 'rights') owing much to South Africa's past. Such a coexistence requires a more fine-grained analysis of how state agents and non-state actors interrelate and diverge.

Notes

This chapter is based on research that was partly funded by the Economic and Social Research Council of the UK through a project entitled 'Property, Community and Citizenship in South Africa's Land Reform Programme', grant R000239795. Opinions expressed are the author's own. Thanks to all I interviewed, and to the organizers and participants at various workshops where earlier versions of this chapter were presented.

1. This has been a pattern in respect of matters such as health and education as well as land (see James 2002).
2. The Bantu Authorities Act of 1951 laid the basis for imposing so-called traditional chiefs in the homelands, planning agricultural development – so-called betterment – within the homeland areas, replanning villages, removing their inhabitants to new residential areas, culling their cattle and rationalizing their use of agricultural land.
3. Interview with Philip Mbiba of the Commission for the Restitution of Land Rights (CRLR), Nelspruit, 26 January 2001. This subdivision also obscures the intricate inter-connections between rural and urban forms of identity that have resulted from South Africa's exceptionally rapid transition to capitalist industry and agriculture (Bernstein 1996: 41). Many Africans domiciled in the rural and/or homeland areas have also had experiences as members of the unionized workforce, supporters of urban-based political parties, Christian town-dwellers, and occupiers or even owners of urban property. Whatever tenure rights they possess or property claims they make within their country domiciles must be – but have not been, by the land reform programme – assessed in relation to town-based shifts in property relations and residential arrangements that affect them as urban wage-earners (James 2007: 177, 180–184).
4. The model was not a new phenomenon: it had multiple historical precedents, including nineteenth-century contestations between colonial-era chiefs and native administrators over the most appropriate way to conceptualize and legislate African landholding (Chanock 1991).
5. The top civil servant, equivalent to a permanent secretary in the UK system of government.
6. Interview with Geoff Budlender of LRC, Johannesburg, 16 January 2001.
7. Ibid.
8. Interview with Tony Harding, formerly of the Commission for the Restitution of Land Rights (CRLR), Johannesburg, 21 August 2001.
9. In swift political changes following the ousting of Mbeki, two further ministers of land affairs were appointed in quick succession.
10. Interview with Geoff Budlender of LRC, Johannesburg, 16 January 2001.
11. The quotes in this section were recorded by me when I attended the ESTA workshop held by TRAC-MP in Nelspruit, on 14 November 2002.
12. Interview with Dan Mabokela, Nkuzi, Pietersburg, 22 August 2001.
13. Interview with Siphiwe Ngomane, Nkuzi, Pretoria, 3 September 2001.
14. In similar vein, TRAC-MP has succeeded in holding white landowners in Mpumalanga to their legal obligations, insisting that anyone wishing to evict a tenant or worker is obliged to provide a 'suitable alternative' for resettlement that would include access to firewood, building materials, hunting and harvesting of medicinal plants. In one case, TRAC managed to force a farmer to pay ZAR 155,000 in compensation to three labour tenant families; the DLA then combined this with government grants to buy them a property for ZAR 650,000 (Chris Williams, personal communication).

References

Adams, M. 2000. *Breaking Ground: Development Aid for Land Reform.* London: Overseas Development Institute.

Barrell, H. 2000. 'Class, Not Race, behind Dolny's Departure', *Daily Mail and Guardian*, 7 January.

Bernstein, H. 1996. 'South Africa's Agrarian Question: Extreme and Exceptional?' *Journal of Peasant Studies* 23(2/3): 1–52.

———. 2003. 'Land Reform in Southern Africa in World Historical Perspective', *ROAPE* 30(96): 203–226.

Bond, P. 2000. *Elite Transition: From Apartheid to Neoliberalism in South Africa*. London: Pluto Press.

Bozzoli, B. 2004. *Theatres of Struggle and the End of Apartheid*. Edinburgh: Edinburgh University Press.

Chanock, M. 1991. 'Paradigms, policies and property: a review of the customary law of land tenure' in K. Mann and R. Roberts (eds.) *Law in Colonial Africa*, Oxford: James Currey, pp. 61–84.

———. 2001. *The Making of South African Legal Culture, 1902–1936: Fear, Favour And Prejudice*. Cambridge: Cambridge University Press.

Claassens, A. 2000. 'Land Rights and Local Decision Making Processes: Proposals for Tenure Reform', in B. Cousins (ed.), *At the Crossroads: Land and Agrarian Reform in South Africa into the 21st Century*. Cape Town and Johannesburg: University of the Western Cape and National Land Committee.

Cousins, B. 2002. 'Legislating Negotiability: Tenure Reform in Post-apartheid South Africa', in C. Lund and K. Juul (eds), *Negotiating Property in Africa*. London: Heinemann, pp. 67–106.

Crush, J. and A. Jeeves. 1993. 'Transitions in the South African Countryside', *Canadian Journal of African Studies* 27(3): 351–360.

Ferguson, J. and A. Gupta. 2002. 'Spatializing States: Toward an Ethnography of Neoliberal Governmentality', *American Ethnologist* 29(4): 981–1002.

Hall, R. and G. Williams. 2003. 'Land Reform in South Africa: Problems and Prospects', in M. Baregu and C. Landsberg (eds), *From Cape to Congo: Southern Africa's Evolving Security Architecture*. Boulder, CO.: Lynne Reiner, pp. 97–129.

Hann, C. 1998. 'Introduction: The Embeddedness of Property', in C. Hann (ed.), *Property Relations: Renewing the Anthropological Tradition*. Cambridge: Cambridge University Press.

Hart, G. 2002. *Disabling Globalisation: Places of Power in Post-Apartheid South Africa*. Berkeley: University of California Press.

James, D. 2002. '"To Take the Information Down to the People": HIV/AIDS Peer-educators in Durban', *African Studies* 61(1): 169–191.

———. 2007. *Gaining Ground? 'Rights' and 'Property' in South African Land Reform*. London: Routledge; Johannesburg: Wits University Press.

———. 2012. 'Money-Go-Round: Personal Economies of Wealth, Aspiration and Indebtedness in South Africa', *Africa* 82(1) 20–40.

Kipnis, A. 2007. 'Neoliberalism Reified: *Suzhi* Discourse and Tropes of Neoliberalism in the People's Republic of China', *Journal of the Royal Anthropological Institute* 13: 383–400.

Lahiff, E. 2000. 'The Impact of Land Reform Policy in the Northern Province', in B. Cousins (ed.), *At the Crossroads: Land and Agrarian Reform in South Africa into the 21st Century*. Cape Town and Johannesburg: University of the Western Cape and National Land Committee.

Levin, R.M. 1996. 'Politics and Land Reform in the Northern Province: A Case Study of the Mojapelo Land Claim', in M. Lipton, F. Ellis, M. Lipton and M. de Klerk (eds), *Land, Labour and Livelihoods in Rural South Africa*, vol. 2: *KwaZulu-Natal and Northern Province*. Durban: Indicator Press, pp. 357–392.

Lewis, D. 2008a. 'Crossing the Boundaries between Third Sector and State: Life-Work Histories from Philippines, Bangladesh and the UK', *Third World Quarterly* 29(1): 125–142.

———. 2008b. 'Using Life-work Histories in Social Policy Research: The Case of Third Sector/ Public Sector Boundary Crossing', *Journal of Social Policy* 37(4): 559–578.

Long, N. 2001. *Development Sociology: Actor Perspectives.* London: Routledge.

Marais, H. 2001. *South Africa: Limits to Change: the Political Economy of Transition,* 2nd ed. London: Zed Press.

Murray, C. 1992. *Black Mountain: Land, Class and Power in the Eastern Orange Free State 1880s–1980s.* Johannesburg: Witwatersrand University Press.

———. 1996. 'Land Reform in the Eastern Free State: Policy Dilemmas and Political Conflicts', *Journal of Peasant Studies* 23(2/3): 209–244.

Palmer, R. 2001. 'Lawyers and Land Reform in South Africa: A Review of the Land, Housing and Development Work of the Legal Resources Centre (LRC)'. Mimeo.

Robertson, A.F. 1984. *People and the State: An Anthropology of Planned Development.* Cambridge: Cambridge University Press.

Sanders, T. 2008. 'Buses in Bongoland: Seductive Analytics and the Occult', *Journal of Anthropological Theory* 8(2): 107–132.

Seekings, J. and N. Nattrass. 2006. *Class, Race and Inequality in South Africa.* New Haven: Yale University Press.

Selznick, P. 1949. *TVA and the Grass Roots: A Study in the Sociology of Formal Organization.* Berkeley: University of California Press.

Sender, J. and D. Johnston. 2004. 'Searching for a Weapon of Mass Production in Rural Africa: Unconvincing Arguments for Land Reform', *Journal of Agrarian Change* 4(1/2): 142–165.

van Onselen, C. 1996. *The Seed Is Mine: The Life of Kas Maine, a South African Sharecropper, 1894–1985.* Cape Town: David Philip.

van Zyl, J., J. Kirsten and H. Binswanger (eds). 1996. 'Introduction', in J. van Zyl, J. Kirsten and H, Binswanger (eds), *Agricultural Land Reform in South Africa: Policies, Markets and Mechanisms.* Cape Town: Oxford University Press.

Wotshela, L. 2001. 'Homeland Consolidation, Resettlement and Local Politics in the Border and Ciskei Region of the Eastern Cape, South Africa 1960–1996, PhD dissertation. Oxford University.

Public officials face intense questioning over plans for the 2014 World Cup by residents of Bairro da Paz in a public meeting convened by the Forum of Social Entities. Source: John Gledhill

Chapter 5

REDEEMING THE PROMISE OF INCLUSION IN THE NEO-LIBERAL CITY

Grassroots Contention in Salvador, Bahia, Brazil

John Gledhill

The democratic constitution that Brazil adopted in 1988 after two decades of military rule promised a revolution in urban planning. Modernist planners and real estate developers alike had shared a dream of creating rationalized capitalist cities fit for expanding middle classes to live in, a vision that had no place for the irregular settlements of the poor, many still recent rural migrants. Yet Brazil's public housing programmes, limited in scope by fragile public finances and distorted in resource allocation by logics of political clientelism, remained economically inaccessible to the poorer sectors of the population (Gordilho 2000; Valença 2007). Even when access to a ready-made home in a serviced planned settlement became an option for some, it could prove less satisfactory than self-construction of a residence on invaded land, since the modular housing complexes that planners deemed appropriate for Brazilian working people were ill adapted to the social reproductive processes of their families, a general problem discussed in depth by Robertson (1991, 1996). So urban land invasions continued through the 1980s, and the non-viability of policies of forced eviction and relocation in public housing projects was increasingly recognized.

After 1988, a new policy language focused on the right of the poor not simply to have a place in the city but also to participate in a democratic process of 'urban self-management' (Caldeira and Holston 2004; Texeira 2001). This change was not simply a result of new thinking at the top of Brazilian society about how to combine 'progress' with 'order' in a country with stupendous social inequalities. Much less was it merely a consequence of the 'populism' of politicians such as the leftist leader Leonel Brizola, who, returning from exile in the twilight of military rule to become governor of Rio de Janeiro state in 1983, replaced eviction and repressive policing with efforts to provide services to the city's *favelas* (slums).[1] It also reflected the demands of combative urban popular movements, backed by allies that included liberation theology–oriented Catholics and middle-class professionals. As time went by, continuing demands for inclusion gave more substance to 'popular participation' in city government. But grassroots movements could still be corrupted by the clientelist strategies of political parties. As we will see in the case of Salvador, Bahia, Brazil's third largest metropolis, populist discourse has also been a legitimating tactic in elite modernization projects deeply inimical to lower-class interests. Yet during the 1990s Brazil's new policy language resonated ever more strongly with 'progressive' international trends.

In 2001, Congress approved a new City Statute (Federal Law 10.257). This legislation proposed a new partnership between federal government, municipal governments (which have primary legal responsibility for urban development and management) and 'civil society'. It aimed to give practical substance to the pluralistic social control over urban planning promised by the urban chapter of the 1988 Constitution and the global agenda of the United Nations Human Settlement Programme (UN-Habitat), which hailed the Brazilian law as an exemplary recognition of the 'right to the city' possessed by the poor. In the classic book that launched that concept, Henri Lefebvre argued that cities are a social project shaped by different groups' struggles to establish their right to inhabit urban space, struggles that are central to realization of full citizenship. The 'bourgeois city' denied urban society's true potential. With the rights of citizens to participate restricted to the periodic election of political representatives and urban planning simply a matter of technical experts implementing instructions received from government, it was dominated by a class uninterested in making the city a socially and culturally diversified space produced by all its inhabitants on the basis of equal rights of participation and appropriation (Lefebvre 1968: 174).

The City Statute, however, is legislation from the neo-liberal era. Abandonment of the developmentalist state model has not rendered the Brazilian government' participation in economic and social development inconsequential, although in tackling issues of poverty and inequality, many politicians of the Left have accepted neo-liberal ideas such as targeted conditional cash transfers (as distinct from universal benefits) and a leading role for private-public partnerships. I therefore endorse the argument that James makes in this volume against adopting a monolithic view of 'neo-liberal governmentality' that obscures how points of tension and dispute between state and non-state actors vary between different contexts. In Latin America, neo-liberal promises to liberate an 'active' civil society from the dead hand of corporatist government and enable those who have been excluded by poverty and racial and ethnic discrimination to realize their citizenship rights led to the enrolment of many previously dissident political actors in the neo-liberal project. Yet the kind of capitalist development that project furthered could scarcely fail to provoke contradictions in a climate of heightened expectations. Bolivia offers a dramatic example of that (Postero 2006), but also of the difficulties of ending the coloniality of power in a society where regional elites still wedded to both capitalist freedoms and racial hierarchy are the ones demanding 'autonomy' (Gustafson 2009), while much of Latin America still seems far from becoming even ambivalently 'post–neo-liberal'. Brazil poses the question of whether the neo-liberal city exacerbates the class bias in urban development that Lefebvre identified in the bourgeois city, under the cover of practices of inclusion, participation and respect for difference that are tools to manage rather than reduce or resolve social problems.

The anthropology of development literature has produced much critical ethnography of the practices of 'popular participation'. At the micro-level are issues such as who, if anyone, gets empowered, and how differentiated community actors learn to navigate participatory structures and make demands that seem appropriate to the apparatus that is reaching out to them (Mosse 2005). Since the personnel who implement projects are not as all-powerful or socially and ideologically homogeneous as the more monolithic accounts of the power of the development apparatus that dominated anthropological literature in the 1990s suggested, there is no compelling reason to think a priori that 'participatory' policies can offer nothing of practical value to poor people who engage with what is on offer, even if the actual result of participation remains quite distinct from what policy texts suggest it should be. Still, two critical perspectives seem particularly compelling in the context of urban development, given that participation in urban planning involves a range of power-differentiated stakeholders.

First, even if more professional planners opt to join the ranks of the community activists, city councillors, schoolteachers, unemployed and retired people and mothers who participate in the vernacular 'insurgent planning' that disrupts dominant models of desirable urban futures by valorizing the homes and communities that poor people have created and wish to defend (Miraftab 2009), the most powerful of the private-sector stakeholders generally exercise disproportionate influence over government. In Brazil the interests of poor working people still seem of limited significance in shaping patterns of urban development, let alone in any new thinking about how to create a more 'liveable' urban society. The privatized, securitized city oriented to the interests of developers, big business and citizens with consumer power is itself more of a social problem than a solution (Caldeira 2000; Fix 2001), and a problem that could only be aggravated, particularly in Rio de Janeiro but also in other metropolitan cities, by new processes of eviction and relocation associated with Brazil's hosting of the 2014 World Cup and 2016 Olympics.[2]

In an analysis that puts cities such as São Paulo into a global context, Neil Smith (2002) emphasizes not only the class bias behind the term 'urban regeneration', which so often means 'retaking the city for the middle classes', but also the centrality of real estate development to the productive economy of cities in a neo-liberal 'third wave' of gentrification in which private finance plays the leading role. If struggles over social reproduction become heightened everywhere under this new form of urbanism, so, Smith argues, does authoritarian policing to make the streets safe for gentrification by repressing social movements campaigning against lack of affordable housing (Smith 2002: 442). In São Paulo, workers consigned to the urban periphery endure arduous and expensive commutes to work imposed upon them by 'the pitiful wages on which this capital centralization is built' (Smith 2002: 435–436). Residents of more centrally located favelas in Brazilian cities build yet another storey on top of their houses to avoid relocating to more peripheral areas, despite the fact that this exacerbates the conflicts between neighbours and drug-related violence afflicting their overcrowded settlements (Handzic 2010: 15). At one level they are simply trapped by the cost structures that the wider economy imposes on them and by their own investments in self-built housing. Yet having made those investments, they too have a material stake in contesting their place in the city. I will argue that Smith is unduly pessimistic in suggesting that Lefebvre's announcement of an urban revolution redefining urban struggles in terms of social reproduction has 'faded into historical memory' because 'the dramatic urban expansion of the twenty-first century will be unambiguously led by social production rather than reproduction' (Smith 2002: 436). There is, however, no doubt that the contemporary drivers of urban development, including sports mega-events, pose new problems for stigmatized lower-income groups.

Second, we need to ask whether 'participation' as an artefact of neoliberal rule plays an exceptionally important role in *urban* governance. The Brazilian urban poor have shown a persistent historical capacity for mobilization and organization. This is not entirely *self*-organization, since 'external actors' from other social classes have always been involved (Assies 1999). In the case of Salvador, a city whose population is 80 per cent Afro-descendent, these external actors were also predominantly 'white' in the past, but today's foreign NGO and transnational activist networks include United States–based militant black organizations intent on challenging Brazil's ideologies of racial democracy and implanting a new politics founded on the principle of historical restitution for slavery (Costa Vargas 2006). Elites therefore face a real problem of institutionalizing popular demands and keeping them within politically manageable limits.

Despite pervasive crime, violence and insecurity, Brazil remains an apparently 'well-governed' society. Contained in their favelas by a policing system that combines extra-judicial violence with corruption and victimizes a working population stigmatized by images of criminality and the 'racialization' of poverty, slum-dwellers have arguably never presented a threat to the established order of things. This seemed truer after 2008, when Rio de Janeiro began to implement new public security policies. Following an initial occupation by the police or military to arrest or expel armed traffickers, specially trained "pacificatory police units" (UPPs, Unidades de Polícia Pacificadora) were installed on a permanent basis in Rio favelas located next to more affluent areas in an arc around the city's main football stadium.[3] Yet favela residents have shown a growing capacity to contest their stigmatization. Up to a point, neo-liberal governmentality can canalize these popular sentiments in directions that are 'productive' from the point of view of creating the 'right' kinds of social subjects and drawing a line between the acceptable and the excessively 'radical' (Hale 2002). Anti-racist legislation can be combined with programmes to foster individual 'self-esteem' and 'black role models' that embody a spirit of enterprise. Promotion of black music and culture provides individuals with livelihood opportunities that enhance an urban environment catering for global tourism. Partnerships between community organizations and public, private and third-sector organizations reduce the cost of social service delivery and training programmes. They also 'frame' social problems in terms of normative standards imposed from above on what constitutes a 'desirable' pattern of family organization, justifying deeper interventions in the intimate lives of people and communities. Yet intervention strategies complemented by rituals of participation have more power than top-down measures alone to create a sense of grassroots 'ownership' of policies that often evolve in a transnational sphere that is extremely distanced socially from the groups whose conduct is to be governed.

On the wrong side of the line drawn by neo-liberal governmentality projects are demands for the creation of urban *quilombos*[4] and major public interventions in the property regime that condemns the working poor to an overcrowded existence on the margins of urban land allocation. So are demands to change an urban spatial architecture that prioritizes the residential, service, transport and security needs of upper-income residents.

Nor is this a purely spatial issue in a city such as Salvador, whose conservative modernizing elite promoted development based on financial, administrative and commercial services and global tourism as a complement to industrial development based on petro-chemicals and capital-intensive multinational plants that generated comparatively little employment. Although unemployment fell to historic lows and the proportion of workers enjoying state protection and benefits increased to historic highs as the Brazilian economy boomed at the end of the first decade of the twenty-first century, Salvador remains a city in which many of the working poor still find 'informal' economic activity more attractive than low-wage employment.

The case I am going to describe here suggests, however, that once governance is couched in the idiom of popular participation, the objects of these governmentality projects re-appropriate the categories within which they are encouraged to express their demands, learn rapidly about the constraining effects of the new power relations to which they are subject, contest the bases of certain kinds of interventions and raise their expectations in a way that may yet realize more of the promise of the City Statute. The actors in this story have internalized certain ways of framing demands and negotiating with state agencies, but they have not become docile subjects of neo-liberal governmentality. One reason for this is that while they continue to fight various internal political battles, they do so within a context shaped by a struggle to defend a foothold in the city that retains the goal of working together, despite central differences in their engagements with public power. The centre-periphery framework of Smith's model of neo-liberal urbanism is too simple to capture the spatial, political-economic and political dimensions of the case I will describe here, in which the 'centre' has now come to the 'periphery' as what was once a peripheral space occupied by land invaders has become one of the most dynamic and valorized areas of an expanding twenty-first-century capitalist city, whilst the political opportunities of this 'marginalized' population have also changed significantly as a result of national developments in the politics of 'race'.

Modernizing Salvador

Founded in 1549, Salvador became the hub of an Atlantic economy based on the enslavement of Africans and the export of sugar and other plantation products. The colonial city's spatial organization resembled that of Lisbon. Most of its population, free and slave, rich and poor, lived in the administrative and religious centre of the 'upper city', built on the cliffs overlooking a 'lower city' containing financial, port and market facilities, built along the edge of All Saints Bay. The colonial city involved some so-cial intimacy between classes and races since hierarchy was not expressed by spatial segregation but vertically: slaves lived on the lower floors of buildings occupied by their masters (Bacelar 2001). Although urban–rural social distinctions remain as important in Bahia as in the case of southern Peru analysed by Lund in this volume, they are configured in a different way historically. The only Afro-Brazilians to live in self-governing com-munities were the runaway slaves who formed *quilombos*; rural land re-form remains limited and contested, making it difficult to link claims to invaded urban land to principles of agrarian social justice through land redistribution. Yet even servitude did not prove a barrier to 'autonomous' organization, whilst 'civilized' white elites have never managed to segre-gate themselves completely from the black and mulatto majority occupy-ing Salvador's urban space.

Significant transformations of the social geography of Salvador in the decade before military rule did, however, reflect efforts to achieve greater segregation as better-off families began to move out of the decaying historic centre of the upper city towards the Atlantic coast, abandoning it to lower-class residents. As the city expanded over the hills and ridges that charac-terize the abrupt topography beyond the original colonial settlement, poor Afro-Brazilian families colonized the unoccupied low-lying valley floors. Yet given low incomes, high rents for private housing, and a dearth of public housing, settlements were already being formed by land invasions around the old city before 1950, and invasions extended to the Atlantic coastal strip itself during that decade (Gordilho 2000: 195). In practice, it has never proved possible to transform a mosaic of urban settlement in which poor citizens live in close proximity to better-off neighbours. Physi-cal and social barriers have been strengthened by the upper and middle classes' shift to condominium living and stronger policing of boundaries, but even before military rule ended, new invasions were filling in all re-maining pockets of vacant land wherever they were to be found.

Initially, however, the advent of military rule saw determined efforts to end unplanned urban expansion and construct instead a city adapted to new paradigms of capitalist modernity. Appointed city Prefect in 1967 as a protégé of the dictatorship, Antônio Carlos Magalhães (popularly known as ACM) was to dominate Bahian politics for the rest of the twentieth cen-tury, serving three terms as state governor and holding ministerial offices in the federal government. ACM's first act as prefect was to take personal charge of eviction of illegal settlers from the coastal strip. Although he of-fered a populist justification for his actions as a move against privileged, middle-class people who had disobeyed the law, promising resettlement on publicly owned land to any poor families that had lost their homes, the removal of visible poverty from this emerging 'exclusive area' (*área nobre*, literally 'noble area' in Portuguese) was desirable not simply from the point of view of real estate development targeted at higher-income residents but also as a means of developing the city's beaches for upscale national and international tourism (Dantas Neto 2006: 306). ACM also eventually realized his long-standing ambition to rehabilitate Salvador's historic centre, the Pelourinho, although its 'return to the city' via the eviction of most of its lower-class residents had to wait until his final term as governor, when it became possible to secure the funds required because UNESCO had declared the Pelourinho a World Heritage Site (Collins 2004; Dantas Neto 2006: 307).

Accumulation by dispossession (Harvey 2005) was equally central to another key aspect of ACM's initial modernization programme, the construction of interior highways to connect the zones in which new economic developments were taking place, since these passed through the valley areas hitherto occupied by poor Afro-Brazilians. By obliging occupants to buy, ACM's Law of Urban Reform ended an antiquated leasehold system that allowed private citizens to acquire perpetual control of public lands for a fixed annual payment. Large landholders could pay by returning part of their holdings to the city. Once again, ACM put a populist 'spin' on his measure, suggesting that it would dismantle the large private estates that had developed on public lands and enable 'the popular classes' to acquire full property rights to their dwellings. A policy of allowing land invaders the right to acquire permanent property rights over publicly owned land was already being discussed as a solution to 'urban disorder' by the end of the 1950s, by which stage middle-class city residents facing high rents were also pressing for reform of the land tenure system, adding to the political pressure on landholding elites (Dantas Neto 2006: 323). Here there is a limited parallel with the situation Lund describes for Peru, but removal of invasions continued to be justified in Bahia in this period on grounds of 'public hygiene' and the need to ensure more attractive living conditions for the growing urban middle classes. Property developers were the main beneficiaries of the Law of Urban Reform, and the populist discourse was but a cover for a process driven by a different logic (Dantas Neto 2006: 336). This history is important, because residents of poor neighbourhoods saw it potentially repeating itself after the city government that defeated ACM's political machine endorsed processes of 'urban renewal' that threatened them with dispossession 'in the public interest'.

One of ACM's most significant strategies as governor was to construct the state government's new Administrative Centre (CAB) on the Avenida Paralela, halfway between the old commercial zone in the lower city and the airport. Relocation of government buildings to this zone unleashed a boom in land valorization between the site of the CAB and areas that were forming a new commercial centre for the 'modernized' city. By the end of ACM's second term as governor, many firms were relocating their offices from the old port area to the new central business district surrounded by upscale vertical condominiums developed around Iguatemi, the site of the city's first shopping mall (founded in 1975), a hypermarket and a new bus terminal (Almeida 2006: 39). The Avenida Paralela also opened the way to the further development of the northern coast of Bahia as a location for weekend homes and tourist resorts, offering rapid access to the city centre and upscale residential districts beyond Iguatemi.

So in 1982, when invaders began to occupy a site on the Avenida Paralela six kilometres beyond the CAB, they were inserting themselves into the principal future path of expansion of the capitalist city.

From the Malvinas to Bairro da Paz

Although the pioneer settlers rebuilt their precarious shelters after they were demolished, in 1983 the prefecture combined forced removal tactics with an attempt to negotiate the settlers' permanent relocation to public lands in another, distant area (Hita and Duccini 2007), at the very moment when the accession of Brizola to the governorship of Rio brought a halt to the policy of forced removal there. Many settlers, finding the alternative location a poor one in terms of environment, transport and access to jobs, returned to the Avenida Paralela site. An organized hard core resisted relocation, and the invasion continued to attract new families. The militancy of the invaders' resistance earned this community the sobriquet 'the Malvinas', a reference to the contemporary war between Britain and Argentina over control of the Falkland Islands. The invaders secured support from politicians of the Left, the Movement for the Defence of Slum Dwellers, and Catholic Church organizations. Of the latter, the most important was CEAS (Centre of Studies and Social Action), a liberation theology-oriented Jesuit NGO created in 1967 to engage in politico-educative activity throughout the Brazilian Northeast.

As democracy was slowly restored, political opportunities began to change. ACM's political machine suffered a temporary reverse in the 1987 state elections – the first truly democratic elections after military rule – when Waldir Pires won the state governorship, standing for the centrist Party of the Brazilian Democratic Movement. Although Pires's tenure was brief, it was sufficient for the area of the Malvinas invasion to be declared suitable for human habitation. The invaded lands' official owners, the Visco family, transferred their rights over the property to the city government to offset accumulated unpaid taxes, and the prefecture issued the residents provisional permission to use it (Hita and Duccini 2007). By

1988, the city government had promised the renamed 'Bairro da Paz' basic infrastructure works, and the Viscos had transferred a further tranche of land to the prefecture for distribution as housing lots.

The transformation of the Malvinas invasion into an officially recognized neighbourhood of the city, even if its legal situation and infrastructure remained precarious, reflected the broader conjuncture of change embodied in the 1988 Constitution, outlined at the start of this chapter. The problem was that the resources required to implement these new ideas remained limited under conditions of economic stagnation and crisis that continued well into the 1990s.

Waldir Pires prided himself on having made housing for low-income families a priority for the first time in the history of Bahia. Past public housing programmes had excluded poorer families by designating a cut-off point of an income equivalent to three minimum salaries, obliging most people to seek to solve their housing problems by land invasion and self-construction (Gordilho 2000). Under a new national programme, benefits promised to Bairro da Paz included a regularized electricity supply and public buildings such as a crèche, church, school, medical post and building for the Residents' Association. In practice, government delivered few improvements to this community between 1988 and 2000. What money was available was concentrated on other poor areas of the city. A new urbanization programme drawn up in 1999 was to be realized as a partnership between the Italian NGO Association of Volunteers in International Service and the state government development corporation, with World Bank funding, but it was not carried through.

Given limited availability of public funds, the bulk of improvements during the 1990s were delivered through Catholic NGOs, or partnerships between these NGOs and city authorities, under the centre-left administration of Lídice da Mata, the city's only female prefect to date (1993–1997) and later leader of the Brazilian Socialist Party group in the federal senate, and Antônio Imbassahy (1997–2004), then aligned with ACM's Party of the Liberal Front, although he later became a federal deputy for the Brazilian Social Democracy Party. The very marginality of Bairro da Paz increased its attractiveness for NGO investment, and under the Imbassahy administration, more public funding also flowed in. By 2002, a bus line connected the *bairro* to the city centre, four doctors staffed the medical post and a state primary school had finally been inaugurated, albeit it offered only the first four years of primary education. By 2007, with a population now reaching 60,000, the community possessed not only a health centre but also three primary schools, a provisional and badly equipped secondary school and a 'digital inclusion' *Telecentro* connected to the Internet. Some of the community crèches organized by religious associations received support from public funds. The Living Together Centre, which had opened in 2005, offered various kinds of training activities funded by the investors behind the upscale Alphaville condominium developments built in the surrounding area, in partnership with a private university, the Faculdade de Tecnologia e Ciências.

An important part of the negotiations that transformed the Malvinas invasion into a recognized neighbourhood of the city was that the prefecture's assent to allowing the community to remain was conditional on the Residents' Association's agreeing to help limit the numbers of new settlers. Although this did not halt long-term growth of the settlement, it did mean that in 1991, the density of occupation in Bairro da Paz, at 200 inhabitants per hectare, remained far below both that of zones invaded earlier and the city average of between 300 and 599 inhabitants per hectare (Gordilho 2000: 148). This, together with the availability of work in construction and in the surrounding upper-income condominiums developed in the area, made Bairro da Paz a relatively attractive place to live. At the same time, the protracted struggle against eviction created a collective identity built explicitly around the idea of militant 'resistance' (Hita 2012).

No Docile Subjects Here

In the 1990s, the newly created 'neighbourhood' was colonized by both ACM's clientelistic political machine and more conservative service-delivery Catholic NGOs, complemented by other religious organizations such as Candomblé temples (*terreiros*) and evangelical churches. The Residents' Council – which had replaced the earlier Residents' Association in 1993, when the latter's leadership came under attack for failure to hold elections and personal enrichment – became the most significant community organization, although it faced challenges from rival leaders. One of the most significant was Ronaldo, founder of the Luiz Eduardo Magalhães Association named after the deceased younger son of ACM, groomed as his political heir in preference to his elder brother Antônio Junior, who preferred to manage the business interests the family had accumulated in the course of ACM's political career. Ronaldo's association has now been completely eclipsed by the Residents' Council, which he accused of using its partnerships with private, public and third-sector organizations to subsidize 'internal mafias'. In the past, Ronaldo's close relations with Prefect Imbassahy strengthened his influence over the flow of projects into Bairro da Paz, but despite his involvement in the initial negotiations with the Faculdade de Tecnologia e Ciências and the Alphaville condominium developers, control of this initiative passed to the Residents' Council as political patronage networks shifted following the defeat of ACM's candidate in the 2005 municipal elections.

Ronaldo's organization was not alone in criticizing the Residents' Council. Contention at the grass roots is inevitable, given the inequalities existing with the *bairro* and the difficulties of securing sufficient resources to meet the needs of the entire community. 'Urbanization' in the form of street paving, lighting and improved sanitation was concentrated in the central zone of the community, where the main Catholic Church, other key public buildings and bigger shops were located. Residents of the zones beyond the centre not only resented this somewhat, but also found themselves in a particularly precarious legal situation because the prefecture only conceded rights to occupy land – without immediate issue of property titles – to residents in the central zone of the original invasion, defined as the 'polygonal', although improvements in the form of schools and plazas have now been extended to additional areas.

The absence of formal property titles in favelas has not, however, proved a barrier to the development of lively informal land markets, which reflects an important consequence of states' tendency to condone illegal activities that 'unfold within prescribed limits' as Lund emphasizes in this volume. In Rio, the development of such markets has pushed up the costs of acquiring land or renting space in what Cavalcanti (2009) calls 'consolidated' favelas: centrally located settlements that boast mature housing stocks improved by residents' investments and also have benefited from public investments in infrastructure, including the 'Favela to Neighbourhood' slum-upgrading programmes of the 1990s. Critiquing the enthusiasm for private property titling, shared by neo-liberals such as Hernando de Soto (2000) and many favela residents themselves, Handzic (2010) argues that retention of land in the public domain, with legalization restricted to rights of use, offers a valuable regulatory instrument that can actively serve the interests of social justice by protecting the economically vulnerable from displacement from consolidated favelas and excluding wealthier outsiders from entry into the land market that favelas constitute even in a situation of 'informality'.[5] These issues are important in Bairro da Paz because, in contrast to some other low-income neighbourhoods in Salvador, no regulations are in force to prevent outsiders from buying up and combining adjacent tracts of land sold by existing residents.

The functioning of the public property regime is determined by the broader politics of urban planning. In the past the *bairro*'s land tenure situation provoked fears, not only of the municipal government's eviction of families living beyond the polygonal, but also of creeping informal community decomposition from within, should developers acquire land from existing residents in weaker economic positions by making tempting offers for assets whose value was rising following the construction of more condominiums, a shopping mall and a technology park in the zone. Anxieties rose to a new pitch in late April 2010, when councillors from the political opposition revealed the enabling decrees for the city's urban renewal plan. In areas subject to expropriation, 'planning blight' (uncertainty about the future) would leave all property owners with devalued assets, but Bairro da Paz faced particularly serious threats, including the prospect of a major new highway passing through the heart of the community. Even residents inside the polygonal now became nervous.

The immediate reaction was renewed mobilization, whose bases I will now explore in more detail. Catholic service-delivery NGOs have played a particularly prominent part in community life and the formation of community associations. The political positions of Catholic actors range from a relatively conservative charitable posture to more radical projects inspired by liberation theology. The Dom Avelar Foundation (FDA), coordinated by Clementina, an Italian missionary, stands at the centre of the Catholic intervention network. It works with Bahia's Santa Casa de Misericórdia to fund the six biggest community crèches and, to provide educational and artistic courses to young people, with the Cidade Mãe (Mother City) Foundation, launched in 1993 under the Lídice da Mata administration with UNICEF funding. Figures associated with the Santa Casa do not, however, have homogeneous views.

From the perspective of the Catholics inspired by liberation theology, the FDA represented a paternalistic approach incompatible with the consciousness-raising, empowering, participant-democracy project CEAS sought to promote. According to one CEAS activist, Clementina used her foundation's economic power 'to buy everything and everyone', obliging even the Residents' Council to bend to her will. Nevertheless, the CEAS-FDA conflict did not straightforwardly map itself onto the council's internal politics. Marivaldo, its vice-president in 2007, was closely tied to Clementina, not only as her subordinate in the FDA but also as a self-proclaimed admirer of her work. Yet he publicly articulated ideas more easily associated with the radical posture of CEAS, consistently arguing the need to reject the 'impositions' of government institutions and NGOs alike in favour of a more combative and autonomous stance of demand-making consistent with the community's long history of militant struggle. Repeatedly raising the spectre of plans to evict the community, Marivaldo regularly advocates resort to its trump card in direct action – its ability to paralyse the city by blocking traffic on the Avenida Paralela with a mass sit-down protest. The road was duly blocked after the decrees enabling land expropriation were promulgated in 2010. Although mobilizations elsewhere in the city led to revocation of most of them, this did not happen in the case of Bairro da Paz, and tensions remained despite the city government's offers to negotiate.

CEAS itself disengaged from the Residents' Council to focus on supporting youth groups, whose leaders were often critical of the way the Council was run. Bairro da Paz is home to several *capoeira*[6] groups; reggae, hip-hop and rock groups; *pagode*[7] and *forró*[8] groups; groups dedicated to various styles of dance, including the Afro-Brazilian *Maculelê*; and theatre groups. Much of this activity is linked to sponsored 'cultural valorization' projects, such as Afrodance and Youth in Action, which bring together dance, *capoeira,* theatre and hip-hop. 'Cultural valorization' resonates with efforts by NGOs active in the *bairro* to promote self-esteem and 'capacity for citizenship' among young people. As young people emerge as community political actors, we see that these programmes sometimes have impacts beyond those their sponsors envisaged. Youth in Action became particularly critical of the Residents' Council, withdrawing from it completely in 2003.

Although Afrodance developed out of the *capoeira* group of the internationally famous *mestre* Paulo dos Anjos, a Bairro da Paz resident, few of these groups enjoy any sustained sponsorship. This encouraged them to come together to discuss their common problems and interests outside the established associational institutions of the community, although divisions still exist within as well as between these different groups, and many of their members simply want a chance to perform and gain a livelihood. Nevertheless, in an environment in which Afro-Brazilian cultural performance is strongly associated with an enhanced public policy emphasis on the promotion of racial equality, and programmes focused on the 'institutional empowerment' of black youth continue to multiply, young people have become strongly aware that they have more voice and potential influence.

Despite high levels of internal contention over power and objectives between different kinds of community leaderships, which have always included a significant number of women as well as men, Bairro da Paz produced an overarching organization called the Permanent Forum of Social Entities that sought to counteract the fragmentation produced by past political and NGO interventions and social and religious differences, thus fostering a unified approach to forcing public authorities to pay greater attention to the community's continued deficits of security, employment, educational and leisure facilities, public spaces and basic infrastructure. Having captured the imagination of the youth group leaderships, the forum has brought them back into dialogue with the leadership of the Residents' Council and a diversity of other community political actors, including a veteran leader from the days of the original Residents' Association. It has now held several public events at which representatives of state and municipal government were asked to respond to the community's own diagnoses of its problems, and representatives of the different member associations and groups meet regularly through the year to develop actions.

There is genuine demand-making here. Functionaries are being forced to explain why past urbanization and health service plans were not implemented. The issue of policing that victimizes rather than protects residents is forcefully articulated. The forum attracts media attention in ways that have advanced the campaign to contest the *bairro's* stigmatized public image as nothing more than a nest of drug-traffickers. The youth groups have made the most of opportunities to stage public events, funded by affirmative action programmes, that they politicize in their own ways because their lived experience of discrimination and police violence transcends the bounds of neo-liberal multiculturalism. Most, however, are more interested in asserting their right to respect than in 'racializing' the political process.

A telling event was a public meeting early in April 2010, to which functionaries were invited to explain how the community might be affected by plans for the 2014 World Cup. When they expressed ignorance of the expropriation decrees shortly to be made public, suggested that it was inconceivable that a community of 60,000 people that had received significant public investments could possibly be slated for relocation, and in one case questioned the representativeness of the forum, the aggressive interventions of ordinary residents as well as community leaders clearly took them by surprise, to the point of disturbing a few older and more conservative members of the forum itself.

The forum emerged internally stronger from this encounter, but the power networks that bind community actors into wider systems remain significant. João Henrique Carneiro, re-elected to a second term as prefect of Salvador in 2008 after changing his party affiliation from the Democratic Labour Party founded by Leonel Brizola to the centrist Party of the Brazilian Democratic Movement, is an evangelical. This gave actors in the community who shared his religious outlook some leverage, although Catholic activists retain a broader range of external networking opportunities. The overall pattern is a proliferation of grassroots political subjects embracing new ways of doing grassroots politics, at least some of which represent a re-appropriation of neo-liberal multicultural agendas to press more radical demands for social justice.

Conclusion: Struggling through Contradictions

One of the Bairro da Paz story's most interesting aspects, central to understanding the kind of grassroots politics that has developed in this settlement, is the neighbourhood's location in a space of leading-edge capitalist

transformation. Amongst those who favoured removal of the original invasion were environmentalists, who argued that preservation of the Atlantic
Forest in the zone should have priority over human habitation. In this respect, the fact that the invaders succeeded in establishing themselves was
highly convenient for the property developers of the Alphaville group,
whose closed horizontal condominiums represent the upper end of the
market in terms of secure and luxurious living beyond inner-city bustle.

For a time, Alphaville's vision of urbanism was neatly encapsulated in
a graphical map on its corporate website. Designed to emphasize the environmental sensitivity of Alphaville projects, it depicted a route that started
with the iconic tourist attractions of the old city, Bonfim Church and the
Pelourinho. Leading outwards to the new, the Alphaville urban vector
marks the major shopping malls en route, then the CAB, before arriving
at Alphaville itself, the ultimate bourgeois – and green – utopia. There is
no place for Bairro da Paz in such a representation. Yet the Alphaville developers found it politically expedient to demonstrate their social responsibility by offering training courses to young people from the slum. Other
consortia involved in the development of the areas around Bairro da Paz
have followed suit, working hard to find allies amongst community leaders, but these moves have not convinced most residents of the *bairro* that
the developers have their best interests at heart. In 2007, a government
spokesperson suggested that developments such as Alphaville demonstrated that the rich would inevitably prove better guardians of nature
than the inhabitants of Bairro da Paz. Such discourses apparently foreclose on the possibilities of future planning models that might promote
lower-density, leafier places in the city for poor people. They might even
signal a desire to deny the next generation a place in the city altogether.
This official's remarks reawakened what became a growing concern,
among residents ever more encircled by condominiums, that the agenda
remained their removal rather than the hardly impractical alternative of
assisting their ascent into the lower middle class.

It would be a historical irony if the rich ended up invading the land
of the poor, but this would not really be unusual in Brazil. The lingering
threat makes the conversion of Bairro da Paz into a community of docile
neo-liberal subjects unlikely. This is more than simply a defensive stance.
The children and grandchildren of the growing population of the urban
periphery will have to fight for their right to the city, and they will do so in
plain sight of the fact that another world exists for the favoured few.

This chapter has focused on one favela in Salvador that demonstrates
that 'hope' does not necessarily die in socially stigmatized spaces, and that
their residents can remain politically astute actors capable of struggling
for their rights. This community's struggle is strengthened by the way in
which young people involved in Afro-Brazilian cultural projects, as well

as production cooperatives and skills training programmes, have become targets of state, private-public partnership and NGO interventions that have given them a new kind of 'voice' in community – and broader urban – politics. Such developments stimulate movements to counter the city government's talk of 'rehabilitating' areas of urban degradation, which evokes memories of past dispossession. Meanwhile, we need to recognize that even limited success in community development breeds social differentiation: leaderships in Bairro da Paz frequently allude to the disintegrating force of what they themselves term 'individualism'. Even best-case scenarios in a neo-liberalized market society display contradictions, and it is necessary to acknowledge that the situation in some of Salvador's low-income neighbourhoods echoes that in many favelas of Rio de Janeiro.

Cavalcanti (2009) has argued that the residents of Rio's consolidated favelas are trapped in a double bind. Because favelas were stigmatized places seen as threatening the order of the city, they obtained sufficient leverage in city politics to receive material improvements. Yet their stigmatization and the everyday violence that both traffickers and police perpetrated within them seriously reduced their 'liveability'. The tragedy facing residents is that although their lives have been improved materially by their investments in housing – which, for the older generation, is the fruit of their struggle to defend their right to the city as well as to build the home itself (Cavalcanti 2009: 74) – the invidious social distinction between 'favela' and 'asphalt' is ever stronger in Rio. Bairro da Paz itself may yet face more of the violence of Smith's 'revanchist' neo-liberal city, already manifest in evictions elsewhere in the country; community leaders may be co-opted, and collective resistance may be weakened by individuals deciding to sell up and leave. Yet this case study shows that organized struggle against these oppressive conditions remains possible and can yield positive results, not least because its 'insurgent citizens' (Holston 2008) can make their own diagnoses of the contradictions their actions must transcend.

Notes

Much of the ethnographic data used in this essay was collected by the team responsible for the project Poverty, Social Networks and Mechanisms of Social Inclusion/Exclusion, directed by Maria Gabriela Hita of the Federal University of Bahia and financed by the Bahian State Research Council (FAPESB) and the Centre for Studies of the Metropolis of the Brazilian Centre for Analysis and Planning (CEBRAP) as part of a comparative study with low income-settlements in São Paulo and Rio de Janeiro. I am very grateful to Dr Hita for sharing this material with me and inviting me to participate in the team's work in support of the development of the Forum of Social Entities.

1. The political Right blames Brizola not only for the continued growth of favelas but also for the consolidation of the power of drug-trafficking gangs within them. This perspective abstracts from the sustained lack of affordable housing for the poorer sections of Brazilian society and the failure of a more violent policing to improve matters. Residents recently found their lives made even more miserable by the extortion perpetrated by paramilitary militias that took over some Rio favelas, under the patronage of politicians arguing for a 'zero tolerance' approach and recruiting former or serving police officers to do the dirty work (Zaluar and Conceição 2007).
2. On 26 April 2011, Brazilian urban planner Raquel Rolnik issued a statement on these problems in her role as UN Special Rapporteur on adequate housing as a human right. She reported allegations from many Brazilian cities of a lack of transparency, consultation, dialogue and negotiation in evictions already undertaken or being planned. The financial compensation offered to affected communities seemed ridiculously low given the rise in real estate values created by redevelopment, and people were being relocated to sites without services, infrastructure or access to jobs. The text is online at http://www.ohchr.org/EN/NewsEvents/Pages/DisplayNews.aspx?NewsID=10960&LangID=E, accessed 5 May 2011.
3. The first UPP in Salvador was established in April 2011, but in Bahia the units are called 'Community Security Bases', a semantic difference perhaps intended to persuade sceptical residents that the new policies aim to improve their security rather than simply that of their higher-class neighbours. By February 2012, five such bases had been established, with twelve more projected for later in the year, one of which will be located in Bairro da Paz, the neighbourhood that is the principal focus of this chapter.
4. *Quilombo* originally denoted a community created by runaway slaves, but the 1988 Constitution granted *quilombos* the same rights Indian communities have to collective landholding, although such claims must be validated through a tortuous legal process before land is officially titled. The more radical idea of demanding recognition of new urban *quilombos* as recompense for the historical crime of enslavement has caught on with some young people despite the restricted success of militant black politics in Brazil, because it is a symbolically powerful way of morally grounding rights to occupy land and a broader right to the city.
5. State interventions also have unplanned consequences. For example, the regularization of conduct within favela space that the UPPs introduced in Rio de Janeiro has increased residents' living costs by combating illegal connections to the electrical grid, obliging some to move elsewhere.
6. A combination of balletic performance and martial art.
7. A subgenre of the samba music of Rio.
8. The dance music of the interior zones of the North-east, derived from European antecedents.

References

Almeida, P.H. 2006. 'A economia de Salvador e a formação de sua Região Metropolitana', in I.M. Moreira de Carvalho and G. Corso Pereira (eds), *Como anda Salvador e sua Região Metropolitana*. Salvador: Edufba, pp. 11–53.

Assies, W. 1999. 'Theory, Practice and "External Actors" in the Making of New Urban Social Movements in Brazil', *Bulletin of Latin American Research* 18(2): 211–226.

Bacelar, J. 2001. *A hierarquia das raças: negros e brancos em Salvador*. Rio de Janeiro: Pallas Editora.

Caldeira, T.P. 2000. *City of Walls: Crime, Segregation, and Citizenship in Sao Paulo*. Berkeley: University of California Press.

————. and J. Holston. 2004. 'State and Urban Space in Brazil: From Modernist Planning to Democratic Intervention', in A. Ong and S.J. Collier (eds), *Global Assemblages: Technology, Politics and Ethics as an Anthropological Problem*. Malden, MA: Blackwell, pp. 393–416.

Cavalcanti, M. 2009. 'Do barraco à casa: Tempo, espaço e valor(es) em uma favela consolidada', *Revista Brasileira de Ciências Sociais* 24(69): 69–80.

Collins, J. 2004. 'X Marks the Future of Brazil: Protestant Ethics and Bedeviling Mixtures in a Brazilian Cultural Heritage Center', in A. Shryock (ed.), *Off Stage/On Display: Intimacy and Ethnography in the Age of Public Culture*. Stanford, CA: Stanford University Press, pp. 191–222.

Costa Vargas, J.H.C. 2006. 'When a Favela Dared to Become a Gated Condominium: The Politics of Race and Urban Space in Rio de Janeiro', *Latin American Perspectives* 33(4): 49–81.

Dantas Neto, P.F. 2006. *Tradição, autocracia e carisma: A política de Antonio Carlos Magalhães na modernizacão da Bahia (1954–1974)*. Belo Horizonte: Universidade Federal de Minas Gerais.

de Soto, H. 2000. *The Mystery of Capital: Why Capitalism Triumphs in the West and Fails Everywhere Else*. New York: Basic Books.

Fix, M. 2001. *Parceiros da exclusão: Duas histórias da construção de uma "nova cidade" em São Paulo*. São Paulo: Boitempo Editorial.

Gordilho Souza, A. 2000. *Limites do habitar. Segregação e exclusão na configuração urbana contemporânea de Salvador e perspectivas no final do século XX*. Salvador: Edufba.

Gustafson, B.D. 2009. *New Languages of the State: Indigenous Resurgence and the Politics of Knowledge in Bolivia*. Durham, NC: Duke University Press.

Hale, C. 2002. 'Does Multiculturalism Menace? Governance, Cultural Rights and the Politics of Identity in Guatemala', *Journal of Latin American Studies* 34(3): 485–524.

Handzic, K. 2010. 'Is Legalized Land Tenure Necessary in Slum Upgrading? Learning from Rio's Land Tenure Policies in the Favela Bairro Program', *Habitat International* 34(1): 11–17.

Harvey, D. 2005. *A Brief History of Neoliberalism*. Oxford: Oxford University Press.

Hita, M.G. 2012. 'From Resistance Avenue to the Plaza of Decisions: New Urban Actors in Salvador, Bahia', in J. Gledhill and P. Schell (eds), *New Approaches to Resistance in Brazil and Mexico*. Durham, NC, and London: Duke University Press, pp. 269–288.

————. and L. Duccini. 2007. 'Da guerra à paz: o nascimento de um ator social no contexto da "nova pobreza",' *Caderno CRH* 20(50): 281–297.

Holston, J. 2008. *Insurgent Citizenship: Disjunctions of Democracy and Modernity in Brazil*. Princeton, NJ: Princeton University Press.

Lefebvre, H. 1968. *Le droit à la ville*. Paris: Ed. Anthropos.

Miraftab, F. 2009. 'Insurgent Planning: Situating Radical Planning in the Global South', *Planning Theory* 8(1): 32–50.

Mosse, D. 2005. *Cultivating Development: An Ethnography of Aid Policy and Practice*. London: Pluto Press.

Postero, N.G. 2006. *Now We Are Citizens: Indigenous Politics in Postmulticultural Bolivia*. Stanford, CA: Stanford University Press.

Robertson, A.F. 1991. *Beyond the Family: The Social Organization of Human Reproduction*. Berkeley and Los Angeles: University of California Press.

————. 1996. 'The Development of Meaning: Ontogeny and Culture', *Journal of the Royal Anthropological Institute RAI* 2(4): 591–610.

Smith, N. 2002. 'New Globalism, New Urbanism: Gentrification as Global Urban Strategy', *Antipode* 34(3): 427–450.

Texeira, E. 2001. *O local e o global: limites e desafios da participação cidadã*. São Paulo: Ed. Cortez.

Valença, M.M. 2007. 'Poor Politics, Poor Housing: Policy under the Collor Government in Brazil (1990–92)', *Environment and Urbanization* 19(2): 391–408.

Zaluar, A. and I.S. Conceição. 2007. 'Favelas sob o controle das milícias no Rio de Janeiro', *São Paulo em Perspectiva* 21(2): 89–101.

Source: Richard Baxstrom

– Chapter 6 –

EVEN GOVERNMENTALITY BEGINS AS AN IMAGE

Institutional Planning in Kuala Lumpur

Richard Baxstrom

I think that most of their reports are simply bullshit!
— City planner, Dewan Bandaraya Kuala Lumpur
(referring to visions of 'the future' asserted in formal planning reports)

Velocity without Destination

Kuala Lumpur is always in motion. This fact is so widely cited it qualifies as a cliché. Yet in acknowledging the common sense of the statement, I cannot help but think that we seldom contemplate its wider effects on the everyday lives of Kuala Lumpur's urban population. Is the direction of this moment really clear? What are the outcomes of a form of urban living that is premised on never coming to rest? Can we anticipate what 'the future' will bring? Importantly, it appears that a particular form of urban life is discernibly coming into being in Kuala Lumpur. This form of life resembles life in other cities in the region (Singapore, Hong Kong, Jakarta) and arguably throughout the world, but Kuala Lumpur differs from these cities in the way urban living relates to time and experience.

The complexity of this form of life becomes clearer when one directly engages specific domains within this environment that work to shape and bring forth particular forms of urban existence. In this chapter, I will engage this complex field through a consideration of *planning* and *the plan* itself as a thing in the world. My argument is that the plan functions as a vehicle for action in the present that does not, in a formal sense, require a singular vision of the future in order to succeed on its own terms. As I will demonstrate, while the plan must gesture to '*the* future', this gesture does not often require the specification of '*a* future' in order to function in a highly effective manner in the present. While it would be empirically suspect to de-emphasize the elements of power and discipline essential to any institutional plan and its effects within a wider population, the evidence from Kuala Lumpur that I will present indicates that the primary effectiveness of the plan largely relates to its status as a virtual object in the present. As such, these virtual plans bind subjects to the conditions of the present within the desires and limits asserted by the institutions seeking to dominate contemporary life in the city. This domination, while often quite totalizing in its aspiration, is never absolute, singular or complete.

The multiplicity inherent in what a plan is and what a plan can do becomes clearer through the examination of two examples of recent institutional plans devised to address issues of the present in Kuala Lumpur. One, the National Integrity Plan, is grand and national in scope; the other, KL Monorail's plan for the Jalan-Jalan Leisure Park in the Brickfields area of the city, is specific to a particular urban development initiative. Through an examination of these plans, woven together with some consideration of the dispositions of individual bureaucrats responsible for the specific implementation of plans of this type, I intend to clarify my claims that the plan primarily exists as a virtual object in the present and that one can only explain the role of plans within governance and the life of the city by accounting for this relatively precise ontological status. While I draw exclusively from evidence gained in Kuala Lumpur, I hope that the detailed discussion that follows engages wider debates about urban planning throughout the world and contributes to our general understanding of what 'a plan' is in a variety of contexts.

Current Prime Minister Najib Tun Razak appears to have captured the manifold sense of life in contemporary Malaysia with his highly effective 1Malaysia campaign. In the wake of the commonly understood failure of Abdullah Ahmad Badawi's time as Prime Minister (2003–2009), Najib rose to the leadership of the country behind the slogan '1Malaysia. People First, Performance Now'. With its emphasis on inclusiveness, equality and promises to address a perceived drift in the country since the end of Mahathir Mohamad's long tenure as PM, Najib's slogan (devised by public relations experts) not only succinctly captured the mood of the country but also appeared to address itself to the very texture of everyday living in the country. It has been pointed out that Najib's 1Malaysia slogan has not coalesced into an objectively concrete plan of action, but perhaps this criticism misses the point (Chin 2010). 1Malaysia as an image has provided the ground on which the ruling Barisan Nasional ruling alliance, a coalition perceived to be greatly weakened by perceived mismanagement in the Badawi era, has been able to reassert itself as the dominant political force in the country. Despite Barisan Nasional's loss of its two-thirds majority in the parliament for the first time in its history, under Najib it has managed to forcefully affirm its rule in Malaysia. These political feats were achieved notwithstanding the vagueness of 1Malaysia in terms of specific goals and desired outcomes. Abstractly, Najib's programme seems a failure as a plan; objectively, however, it is evidently effective as an instrument of rule and of directing the country towards 'the future'.

How is this possible? To address this question, one must address the wider issue of the plan in general and the act of planning in relation to notions of proper governance, urban development and the seemingly strange disavowal of the near present that appears to mark contemporary institutionally based planning efforts such as 1Malaysia. By analysing several similar plans in this chapter, I aim to partially illustrate the character of urban life in contemporary Kuala Lumpur and the people who work on a daily level to formulate and execute such initiatives. Despite the wide proliferation of plans, it seems that life in Kuala Lumpur is always moving fast but never actually going anywhere, with individuals and institutions alike increasingly unwilling or unable to address themselves to the near present (Guyer 2007). To phrase the question more precisely, how is it possible to imagine or plan for a future that may never actually come in what increasingly feels like a zone of the infinite present?

The Plan as a Virtual Object

> [O]ur action will dispose of the future in the exact proportion in which our perception, enlarged by memory, has contracted the past.
> —Henri Bergson

At the level of the everyday in urban Malaysia, questions of past, present and future seem to matter a great deal. The overflowing abundance of plans appears to indicate that Malaysians are obsessed with the future. Draft structure plans, development plans, National Integrity Plans, the New Economic Policy, the National Development Policy, Wawasan 2020, Mission 2057 – getting to some imaginary future outpost appears to be a national obsession, a hangover from the space-age, progressive, prosperous piety of the Mahathir epoch. In this official version, the forward-looking, progressive Malaysian citizen 'respects' tradition but moves boldly into the future, and does so *according to plan*.

That such plans exist at the level of metaphysics in Malaysia becomes plain when one tries to determine the function of the plan. Typically, plans follow a simple structure of marking a domain of action, isolating a problem within that domain, formulating a procedure for addressing that problem within the specified domain and (importantly) specifying a set of projected/desired outcomes. Formal plans in Malaysia have historically followed this formula, but at the level of outcomes, an abyss often separates the ideal of the plan from the reality of its execution. Specifically, most empirical evidence suggests that the classic notion of a projected future outcome exists in such plans only as a formal gesture to the ideal of 'the plan' itself; in reality, the plan *effectively* functions as only a variable in the present, one factor amongst many in the everlasting horizon of the now in Malaysia.

Jomo K.S. points out that this relative gap concerning planning has a history in Malaysia. Although his focus is primarily on governmental economic planning when he observes that 'post-colonial economic planning has not provided much more than limited blueprints for industrial, agricultural and other economic development', his critical analysis of planning in Malaysia also reveals a pattern of oscillation between broadly defined 'blueprints' and more specifically oriented plans for change or action (Jomo 1999: 88). Early attempts at large-scale planning, such as the late-colonial era Draft Development Plan (1950–1955) and the post-independence Five Year Plans, were quite open in their projected outcomes: they tended to set a particular tone, but they did not necessarily possess more than a gestural relation to the future. As Malaysia moved aggressively to modernize its economy from the early 1970s on, more detailed and prescriptive plans like the wide-ranging New Economic Policy began to dominate spheres of governance, with specific efforts such as the creation of the Federal Land Development Authority exemplifying this particular approach to national-scale planning. As the country moved through the long Mahathir era (1981–2003), the character of planning began to swing back towards the more general 'blueprint', as typified by the introduction of VISION 2020 as part of the 6th Malaysia Plan in 1991 and the subsequent formation of related plans such as the National Integrity Plan, which is discussed in detail below (Jomo 1999; Gomez and Jomo 1999).

In light of this general history of institutional planning in Malaysia, the obvious question is how one can come to terms with the fact that in urban environments such as Kuala Lumpur, the past and the future have apparently receded from view without recourse to a framework of 'the end of history' or what Derrida identified as 'the apocalyptic tone in philosophy' (Derrida 1994; see also Geroulanos 2010). Getting at these issues requires a closer examination of two related questions that may strike the reader as naively simplistic. First, *what is a plan?* Secondly, and related to the first, *what is the function of the plan?*

As previously outlined, my argument is that the plan functions as an instrument of action in the present whose efficacy does not, in real terms, require a future in specific terms. This claim is linked to the ontological status of plans as *virtual objects* originating within images of thought that allow one to 'think' the condition of the present. The ontological status of the plan as such must be distinguished from the content or aspirations of specific plans. Thus, plans exist concretely as objects in thought that catalyse action. They operate discursively, both as evidence of mastery or aptitude of particularly fluid situations in the present, and as forms of strategy and hope that direct the agent towards movement, albeit seldom movement into 'the future' in a teleological sense. Taking some inspiration from Georges Canguilhem, my approach does not regard the plan as a form of knowledge or action that exists separately from life; rather, the plan, from its origins as a virtual object in thought, is concretely embedded *in* life[1] (Canguilhem 2008). Thus, the plan is material from the moment of its inception, embodies a process of becoming that accounts for its efficacy as an instrument of action in the present and (as all objects do in the ontological sense) generates a multiplicity of possible outcomes and uses, regardless of the specific discursive content of any one specific plan.

The multiplicity of aspects or characteristics within the plan as such must be understood as differences in *kind* rather than *degree,* so my analysis of the ethnographic evidence will necessarily tack back and forth between demonstrating how the specific plans described existed as objects and how they functioned discursively as vehicles of action in particular domains of everyday life in Kuala Lumpur. Such an understanding of multiplicity in plans only makes sense, however, if we consider the ontological status of the plan as such, putting aside for the moment the specificity of particular plans. Therefore, before addressing the question of what a plan *does,* we must consider what a plan *is*. Before a plan exists as discourse, within institutions, as documents or flow charts or budgets or manifestos, it exists as a virtual object, grasped within thought as *potential*. This image is not abstract but is perceptible as such: a Bergsonian object, existing in the interstices between the actual and the virtual. This complex theme is developed further in *Matter and Memory*: 'I call *matter* the aggregate of images, and *perception* of matter these same images referred to the eventual action of one particular image, my body' (Bergson 1991: 22, emphasis in original).

Bergson goes on to explain that matter does not possess some 'occult or unknowable power' and thus can be assimilated to the image as he defines it (Bergson 1991: 73). No doubt there can be more in matter than in the image we have of it, but there cannot be anything else in it, of a different kind. Thus, the presence of such images in consciousness, in a brain that exists as an image among images, is not essential to their perception as objects. Bergson is clear regarding the relation of such virtual objects to matter and to the actual. Understanding the plan as an image of the material, itself and at the same time material, reveals its potential as a vehicle of action regardless of the plan's specifics. At this basic level, the formulation of the image, or of the plan itself in this context, is the crucial point. The execution of the discursive content of the plan is immaterial to the plan's status as an object that generates movement in the world.

This is not to argue that the characteristics that give 'the plan' force and those that animate specific plans are opposed or exist within this object as discrete aspects. Indeed, the multiplicity of the plan as such is a powerful argument against simplistic binaries or dialectics. 'The virtual' should not be confused with 'the abstract', and to oppose the plan as an object to its content performs precisely this abstracting operation, confusing the issue of what gives a plan force as a particular kind of object among others in the world. As Deleuze has noted, 'Bergson criticizes the dialectic for being a *false movement,* that is, a movement of the abstract concept, which goes from one opposite to the other only by means of imprecision' (Deleuze 1991: 44, emphasis in the original). What this implies for my argument here is that the essential issue at stake in understanding what a plan does cannot be ascertained by comparing the plan with negative forms such as 'disorder' or 'non-planned', for such dualistic comparisons ultimately do not address multiplicity as an essential aspect of what a plan *is.* Following Bergson, the task is to think multiplicity independently of conceptual negations (Deleuze 1991). Only thusly can we gain understanding of what a plan is and how it functions.

In summary, understanding the plan as originating as a virtual object – an image of thought that exists as an object and subsequently provides the ground for a range of acts and outcomes over time, and particularly in the present – allows for more precise determinations of the variety of possible effects and outcomes that particular plans have in specific contexts. Starting from this point thus acknowledges the power that specific plans have or the mechanisms of power that are embedded in the execution of these plans, particularly at the level of state governance (Scott 1998; see also Herzfeld 2005; Li 2005). Clearly, however, even governmentality begins as an image: a perceptible virtual object that then proliferates through institutions, through discourse and, in the case of many large-scale, institutionally driven plans, directly and concretely into people's everyday lives. While such plans must discursively address themselves to both the future and the past, the zone of their true efficacy can only be the present. Thus, referring to Guyer's argument about time and the phenomenon of the near future seeming to recede into an ever-expanding zone of the present, the plan logically does not require a particular future in order to exist as an object or produce effects, intended or not, in the present.

Better Living through Planning: The National Integrity Plan

The National Integrity Plan (NIP) was announced with great fanfare by then Prime Minister Abdullah Ahmad Badawi in April 2004. Launched in conjunction with the founding of the Integrity Institute of Malaysia, the plan sought to reduce corruption, increase the efficiency of public institutions, enhance business ethics, strengthen family institutions and improve the quality of life for all Malaysians. Originally generated in response to an earlier report entitled 'Public Perception of Corruption in Malaysia'[2] the NIP sets quite laudable goals that appear necessary to everyone, probably even to the 'criminals' themselves. Reading carefully through the plan in the years since, however, one cannot but notice that, as high-minded as the general goals were, the plan outlines almost no concrete strategies to achieve these goals in any specific domain of public life within a definite period of time.

The NIP gestures towards the formal structure of any plan by including a 'strategies for implementation' section in the report. These gestures are referred to specifically as 'Integrity Agendas' (Government of Malaysia 2004: 41–47). Yet these agendas are anything but concrete sets of strategies for increasing the integrity of public or social institutions. Rather, the integrity agendas serve merely to amplify the need to 'enhance' integrity in families, businesses and government. Specific initiatives are deferred *infinitely* in these agendas and in this plan as a whole. Thus the projected outcomes and the strategies for achieving these goals become folded into each other in a breathtakingly tautological fashion. Paraphrasing the report, Malaysians must enhance the integrity of civil society by displaying noble values that will enhance the integrity of civil society.

Scrutiny of the specific 'Action Plans' outlined in Section IV of the report reveals further amplification of the NIP's circularity and lack of concrete goals and outcomes. In this section, the NIP looks to provide precise courses of action to address itself to eight specific social domains, including family, religion and politics. Yet the action plans themselves are hardly more specific than the generalities in the rest of the NIP. For example, the objectives and strategies for addressing integrity in 'the community' are as follows:

OBJECTIVES

Objective 1: Strengthening of good neighbourliness and community values

Objective 2: Strengthening of grass roots organizations and institutions in the community

Objective 3: Strengthening of patriotism and inter-ethnic unity as well as awareness for [sic] environmental protection

STRATEGIES

Strategy 1: Inculcate noble values through neighbourliness and community activities

Strategy 2: Establish networking between community and other organizations

Strategy 3: Strengthen patriotism and inter-ethnic relations

Strategy 4: Enhance awareness on [sic] environmental conservation

(Government of Malaysia 2004: 71)

Setting aside the conjoining of patriotic and environmental concerns in Objective 3 and their subsequent disaggregation in Strategies 3 and 4, it is starkly obvious that strategies and objectives in the NIP are collapsed into one another. This peculiar merging of objectives (future desires) and strategies (present action) is prevalent in the action plans for all social domains that this plan marks as requiring specific attention. In the pages that immediately follow this outline of objectives and strategies for 'community', some suggested actions do become marginally more concrete. They include the organization of campaigns to obtain community support for the Integrity Institute of Malaysia (IIM); an 'early warning system' to detect 'social ills and crimes', to be administered by the IIM; and formation of a database of 'resources persons' who would act to 'disseminate noble values'. Like the other suggestions, this database would be implemented by the IIM (Government of Malaysia 2004: 74–75).

A close reading uncovers one exception to the infinite deferral of action devoted to concrete future outcomes in the NIP: time and again, the NIP calls on institutions (such as the IIM) to continue to formulate plans for the implementation of the NIP. In other words, the only specific outcome of the NIP seems to be the proliferation of plans designed to inculcate noble values and integrity among Malaysians. Here, the actual orientation of the NIP becomes clear: as a plan that exists as an object in the present, it is a vehicle to simply generate more plans. Perceived issues of the present are acknowledged and creatively engaged, which in turn generates movement in the now without the actual burden of living with a future that may not come. Perusing the IIM's website confirms this: nearly a decade after its founding, nearly all of the IIM's activities and accomplishments consist of devising 'plans', 'roadmaps' and 'agendas' related to integrity

(Integrity Institute of Malaysia 2013).[3] 'The plan' and 'the outcome' thus become one, unified as an object that becomes powerfully operational within the common sense of an everlasting present, where time is experienced as an index of movement but does *not* presume succession. In turn, action becomes the ability to creatively index and mediate the conditions of the present rather than control the trajectory of a successive movement into a concretely imagined future (Deleuze 1993).

The Plan Outruns Its Planners: The Dewan Bandaraya Kuala Lumpur

It is extremely difficult to gain access to those who make and carry out institutional plans in Kuala Lumpur, a general perception that is not exaggerated (see Baxstrom 2008[4]). Dewan Bandaraya Kuala Lumpur (DBKL, roughly translated as 'City Hall'), which is responsible for the city's development and planning, is no exception. DBKL attached little urgency to fielding questions from anyone on any issue related to planning or the details of urban governance. Goh Ban Lee accurately summarized the general situation over twenty years ago:

> In Malaysia, where power is very concentrated and centralised in the hands of a few people and the culture of sharing power is almost non-existent, it is very difficult to envisage a situation where the public can participate effectively in the development plan making process. It is not only a case of the politicians and the planners not willing to share power, it is also a case where the citizens themselves are not able to make effective representations, having been denied the opportunity to do so for so long. (Goh 1991: 116)

Goh's characterization of the relative lack of public access to decision-making processes in urban development is generally accurate in reference to DBKL. However, his description leaves out the very real ambiguity that government officials themselves face in the process of designing and executing urban planning initiatives. The general lack of procedure that hampers civic efforts to influence or even just understand the process can also represent a zone of indistinctness for officials, forcing them to exercise a great deal of bureaucratic discretion in the present, particularly when dealing with requests or demands from the public. As my own encounters with government officials illustrate, it was important, in the context of urban governance in Kuala Lumpur, to consider how planners make decisions when the proper application of rules or laws is unclear. When I requested an interview with DBKL for my ongoing research project, Dr Guo,[5] a high-level official in DBKL's Master Plan Department, agreed to see me but introduced himself by stating, 'I've only got about ten minutes, so tell me what you want.' The concluding moments of the interview was similarly telling:

RB: Does DBKL have a guiding philosophy or more broadly defined goals in planning how the city should look and what development projects should be pursued or not?

Dr G: City planning in KL is primarily a reactive process. Our planning is really a way to rationalize megaprojects such as KL Sentral. We don't always have a lot of influence until after a big project is underway.

RB: So you are saying that it is the vision of the developers that counts the most here? It's not the local communities or DBKL…

Dr G: [Interrupting] Local communities do not, frankly, have much say in what is happening, or is going to happen, in their neighborhoods.

RB: But there seems to be quite a lot of concern in DBKL documents like the Draft Structure Plans that the public doesn't really participate in this process.

Dr G: Well …there isn't really a process for communities to voice their opinions or complaints. Sure, sometimes there are public hearings, but this isn't really effective. Most people don't know what is going on.

RB: How do you feel about that?

Dr G: I've already told you what my job is. Do you have any more questions, because I have to go now.

(Baxstrom 2008: 105)

Dr Guo asked me to submit my questions to him in writing. The questions I subsequently forwarded were very specific, dealing primarily with timetables for ongoing projects, plans for specific city blocks in the Brickfields area of the city where I was conducting my primary ethnographic field research, and projected changes in vehicular and pedestrian traffic flows. Most of all, I wanted to discuss (or better yet, obtain) DBKL impact studies regarding the KL Sentral and KL Monorail projects. In short, I wanted to know what DBKL's vision of the future was, according to its own plans.

The direct, detailed questions drew a response from one of Dr Guo's assistants, Mr Shunyuan. Interestingly, our telephone conversation was initiated due to a case of mistaken identity:

Mr S: I have your inquiry here … your set of questions. Are you a consultant?

RB: No, I'm an anthropology graduate student. Currently I am doing research for my doctorate in Brickfields. I included some of my bio information on the fax, I think … at the top?

Mr S: Yes, I saw it … are you sure you aren't a consultant? Academics don't ask detailed questions like this. Why do you need such detailed information?

RB: Well, I spoke with [Dr Guo] and he instructed me to be as precise as possible. Also, my work involved the impact of large development projects in the neighborhood, so knowing the details of the project is important to my findings.

Mr S: Yes, ok ... [Dr Guo] asked me to handle this, but I looked at your list and thought that you were a consultant.

RB: Ah, I see. No, no ... just for my research. I'm not working for a company or anything.

Mr S: Well, alright ... hmmm ... you know, I can only answer a few of these you know. Most are not my department ...

(Baxstrom 2008: 105–106)

Shunyuan's primary responsibility was in the traffic division. He ruled out addressing most of my written questions but did answer a few:

Mr S: Ah, here you ask about impact studies. Well, DBKL does do some of its own research, but our studies are quite small. So we tend to rely on the studies that developers submit.

RB: So you don't do independent studies to check against those submitted by the developers?

Mr S: No, not really. We don't have the resources. To tell you the truth, I don't really trust what those guys give us. In fact, I think that most of their reports are simply bullshit! Still, in many cases it is all we have to work with.

RB: Why do you think that? Do you think they are inaccurate?

Mr S: Well ... I don't know. It doesn't matter. Most of these projects are done deals anyway. Especially the ones you are asking about.

RB: Are these reports public?

Mr S: No way!

RB: So I couldn't get a copy of them or a summary for research purposes?

Mr S: [Laughing] I don't think so.

(Baxstrom 2008: 106)

In the absence of laws or guidelines governing officials' contacts with the public, any outside inquiry regarding DBKL policies or plans presented officials with a problem. In our brief telephone interview, Shunyuan avoided answering most of my questions directly. Yet expressed alongside this avoidance was a barely concealed desire to talk. Certainly, this was partly because of my position as a foreign researcher seeking information, and it is safe to say I was able to gain greater access to DBKL officials than that afforded to most Malaysian citizens. In any case, despite the relative failure of my attempt to gain empirical information from these officials regarding ongoing development projects in the city, their ambivalent evasion of my questions and desire at the same time to provide some answer to them is significant. Every request for clarification or information regarding their work outside the internal channels of the state generated an experience of aporia and a grasping for traction that strikingly resembled that of local residents (Baxstrom 2008, 2012). Although government bureaucrats are often understood locally as the 'instruments' through which the state exercises its power, my encounters with these men and women were shaped by many of the same forces that marked and delimited the agency of individuals in setting the trajectories of everyday life in the city. Dr Guo articulated the bind very well when, addressing my request for information from his department for research purposes, he replied: 'There aren't any [rules specifically denying access to DBKL plans], but we have to be careful. If we give out something that someone doesn't want us to, we can be accused of giving out official secrets.' Violating the Official Secrets Act is a heavy price to pay for acting in the absence of formal rules and procedures. In this context Shunyuan's incredulous 'No way!' response to my probing for access to internal impact studies made more sense, as the release of information to a researcher could easily be defined as a crime. Thus, officials at DBKL had to anticipate the possibility that their acknowledgement of a party not formally recognized by the legal procedures in place could lead to their engagement with the law as criminals and representatives of their particular institution simultaneously.

Dr Guo and his assistant alluded to the fact that the decision-making process within DBKL is sharply circumscribed by ministers in the Office of the Prime Minister and by property developers allied with those officials. They did not state this directly during our brief interviews. They did, however, mention that DBKL must often act according to information that they do not credit and that does not seem to strongly refer to a singular result. Both men cited the reactive nature of their work, rooted in strategic movement in the present, and underscored the fact that they were primarily concerned with enacting plans that were already approved, rather than helping to formulate these development projects in relation to future outcomes. Shunyuan mentioned several times that he had no confidence in the accuracy of property developers' reports and implied that he and others at DBKL were well aware that property developers file misleading reports to justify their projects in the present. 'I must say that I don't have very much confidence in these fellows,' Shunyuan restated towards the end of our conversation. 'They have the bottom line in mind and that's it.' Aside from such acidic comments, Shunyuan did not articulate a broad critique of the process. He disclaimed responsibility for the outcomes of his actions by citing the 'real powers' that directed him to act in particular ways, and did so in a way that strikingly resembled the ambiguous, baroque understandings of agency, recognition and justice that city residents articulated regarding their own futures and their relationship to agents of the state (Baxstrom 2012).

Jalan-Jalan: Walking with Nowhere in Particular to Go

The plan as a creative instrument of contingent, momentary action is not limited to government schemes such as the NIP or to the inner workings of DBKL. This is evident when one enters the Tun Sambanthan Monorail station in the Brickfields area of the city. Hanging over the entrance is a puzzling sign that simply reads 'Jalan-Jalan'. Does it refer to the company sponsor of the station? Is it a somewhat odd suggestion (i.e. 'walk around')? As it currently exists, the meaning of the sign simply floats in the air, much like the sign itself seems to. But in fact, Jalan-Jalan is the trace of a plan that lingers in the present of Brickfields in a time of radical change.

In September 2002 I visited the new headquarters of the KL Monorail Corporation to interview a public relations officer about the then ongoing construction of the monorail system for a book about everyday life in early twenty-first-century Brickfields (Baxstrom 2008). Among other things, I was handed a detailed plan for the construction of a leisure park on the banks of the Klang River that was to be associated with the Tun Samban-than station (Kuala Lumpur Monorail Corporation. n.d.). Boat rides, pic-turesque walks, food courts: Jalan-Jalan would bring a new feel to an area that just a few short years before had consisted of urban *kampungs*,[6] local temples, and crumbling 1960s-era apartment blocks. The flashily detailed plan for Jalan-Jalan implied a commitment to community well-being and order in its unambiguous, ambitious vision of a Disney-like river park. According to this plan, the shabby low-cost flats and spiritually danger-ous (and most often illegal) temples of the river would yield to the cheer-ful soft power of development, noble values and wholesome family fun.

The Jalan-Jalan plan served as an important vehicle of local action in the present for the KL Monorail Corporation. In 2002 the company's mono-rail project had run into some serious obstacles. Bizarre, baffling accidents during the testing of the trains had shaken public confidence in the safety of the system before it had even opened. Local residents muttered darkly about the radical, aggressive changes the construction of the elevated tracks had brought to the physical environment of the neighbourhood. The project was way behind schedule. Was KL Monorail really in control of the situation? Could KL Monorail plan effectively?

As it turns out, KL Monorail could plan effectively. The dark mutters audible in 2002 receded into silence long before my return visits to the area in 2006 and 2008. The basic system has been operational for nearly a decade now. But where is the Jalan-Jalan recreational park? Like all contingent strategies, it appears to have served its purpose and gone into the drawer, with the puzzling sign at Tun Sambanthan station currently the only visible trace of such a plan ever having existed. The temples, shabby apartments and polluted river remain largely as they were before (although the *kampungs* have truly disappeared). Perhaps the KL Monorail Corporation will someday pull the plan out of the drawer and dust it off; it all depends on what the present brings.

I emphasize here that, while it is quite obvious that neither the NIP nor the Jalan-Jalan plan has functioned as an instrument for controlling future events or outcomes, it is incorrect to label such plans total failures, given that they generated the ability to act in the present. Echoing James Ferguson, it is important to recognize the productive (in the Foucauldian sense) effects such plans have had, particularly in expanding the reach of bureaucratic institutions (Ferguson 1994; see also Mosse 2005). The task now becomes to specify the differences between such instruments' effects for institutions and their effects on the everyday lives of the people who are subject to planning initiatives. As I have argued elsewhere, the concrete effects of such plans on ordinary people often take the form of ruptures that disorient the experience of urban living (at least temporarily), to the extent that people do not trust their own senses when inhabiting their own homes, neighbourhoods and communities. When the state and its agents make aggressive, unanticipated, sudden moves to radically shape urban environments, seemingly without direct reference to known plans that would provide a mode of imagining future outcomes, the net effect in social terms, I have argued, is that urban dwellers are often denied their *right to the city* (Baxstrom 2008; see also Harvey 1990, 2000; Lefebvre 1991, 2003; Mitchell 2003).

These ruptures can also negatively impact institutions and impair their ability to act in the present. This is what had happened to the KL Monorail Corporation in early 2002; faced with missed deadlines, unexpected accidents and equipment failures and especially an ever-shifting backdoor political terrain, the corporation's ability to execute the monorail project had come into serious doubt. The corporation needed a plan; with Jalan-Jalan, it was able to marshal one that reasserted some measure of control and agency within the situation. That the content of the plan ultimately was largely put aside should not distract from the fact of the Corporation's ability to create such an object (actualized in the various blueprints and press releases generated at the time – secondary objects that remain in my office files to this day), which by itself served as a vehicle for re-establishing mastery over the situation and the space of the neighbourhood. In this sense, Jalan-Jalan was a success.

Without minimizing the concrete disruptive consequences of such situations, it is also important to note that the residents of Kuala Lumpur themselves do not react passively in these contexts. The ethnographic evidence shows that faced with a city that is always in motion, individuals subject to large-scale plans that are seemingly disconnected from the future find innovative ways to shape everyday situations themselves. If the plan is an object, it becomes available (albeit in very different ways) to those well outside the context of its origin. To be sure, the forms of action available to individual urbanites in Kuala Lumpur differ substantially from those available to institutions, but it is nevertheless clear that residents also use plans as instruments of action in the present. In essence, they fold the experience of the city as a *condition* and the logic of the everlasting present into their own modes of everyday living. I have linked these folds to a *baroque disposition* in relation to living in contemporary Malaysia (Baxstrom 2012; see also Deleuze 1993). These 'enfoldings' do not represent the overcoming of their present condition in the Hegelian sense; rather, they are a *surpassing mutation* rooted in ambiguous, creative strategies of action that often run counter to the desires and actions of the state and its agents who seek to operate in the same environments (Attali 2001).

Conclusion

The past will disappear and the future will go next.
—J. G. Ballard

What are the larger implications of the disavowal of the future in everyday urban life in Kuala Lumpur? They remain unclear, but we should not rush to decry this radical mode of living as debased or inauthentic. What is abundantly clear is that the creation and use of plans as a vehicle of action in the present remains an effective mode for, at least in part, domesticating this seemingly uncontrolled and uncontrollable present. When it comes to state or institutional planning, the danger of plans that so completely abolish the past and the future from present living is obvious. On what basis, however, do we judge such plans to be 'successes' or 'failures'?

Based on the evidence presented in this essay, I contend that in the context of making such judgements we must adjust our understanding of what a plan is and what it does. Existing primarily as virtual objects, institutional plans in Malaysia set the relations and limits within particular fields that allow for action in the present. While all plans must gesture towards some notion of 'the future', their relative efficacy appears to have more to do with their success in dominating the present rather than willing any particular chrono-future into being. While plans are obvious instruments of power in local contexts, they do not by definition eradicate multiplicity or complexity in those environments, contrary to what scholars such as Scott (1998) have argued. Rather, it is within these fields, demarcated by the plans but not saturated by them in any absolute sense, that various institutions and individuals are compelled to, or excluded from, action that accounts for the complex relations to time itself that are empirically evident in the visible forms of living in contemporary Kuala Lumpur.

Notes

1. Marrati and Meyers offer a concise summary of Canguilhem's understanding of the relation of knowledge to life in their introduction to the translation of Canguilhem's *Knowledge of Life* (2008: vii–xii).
2. Public Perception of Corruption in Malaysia. 2003. Final report in three volumes submitted to the Special Cabinet Committee on Government Management Integrity.
3. Accessed 10 February 2013. http://www.iim.org.my/en/program
4. The ethnographic material dealt with in this section appears in a longer form and a different context in my book *Houses in motion: the experience of place and the problem of belief in urban Malaysia* (2008).
5. The names of my interlocutors from DBKL who appear in this chapter have been changed.
6. *Kampung* literally translates as 'village', although in this context it refers to illegal 'squatter' settlements that until recently dominated large areas of metropolitan Kuala Lumpur.

References

Attali, J. 2001. 'A Surpassing Mutation', in R. Koolhaas, S. Boeri, S. Kwinter, N. Tazi, H.U. Oberist (eds), *Mutations*. Barcelona: Actar, pp. 268–279.
Baxstrom, R. 2008. *Houses in Motion: The Experience of Place and the Problem of Belief in Urban Malaysia*. Stanford, CA: Stanford University Press.
———. 2012. 'Living on the Horizon of the Everlasting Present: Power, Planning, and the Emergence of Baroque Forms of Life in Urban Malaysia', in L. Chua, J. Cook, N. Long and L. Wilson (eds), *Southeast Asian Perspectives on Power*. London: Routledge.
Bergson, H. 1991. *Matter and Memory*. New York: Zone Books.
Canguilhem, G. 2008. *Knowledge of Life*. New York: Fordham University Press.
Chin, J. 2010. 'Malaysia: The Rise of Najib and 1Malaysia', in D. Singh (ed.), *Southeast Asian Affairs 2010*. Singapore: Institute of Southeast Asian Studies, pp. 164–179.
Deleuze, G. 1991. *Bergsonism*. New York: Zone Books.
———. 1993. *The Fold: Leibniz and the Baroque*. Minneapolis: University of Minnesota Press.

Derrida, J. 1994. *Specters of Marx: The State of the Debt, the Work of Mourning, and the New International.* London: Routledge.

Ferguson, J. 1994. *The Anti-politics Machine: 'Development', Depoliticization, and Bureaucratic Power in Lesotho.* Minneapolis: University of Minnesota Press.

Geroulanos, S. 2010. *An Atheism that Is Not Humanist Emerges in French Thought.* Stanford, CA: Stanford University Press.

Goh, B.L. 1991. *Urban Planning in Malaysia.* Petaling Jaya: Tempo Publishing.

Gomez, E.T. and K.S Jomo. 1999. *Malaysia's Political Economy: Politics, Patronage and Profits.* Cambridge: Cambridge University Press.

Government of Malaysia. 2004. *National Integrity Plan.* Kuala Lumpur: Institut Integriti Malaysia.

Guyer, J.I. 2007. 'Prophecy and the Near Future: Thoughts on Macroeconomic, Evangelical, and Punctuated Time', *American Ethnologist* 34(3): 409–421.

Harvey, D. 1990. *The Condition of Postmodernity: An Enquiry Into the Origins of Cultural Change.* Oxford: Blackwell Publishing.

———. 2000. *Spaces of Hope.* Berkeley and Los Angeles: University of California Press.

Herzfeld, M. 2005. 'Political Optics and the Occlusion of Intimate Knowledge', *American Anthropologist* 107(3): 369–376.

Jomo, K.S. 1999. 'Development Planning in Malaysia: A Critical Appraisal', in *Political economy of development in Malaysia.* Kuala Lumpur: Utusan Publications.

Kuala Lumpur Monorail Corporation. n.d. [released 2002]. *Jalan-Jalan: The New Kuala Lumpur Leisure Experience.* Kuala Lumpur: Kuala Lumpur Monorail Corporation.

Lefebvre, H. 1991. *The Production of Space.* Oxford: Blackwell Publishers.

———. 2003. *The Urban Revolution.* Minneapolis: University of Minnesota Press.

Li, T.M. 2005. 'Beyond 'the State' and Failed Schemes', *American Anthropologist* 107(3): 383–394.

Malaysian Institute of Integrity. 2013. *Programs.* [online] Available at: http://www.iim.org.my/en/program [Accessed: 10 Feb 2013].

Marrati, P. and T. Meyers. 2008. 'Life, as Such', foreword to Georges Canguilhem, *Knowledge of Life.* New York: Fordham University Press, pp. vii–xii.

Mitchell, D. 2003. *The Right to the City: Social Justice and the Fight for Public Space.* New York: The Guilford Press.

Mosse, D. 2005. *Cultivating Development: An Ethnography of Aid Policy and Practice.* London: Pluto Press.

Scott, J.C. 1998. *Seeing like a State: How Certain Schemes to Improve the Human Condition Have Failed.* New Haven, CT: Yale University Press.

Container ships waiting for tide on Hooghly. Source: Laura Bear

Chapter 7

MAKING A RIVER OF GOLD

Speculative State Planning, Informality and Neo-liberal Governance on the Hooghly

Laura Bear

Adam and Groves have described the plans produced within state institutions as 'actively chosen futures for which the outcome is by no means assured' that outline intended futures or promises (2007: 100). Their social effect is that they forge relationships between bureaucrats and citizens in the present through an attempt to bring about a promised future. This is differently imagined and practiced by various participants, producing contestation and unintended outcomes. This chapter uses such a definition of state planning, turning it towards an exploration of how negotiations of the future proceed between state officials and citizens in the neo-liberal networked state. Research by Swyngedouw (2005) in the European Union has suggested that audit practices and calculative rationales extend state schemes into civil society organizations. Yet there has been little examination of how plans and regulations are deployed in the frontline offices that forge the public-private partnerships that characterize neo-liberal state policy. By tracing the effects that governance's emergence beyond the state has had on the practice of state planning by the Kolkata Port Trust on the Hooghly River, this essay illuminates an underexplored aspect of neo-liberal policies (Hibou 2004).

This example will show that governance beyond the state produces a new form of planning. In it, the productivity of state promises is not that they bind citizens and bureaucrats in a centralized public dialogue over the future, but that they create decentralized improvisation and speculation along networks that cross between state and society. These links are not sustained by rule-governed rationales or neo-liberal audit culture alone. Instead, in this case and potentially in many others, relationships between citizens and bureaucrats are forged through the deployment of these rationales alongside forms of ambiguous power, charisma and speculation. As this chapter will show, planning practices produce opaque accountability, growing inequalities and difficulties for targeted political resistance, as Swyngedouw predicts (2005). This is because the effects of state plans are not attributed to bureaucratic action and differ significantly from the effects outlined in their original schemes. The plan, in fact, takes on a new legitimating role that is quite distinct from its actual social effects. It presents a future of productivity and urban development through public-private partnerships. Yet its existence contributes to the growth of exploitative, and in this case informalized, decrepit working environments from which state agencies extract surplus value and revenues. Meanwhile bureaucratic institutions are neither held accountable for these nor seen as responsible for their emergence.

The context in which I will examine this process is in the liberalization governance of the Hooghly River by the Kolkata Port Trust. Before the early 1980s, the Port Trust shaped the waterscape according to five-year plans authorized by the central government Ministry of Surface Transport (MOST). Under this technocratic rule by experts, the future of the river was determined by departmental heads, the Port Trust Board and MOST. Decisions were made centrally and involved no public consultation; instead they were announced as political gifts to the city and nation in official public statements. Alongside this mode of planning, the Port Trust employed a permanent labour aristocracy of unionized employees and provided them with housing and pensions. The role of middle- to low-level bureaucrats was to apply the rules of the port, implement plans and issue tenders to other state agencies. Some limited associations between bureaucrats and the few labour brokers and entrepreneurs who operated on the river existed and sometimes led to personal financial gain. However, these relationships were cultivated entirely for individual benefit in offstage, unofficial liaisons. This situation changed during the 1980s with the gradual political acceptance of neo-liberal policies, along with the contractual obedience to them that followed an IMF loan to the central government in 1991. From 1982 on, MOST gradually took on an extractive role in relation to the Port Trust, seeking to withdraw income from it in a manner that transformed labour, bureaucracy and planning on the river. This intensified in the 1990s, when the central government began to recall vast debts with accrued interest from the Port Trust that it had held in permanent moratorium in the previous era of social investment.[1] Five-year plans

were still made in the 1990s, but these often consisted of broad guidelines on how to generate revenue and achieve public-private partnerships.
There were still no public consultations, but the port set up a publicity
department to encourage entrepreneurial activity on the Hooghly, create
support for its schemes and protect its reputation. Today, the role of bureaucrats on the river is to generate public-private partnerships with entrepreneurs, extract revenue towards the centre and find cheap, fast ways
of accruing income for the state.

In the case outlined here, the extraction of revenues and surplus value
from networks that run between state and society is particularly exploitative. This is because de-unionized, unregulated, casual labour dominates
in the private sector along the Hooghly River, as it does throughout India,
where 83 per cent of workers operate in the informalized sector (Harriss-
White 2003). As a result of the liberalization governance of the Kolkata Port
Trust, the 'shadow state' is being drawn directly into the plans and revenue streams of the official state (Harriss-White 2003: 17). The state directly
stimulates and profits from the long-standing and growing mechanisms
of informality associated with a local 'informal' state and economic forms
characterized by 'accumulative cruelty' (Corbridge and Harriss 2000: 146).
As this chapter will show, this means that low-level bureaucrats now occupy a Janus-faced position, acting to both produce and cross a boundary
between a public, regulated and a private, informalized sector. Like the
Roman god, they produce and look both ways across a boundary enacting both liminality and a distinction between spaces (Van Gennep 1960).
This essay explores the specific practices through which informal labour
is made part of the state, its fiscal relationships and plans while also being held apart from inclusion in the citadel of public employment with its
legal rights and fair wages.

What is important is not that the boundaries between state and society,
informal and formal, illicit and licit are blurred by these new state practices,
but that these realms of action are articulated with each other yet marked
as distinct. So although Elyachar is correct to argue that 'making sense of
the "informal"... is impossible without a parallel story of the state' (2005:
95), it is not true that in Kolkata hybrid forms of the state are emerging in
which it appears 'fuzzy'. Instead the work of liberalization bureaucrats in
India is to ensure constant movement of plans, state tokens, officials and
revenues between domains of formality and informality while maintaining the separation between them. Networks of informality are not always
unmapped or beyond the purview of state institutions, as some authors
have argued (Breman, Guerin and Prakash 2009; Roy 2002). They are an
expanding inner darkness of exclusion from rights within the networks

of the state in India and elsewhere. This example from Kolkata points to the need for further comparative work in the many other urban settings across the world where neo-liberal policies combine with networks of informality (Roy and Nezar 2003). But this chapter's findings also have more general implications for understanding governance beyond the state. The simultaneous deployment of forms of personalized and officialized authority and contradictory goals of public good and private profit is likely widespread. Most importantly, the task facing Port Trust officials – crossing and producing a boundary between public state and private non-state action, which is manifested so acutely in this case – is one they share with most neo-liberal bureaucrats.

This task requires new forms of low-level bureaucratic action and distinct claims to legitimacy. This chapter explores these, suggesting that state authority is no longer derived from the claiming of collective corporate agency and the distancing invocation of the plan, rule or document (Bear 2008; Hull 2003). Nor are personalizing idioms of patronage now associated solely with negotiations for private benefit or 'corruption', as much ethnography of the state has so far assumed. Instead, encounters between bureaucrats and citizens now have an ambiguous polytonality. This essay will show that bureaucrats on the Hooghly River are now using four key practices to articulate state plans and revenue streams with broader networks: speculative state promises, profitable rules, personal promises and the circulation of state tokens into non-official contexts. State plans announced in public have become speculative promises intended to generate entrepreneurial activity. Bureaucratic regulations have become a potential source of revenue – profitable rules. Bureaucrats enfold networks into the Port Trust by making personal promises underpinned by patronage, friendship and religious imagery. State tokens and officials circulate across the boundaries of legality, acting as guarantors of illicit acts or informal networks. These practices likely exist beyond this setting in other offices of the liberalizing state, although they have not yet appeared in accounts of it (Gupta and Sharma 2006; Gupta and Sivaramakrishnan 2011). In addition, they are no doubt relevant to our understanding of how public-private partnerships are forged in contemporary Europe and America.

The ethnographic microcosm through which I will address these issues, the Port Trust's small vessel licensing office (SVLO), provides examples of widespread practices I witnessed during a year of participant observation in the private-sector shipbuilding firms, port offices, barge companies and docks along the Hooghly River.[2] To understand the significance of this setting, we must first turn to the history of recent changes in the governance and planning of this waterscape.

Planning in Liberalization Kolkata:
Public Deficit, Speculative State Promises
and the Official Uses of Informality

Balance-of-payments crises, and pressure from political and business elites for neo-liberal responses to them, emerged in India between 1980 and 1991. Research on the board meetings of the Port Trust shows a hidden consequence of this: the gradual development of an extractive central state that sought to capitalize public resources, divest itself of permanent labour forces and draw back revenue centrifugally to meet its obligations in the repayment of international loans. This process began in 1981, when Indira Gandhi accepted an IMF loan and some limited measures of liberalization to stabilize the economy and gain a wider vote bank among the business classes (Dash 199). Under Rajiv Gandhi in the second half of the 1980s, the central government faced regular balance-of-payments crises caused by the reduction of taxes on the middle classes and business, a spike in oil prices due to the first Gulf War and the collapse of the Soviet Union, India's main trading partner. In 1991 under Narasimha Rao, India accepted an IMF loan of 1.8 million dollars in return for the adoption of economic reforms that would open up the economy to external investors, lessen state control of the market and end public monopolies. This was followed by further reforms that solidified the political response as one in which private business and trading interests were given priority over social investment (Corbridge and Harriss 2000). The resultant changes in the private sector and practices of consumption are a well-known story, but the history of the Port Trust reveals an entirely different and equally significant process: a shift in the practice of the public good away from long-term social investment orchestrated in five-year plans and into a drive to extract revenue through short-term, decentralized actions.

This sea change in the role of the state occurred through a gradual process that was consolidated by a replacement of top-level bureaucratic personnel in 1990 and 1991. The IMF loan of 1981 was successfully repaid by 1985, but only by diverting funds from public investment and extracting resources from state industries such as the Port Trust, a tendency that escalated through the second half of the 1980s and culminated in the period of 1990–1991, when the new reforming finance minister, Mammohan Singh, and his secretary, an ex–World Bank economist, Ahluwalia, assigned top-level posts in the ministries to their allies (Dash 1999), who all had extensive World Bank or IMF experience and would ensure fiscal stringency and the repayment of loans. This shift away from policies of social investment towards the extractive repayment of debts led to a profound restructuring of working-class state employment, bureaucracy and planning that is visible in the recent history of the Kolkata Port Trust.

Crucial to this process was the new agency given to public deficit, which the actions of MOST exemplify. Starting in 1982, it annually reduced its subsidies to the Kolkata Port with the sudden justification that the port owed repayments on costs incurred for infrastructure projects on the river in the 1960s and 1970s. From 1994 on, it plunged the port into perennial fiscal crisis by demanding repayment on loans that had previously been in permanent moratorium. Meanwhile, further loans to the port became decentralized and profit-driven, supplied at commercial rates of interest from other ports or foreign banks. These extractive debt relationships have led to successive financial crises in the port. Each year of accounts shows that the passage of goods has consistently made a profit or broken even, with the cost of labour on the river easily covered.[3] Levels of trade have remained high: for example, in 2008–2009 the absolute volume of cargo moving along the Hooghly was the third highest among Indian ports. The accounts were consistently pushed into the red by the cost of repayments to an extractive state whose new priorities were its own fiscal obligations to international capital and the interests of business classes at home and abroad.

In response to these new policies, the Kolkata Port Trust systematically cut its costs and outsourced work to newly emerging brokers and private entrepreneurs. Between 1981 and 2000, it reduced its permanent work-force from 34,492 to 11,514 employees by cutting working-class and lower-middle-class jobs on the river.[4] Unions resisted this process through the early 1980s, but activism has declined sharply since their central leadership agreed to the IMF loan in 1991 (Dash 1999). This allowed many local leaders to become brokers for access to temporary contractual work on the river, so that rights were protected only for the dwindling numbers of permanent employees. These processes have taken on even greater urgency since 2000, when the Port Trust experienced the most severe financial crisis in its history. A hiring freeze that its chairman instituted on permanent jobs at every level of the port continues to the present. Any equipment that could be sold off was auctioned. All new building or infrastructure replacement projects were discontinued. Repair of vessels and equipment in the port slowed almost to a halt, and the ship-repairing department was closed. For the young men whose fathers had made up the working classes of the river, access to livelihood has become scarce, temporary, informalized and uncertain.

These fiscal crises and central government demands do not appear in the five-year plans publicly issued by MOST. Since the 1990s, these have instead simply generally called for private-public partnerships and the generation of productivity from the resources of the Port Trusts. This has resulted in a decentralized practice of planning led by whatever schemes local-level bureaucrats can conceive of and realize in partnership with entrepreneurs and other local state agencies. Bureaucrats' consequent position in a horizontal and sometimes subordinate relationship to local entrepreurial and political classes in Kolkata is quite distinct from their place in the centralized, government-funded schemes of the past. Outcomes of this form of speculative planning have followed a consistent trajectory. The port proposes plans, disseminated by its publicity department, that follow neo-liberal principles and aim at generating productive entrepreneurship and middle-class river use. Yet after covert negotiations between local state-level bureaucracies, politicians and entrepreneurs, the outcome is the creation of decrepit working-class environments and networks of de-unionized, contractual labour. Here I will focus on the fate of three schemes that show the historical context of the emergence of the current nodal brokering role of the SVLO: the plans for the development of the waterfront, the promotion of shipbuilding and stimulation of inland water trade.

In 1984, the Kolkata Port Trust produced its first large-scale scheme for the profitable use of its landholdings along the river. Under the plan, land along the east bank of the river in central Kolkata was intended for middle-class commercial and residential use. In the 1990s, wishing to generate investment through public-private partnerships, the port's public relations department began to publicize the transformation of the waterfront into private housing, shopping malls and leisure spaces as imminent. Yet the port could not realize its schemes without negotiating the predatory ambitions of local state and political classes driven by their own fiscal constraints at the Kolkata Metropolitan Development Agency (KMDA) and the Kolkata Municipal Corporation (CMC). Both of these agencies drew up their own rival plans for the land and refused to grant environmental permission for its redevelopment by the port. The CMC also delayed deploying police to clear the land of the urban poor, who had settled in the derelict warehouses. Decentralized planning made the port reliant on alliances with local bureaucrats and politicians, who created pressure to hand over the valuable waterfront to them. The resulting stalemate lasted until 1999, when the land was divided up and leased to the KMDA and CMC, with a third section retained by the port. Each organization agreed to 'beautify' its stretch, which meant no more than demolishing old buildings, planting trees and making a path along the river. The CMC and KMDA hoped that this formal leasing would result in more vested rights, under which they could develop their own profitable uses of the waterfront in the future. Only upon the signing of this agreement did the CMC launch a drive with the police to demolish unauthorized structures and evict people living on the land.[5]

The speculative promises in the Port Trust's publicity schemes had evaporated because its decentralized, speculative planning relied on negotiations with other powerful bureaucracies in the city. The waterfront remained a working-class space, part of a semi-legal economy of sex work and mud and sand extraction. The SVLO was moved to this location, and its work has now become to tax and stimulate these trades. None of this process was in the public domain, creating a democratic deficit with no possibility of challenges to it. To the citizens of the city, it appeared that a publicized plan inspired by productive neo-liberal principles had simply failed to be realized. The waterfront and its informal trades were not seen as a consequence of liberalization practices of decentralized, speculative planning.

The outcomes of plans to revive shipbuilding on the Hooghly illustrate a different aspect of liberalization planning – state agencies' systematic promotion of informality to cut the costs of labour. In 1984, the chairman of the port founded the Maritime Industries Development Council, composed of all the state-sector shipyards along the river. Publicly, this was described as a decentralized attempt to coordinate local agencies to work together to promote prosperity and entrepreneurship. With the first meeting of the council, however, it became a forum for coordinating mechanisms to cut the costs of production. Members planned ways to reduce permanent workers and increase out-contracting to small private yards.[6] In 1992 work began to be regularly out-contracted, and in 2000 the port closed its own ship-repairing department. Work that was once carried out by permanent workers in state shipyards was now outsourced to private, unregulated yards. This process produced a chain of small yards along the Howrah side of the river, where de-unionized temporary labourers – including many former port employees and members of the new, younger generation of working-class men – have taken up posts. The labour contractors and private shipyard owners who sought links to and work for the state in the SVLO emerged in the wake of these moves. Once again, a decentralized plan to promote local prosperity had not benefited the working classes on the river. Instead it had led to a high-level coalition of local state industries joined in a systematic attempt to outsource work to unprotected, temporary labour. And once again, the public is unaware that this is the outcome of private negotiations, or that most of the work carried out in the new yards is for the state. The absence of 'prosperity' and development on the river is widely attributed not to the effects of state action, but to the slowness of the private capital flows of liberalization that have not yet reached the Hooghly.

Attempts to revive the inland water barge trade reveal another consequence of the new forms of planning on the river – in this case, a process of de-technologization and promotion of dangerous work environments because of resistance to social investment and reliance on private entrepreneurship. In 2001, newspaper articles and public speeches augured the revival of entrepreneurship on the river through the barge trade. In private, the chairman of the port told his board that the decreasing depths in the river, due to MOST's inadequate public funding for dredging, meant that 'A new kind of port operation is necessary which uses the available draft in the river to the maximum while reducing investment to the bare minimum.'[7] In 2003, both the Government of India and the Kolkata Port Trust announced that they intended to stimulate trade on the Ganges and Hooghly. In January 2004, at a meeting with the secretary of shipping, the chairman and barge operators agreed to turn two out of three jetties at the port into inland barge jetties. Old jute mills, the report to the trustees continued, might develop their sites for handling inland water cargo, and private-sector participation could be brought to bear on the project.[8] But the lack of government subsidies for constructing new jetties and dredging made the project impossible. This project's sole outcome was the encouragement, through tariff reductions by the port, of trade in fly ash waste from local power stations to cement factories in Bangladesh. This trade is entirely dominated by one private firm, which has undercut its rivals by using barges manned by Bangladeshi crews hired on temporary contracts. Because the vessels are so unsafe and the river so increasingly unpredictable, there have been numerous accidents. Participants in this trade also came to the SVLO to broker deals. Once again, a public plan for revival of trade seemed to have simply appeared and disappeared in the sphere of publicity, with no effect. But in reality, this new form of planning, driven by a desire to work with entrepreneurs and carry out minimal investment in infrastructure, has produced a new, higher-risk environment for labour on the river.

These examples have shown how decentralized state planning that seeks to stimulate public-private partnerships and generate revenues to repay public deficits has systematically stimulated and enfolded networks of informality into state practices and revenue streams. It has also produced results quite contrary to those promised in the speculative plans made public by the publicity department. This has made it seem as if these plans have simply failed to be realized or have disappeared. But the situation is quite different: in fact, the plans have set in motion processes of unaccountable behind-the-scenes negotiation and least-cost solutions that often realize the aim of channelling revenue towards the central state. They can therefore be seen as a vital legitimating device for liberalization. They both promise prosperity to the citizenry of Kolkata and hide the links between state action and growing inequality.

In the next section, I will show how the work of middle- to low-level bureaucrats in the Port Trust has now become that of maintaining networks of informality, generating speculation along them and extracting revenues from them. The SVLO run by Mr Bose, is a key site where networks of informality are articulated to current state plans and income generation. Mr Bose does not directly control any of the informal workers who extract sand, ply love boats, transport fly ash or build ships along the river. Nor does he need to help employers evade unionization or employment regulations, as this is achieved by strategies of paying off union officers (many of whom are also labour brokers) and hiring small teams of workers who do not fall under employment law. But his office has come to be a nodal site where new business between the state and informal networks is brokered and stimulated. In addition, through piecemeal actions Mr Bose lends the authority of the state to maintaining the informal networks. He also extracts licence fees from some of these trades and stimulates the development of private business that will serve various state needs for outsourced work. This essay will turn next to the modes by which this is achieved, including Mr Bose's ambiguous promises.

Verbal and Textual Promises: Stimulating Speculation and Enfolding Informal Networks in the SVLO

The SVLO was a long, low, dilapidated building on the waterfront where boat owners, entrepreneurs, crew and labour contractors came to pay fees, register boats, seek redress and negotiate business. Here, along the 'beautified' stretch of the Hooghly, *majhis* (boatmen) who manned small 'love boats' and the female sex workers who made a living in them rested from the night before. Other old cargo boats were tied up at low tide and crews dug the thick grey clay from the bed of the river to sell to brick factories and idol makers. Midstream men in larger boats dug sand to be used for construction in the new town rising on the eastern edge of the city. Breaking the hierarchies of the central Port Trust offices gathered here were *majhis,* wealthy labour contractors, entrepreneurs, local pimps and high-level bureaucrats from state agencies. This open access had been introduced by Mr Bose. Since our first meeting he had encouraged me to come to the office and to accompany him on his inspection tours along the Hooghly. He had told me: 'All the boatmen and people on the river come to share their grief with me. You must accompany me so that you can understand their sufferings like I do.' Here people told me they came to *jogajog kora* or to make connections of useful friendship. Presiding over this space were icons of Kali and Ganesh, and Mr Bose often shared *prasad* (food blessed by these deities) between his assembled clients. He described his work to me in the following terms: 'Yes I make information available, help people to meet and everyone benefits. What is the harm? The port from the end product benefits from business on the river. This is God's work. His reason for putting me here in this chair.'

What was striking from my first encounter with Mr Bose was that like all the medium- and low-level port bureaucrats I met, he saw this work as a continuation of his long public service. Mr Bose was fifty-five when I met him and had spent all his life as a public-sector employee. On the death of his father in 1976, he had left school and become an apprentice shipwright in the port to support his three young unmarried sisters. There he had worked repairing the port vessels, apart from the year from 1981 to 1982, which he spent at the public-sector Shalimar shipyard. In 1991 he took his shipwright exam and joined the SVLO as the assistant, then became the senior officer in 2003. He lived with his teenage daughter and son and wife in a cramped two-bedroom rented flat. Mr Bose hardly spent any time at home, leaving for weekends on long inspection or advisory trips. His mobile phone rang every few minutes even when he was at home. Mr Bose did not attribute his absorption in work to the commercial freedoms of liberalization. He associated it entirely with bringing his now rare technical knowledge and the actions of the state closer to citizens. As he put it:

> The only section that is large now is the PR department, but I do all the PR in my office. I don't just enforce the rules, I make the people understand the rules. They pay something and they have rights. We have to go close to them and explain the meaning of doing it or they will not do it. I could convert the river into a river of gold if they gave me the proper hands to do this.

His actions had in fact brought the networks of informality on the river into a more direct relation with the Port Trust than ever before. His appointment came at a difficult time because in 2003, the current chairman, A.K. Chandra, cut all port fees to generate trade but also demanded that all departments increase their revenues. Mr Bose set about looking for means to gather this income by drawing boat owners, *majhi*s and other entrepreneurs into the orbit of the office. The previous superintendent had turned a blind eye to the illicit nexus of the River Police, boat users, owners and the boat workers' union, running a strictly hierarchical office into which the 'bad characters' on the river were not admitted. Many people explained to me that, as one elderly barge owner put it: 'The owners and *majhi*s used to be treated like nothing. They could not talk to the registration officer. They could not even enter the office nor would the officer listen to them. But Mr Bose is different, he helps us with everything.' A thirty-year-old love boat *majhi* described how before Mr Bose's tenure they were constantly harassed by the River Police, but now they could feel proud to show their licences to them. He added, 'We too are part of the *sarkar* (state) now.'

Mr Bose took two routes to alter the practices of his office. First he increased the number of on-site inspections in the coastal villages along the river. He also used these visits as an opportunity to encourage residents to register their rights: 'I said, "You register your child when it is born. You have the title deeds for your house so why would you not have registered your boat on which your livelihood depends and then no one can take this away from you".' Many owners and *majhis* also told me how significant it was that Mr Bose had come into their village houses.

In addition, Mr Bose persuaded the head of the Marine Department that to increase the port's income he should petition MOST to change the rules so that when an unlicensed boat was seized by the River Police it would be released only if it was first licensed. MOST agreed, and the new law was put in place. Before this, Mr Bose explained, the River Police had had good business from 'seizing the same boat over and over again'. He also stripped the last vestiges of influence from the local boatmen's union, which had already been weakened by the decline of barge trade on the river. As Mr Bose claimed: 'My office has got rid of the need for a union. Actually the union used to intervene in disputes and take money from both parties, but now they do not need the union they can just come straight to my office and talk to me directly.'

Mr Bose also acted to undermine the illicit nexus between the union, River Police and lack of licensing. Before 2003 in the Howrah area, all boats were unlicensed and the River Police were rumoured to be making up to 4 lakhs per month from the 150 sand boats working this stretch. The fees were collected by a *saddhu* (Hindu mendicant) who was said to be the agent of the River Police. One night Mr Bose conducted a raid on him with a journalist from a local paper and the police. He escaped, but after this, the sand boats started to be licensed. So Mr Bose had acted to draw the networks of informalized river labour into the revenue streams of his office. River workers generally welcomed his moves because they felt that unlike the union and River Police, who just wanted bribes from them, Mr Bose supplied them with state-certified documents and rights. These were inalienable and would, as one love boat *majhi* put it, 'secure my future'. Mr Bose seemed to promise them fairness and access to the neutral justice of state tokens that had been long denied to them.

But in spite of these actions, revenues collected from the SVLO were still low because licence fees had been reduced. Thus Mr Bose was constantly on the lookout for other sources of revenue. In fact, all the participants in the newly directed networks on the river had come to understand bureaucratic rules in a new way – not as the distant actions of a legalistic authority on the river, but instead as negotiable potential sources of private and public income, that is, profitable rules.

Mr Bose and his clients liked to discuss future uses of the rules. A common topic of conversation was the pontoon jetties on the river and the ferries that plied from them. The ferry businesses had been entirely cornered by local political party officials, whose supporters now ran them. Mr Bose and his clients often speculated on how they could channel these profits back towards the port. The challenge was, as Mr Bose suggested, to 'look at the value in everything. You even have to know how human value too can be used' to increase the revenues of the port. Conversations between him and clients were directly oriented towards this search for the value in everything, especially current or forthcoming bureaucratic regulations.

Mr Bose and his clients also sought to generate greater revenues for his office and themselves by speculating on entrepreneurial schemes. With his clients and me, Mr Bose often discussed the potential of the silver sand trade, referring to newspaper publicity about the West Bengal government's future infrastructure projects to support expectations. These projects, he suggested, would need good-quality sand for cement, and this was available from the river, which he called 'liquid gold'. He was closely involved with the twenty companies operating up and down the river quarrying this sand, and with the smaller-scale sand boats. Mr Bose also spoke often of how shipbuilding and repair was an endlessly expanding business, especially since his old department in the port had shut down. He had become closely involved with several privately run shipyards as a 'consultant'. Sometimes he recounted schemes that combined elements of all these projects. For example, he imagined a way for the port to raise revenues by outsourcing toll collection to various groups on the river, who could then use the profits to dredge sand from the river and sell it to the construction industry. These verbal speculations were in fact much more than that. They were incitements between himself and his clients to make these things happen.

Very often interests came together around Mr Bose's desk, and he took the opportunity to set up a quid pro quo of brokering of private deals and outsourcing of state work. For example, the following mutual negotiations occurred one afternoon in Mr Bose's office. A first-time visitor, Mr Ghosh, arrived to ask Mr Bose's advice on a silver sand deal. Mr Bose said aggressively that he was a 'public servant not paid for doing this', but that he 'would help out of my own good will, because who will pay me to sort out your problems for you?' Mr Ghosh explained his problem. A *majhi* was demanding advance payment to dig the sand, which the army would use for construction. Mr Ghosh worried that the *majhi* would run off with the advance. Mr Bose told him to bring the *majhi* to his office, where Mr Bose would make him sign a contract with his thumbprint. Meanwhile, a thirty-year-old man, Mr Gupta, had arrived from a shipyard. He gave Mr Bose a verbal quote for building a tourist vessel for the state government. Mr Bose showed him the written state-issued tender requirements for the vessel, adding that 'You should do this job, but you should also cut your costs by subcontracting some of the work to someone else, like Howrah Private Shipyard.' Mr Bose was a 'consultant' with this yard. But then Mr Gupta suddenly asked Mr Bose in turn whether he could help him obtain some cheap silver sand from Mr Ghosh, who had just been dealt with. Mr Bose said he would arrange this for their mutual benefit.

Mr Bose's office was a site connecting the speculative promises of a wide range of state agencies, tiered-out contracting of state work to informalized labour and the calculations of specific entrepreneurs. Here, state textual promises, such as the contract signed with a thumbprint by the *majhi* in front of Mr Bose and the tender document, worked to enable relationships between these various parties. In these transactions, textual tokens were generally associated with the state and the neutrality of disembedded permanent contractual rights. Yet it was clear to the entrepreneurs who entered Mr Bose's office that these documents were always embedded in a network of relationships and verbal personal promises. They were a series of favours extended along these chains of personal relations to the mutual financial benefit of all, including state agencies. The personal verbal promise provided the direction of movement of these state-written promises and brought their power into transactions. But river workers had a different understanding of the new role of state documentation in their lives: they hoped the state document would bring them an inalienable right to justice, work and freedom from the quixotic personalized power of the River Police and unions. That is, they saw these documents as the antithesis of the personal promise or threat. Yet by accepting that the SVLO and its documents had authority and relevance in their lives, they also made themselves subject to the informal networks of influence that emerged from the personal verbal promises between entrepreneurs and Mr Bose. They had substituted the unequal patronage of the unions and the threats of the River Police for another form of inequality – that produced by Mr Bose as a state agent negotiating with entrepreneurs in the interests of the Port Trust budgets and private profits. The next section of the chapter explores how Mr Bose's ambiguous promises worked to build patronage relationships and identifies inequalities that emerged from these relationships.

Ambiguous Power and the Inequalities of Post-liberalization State Promises

In the interest of generating income from informal networks, Mr Bose had to create articulations between the state's projects and those of entrepreneurs, labour brokers and river workers. In this section I will explore how he achieved this through polytonal legitimacy, ambiguous promises and threats. I will also examine the paradoxes of his position and the effects his actions had on structural inequalities on the Hooghly.

Mr Bose's incitement of connection was most visible in his management of the sand boat trade. Usually it was the owners of boats and *golabaris* (literally 'storehouses', the middlemen who started up the business of extraction and sold the sand) who sought help in Mr Bose's office. Owners typically had two or three boats each of which that they rented for 700 rupees per month to a *majhi*. The *majhis* came from rural Bihar or South 24 parganas, and it was their job to recruit the crew of 10–12 men. The crew usually stayed only six months on a boat. The *golabaris* gave the *majhis* interest-free 'loans' that were described as loans by all concerned, but in fact were advances on their labour that they would have to return in the form of sand. The *golabaris* did not expect the *majhis* to ever fully repay the loan; this was the way they kept the boats working for them. Sometimes the *golabaris* joined with the boat owners to coordinate the loan provision because there was nothing to prevent the *majhi* fleeing with the boat and the loan. Mr Bose's official role was simply to inspect the boats during their annual survey and renew the *majhi* licences of the men who were in charge of the boats. But men came to him for advice on starting up their silver sand businesses and enforcing owners' rights over *majhis*. The port had already recently secured the *golabaris*' control of the trade by issuing licences for sand extraction in the most lucrative parts of the river to these middlemen, but not to boat owners or *majhis*.

When he was first approached, Mr Bose gave people in this trade polytonal advice that established his role as a fatherly patron in a situation where he had little actual ability to enforce regulations. For example, when a novice *golabari* approached him for guidance on starting his business on port land, Mr Bose advised him in a paternal but challenging manner. He explained that to get permission, the *golabari* had to follow the government rules so that the port would look on his specific company with favour. Mr Bose then listed an overwhelming number of authorities he would have to approach for permission. The man seemed daunted. Then Mr Bose suddenly asked him if he had been feeling unwell. He said he had and had tried various ritual solutions since his mother died, including wearing astrological stones on his fingers. Mr Bose admonished him, saying these would not help him; only if he started to live and work with his brothers again as a joint family would he become well. He then advised him to take a *Ganga Snan* (ritual bathing in the Hooghly) for this business to be successful. The man left grateful for the multiple forms of help he had received and promised to return when he had advanced his business a little more. The polytonal exchange had confirmed Mr Bose's legitimacy as a paternal counsellor.

But as relationships with owners and *golabari*s developed, Mr Bose began to help them in more direct ways. He had worked out creative techniques for using tokens of the state and his inspection powers to this end. For example, a boat owner asked Mr Bose for help in a situation where he had been intimidated into selling his boat to a gang of 'anti-socials'. They had forced him to sign a deed with a falsely inflated sale price that had been filed in the SVLO. Now his brother, who had had a share in the boat, was trying to get him to pay him half of this imaginary sum. The former owner requested Mr Bose to ask the new owners to give him a bit more money for the boat so he could pay off his brother. A few days later, Mr Bose found a solution to the problem. He left to inspect the boat, intending to use this as an opportunity to negotiate with the new owners, who would fear he would refuse to certify the boat unless they found a compromise with the old owner. As is clear from this example, Mr Bose made his own state powers and tokens relevant to these informal networks by moving them across the boundaries of licit and illicit practices. His illicit use of the legal survey upheld the rights of the wronged old owner, while simultaneously the legal deed filed in the office upheld the rights of the 'anti-social' gang.

Mr Bose had another means of forging connections with networks of informality: allowing his own actions to take on the character of illicit threats. For example, one day an anxious silver sand boat owner arrived in Mr Bose's office and said the River Police had seized his two boats as they made their way to the office for licensing. The police had demanded several thousands of rupees to return the boats because their licences were not on board. The boat owner explained that that morning he had brought all the licences to Mr Bose's office for renewal. Mr Bose assured the boat owner he would phone the River Police and get his boats released for him. But I, the owner and the other clients were left wondering whether this unfortunate event, which seemed so perfectly timed, was such an accident. None of us had any proof, but we were all aware that the distance between the River Police and Mr Bose was not as great as he liked to suggest. The port itself paid the River Police to go on raids on the river, and Mr Bose often accompanied them. But of course this was entirely supposition on our part that could never be proved. Whatever the truth, our doubts greatly increased Mr Bose's perceived power. Precisely this ambiguity about Mr Bose's inspections and official acts was his greatest source of power. His state promises and acts might be threats that would be used illicitly, while his personal promises might be used in the pursuit of licit rights.

The contradictions of Mr Bose's role as a liberalization bureaucrat, to which I turn now, were most clearly manifested in his actions in the fly ash barge and shipbuilding trades. In each of these he acted as both an enforcer of the state's rules on these informalized dangerous businesses and a broker of the businesses' continuing growth. On one of my early visits to his office, I was surprised to meet the three directors and booking agent of the private company that carried out the fly ash trade. They were seeking Mr Bose's advice on how to legally deal with a barge that had run aground and split in two in an undredged part of the river. It was a Bangladeshi government barge that had been leased out for use by a third party, who had then hired it on to the firm. The government wanted the barge repaired and returned, whereas the firm wanted to sell the remains for scrap. The directors were seeking Mr Bose's advice on the legal document that they had drawn up to negotiate the fate of the barge with the Bangladeshi government. Mr Bose explained to me later that he was closely connected to this firm because it had sought his help to find a private salvage operator for an earlier wreck at Baj Baj. A private operator was needed because the port no longer had the facilities or infrastructure to help. When another barge went down, the director of the Marine Department suspended all fly ash trade until safety measures were introduced for loading and operating the vessels. Mr Bose was then made the inspector of the new safety measures on the fly ash barges.

Mr Bose also played a paradoxical role in the private small-scale shipbuilding trade. His job made him responsible for inspecting the construction and installation of pontoons and unpropelled craft on the river. However, his office was at the centre of the process of brokering small-scale construction in the yards along the Howrah bank. He thus served in the contradictory roles of both inspector and outsourcer of this work. One day I arrived in Mr Bose's office to find a fifty-year-old engineer from a private firm showing Mr Bose the plans for a water intake pontoon barge to be built for the West Bengal government. The engineer explained that Mr Bose had helped them already with one such pontoon that had been built by Howrah Private Shipyard. He showed Mr Bose the plans for the jetty to see if he was likely to approve its design in his inspections. When the engineer left, Mr Bose asked me if I would like to see Howrah Private Shipyard where the pontoon jetty was most likely to be built because he had to go there to inspect a barge that was being repaired. As we drove to the shipyard, Mr Bose corrected the plans then engineer had given him.

The shipyard was a stretch of open land featuring a half-constructed concrete building where a planning loft and office would be, and a river dam that created a makeshift dry dock. Mr Bose and the owner, a former labour contractor, explained as we walked around the yard that Mr Bose had advised them to start their business here. He had also helped them get their very first contract. Mr Bose flourished the plans for the water jetty barge in front of the owner, saying, 'This will be your next project.' Mr Bose was acting in line with the outsourcing practices of the port as both inspector and promoter of shipbuilding along the Hooghly. As the blueprints for the water intake jetty and barge approved by the West Bengal government and Port Trust moved between the various hands of the engineer, Mr Bose and the shipyard owner, they were speeded on their way across domains by Mr Bose's moment-to-moment enactment of private promises and state actions. As with the fly ash trade, his private promises had produced the prosperity of Howrah Private Shipyard, with its informalized networks of temporary workers and dangerous conditions, while his state actions guarded the safety of a generic public on whose behalf the Port Trust inspected the products of their labour.

Mr Bose's acts produced another kind of structural inequality on the river. His polytonal patronage had limits, producing inequalities in access to his favours and state tokens. He drew boat owners and entrepreneurs into relationships using his cajoling eloquent Bengali mixed with references in English to regulations. However, a sharp line was drawn most often with *majhis*, with whom he insisted on speaking in domineering, aggressive Hindi.[9] In public offices in Kolkata, this language is often associated with the force of command, often over low-status workers. Like an angry master with a servant, Mr Bose berated *majhis* who stood around his desk. He and his clients often spoke of the comedy of the *majhis'* attempts to beat the official registration system. These conversations harnessed stereotyped certainties about low-caste groups and Muslims to create distance between the actions of *majhis* and those of the other clients negotiating the rules in the office. Clients repeatedly mentioned the bad characters of *majhis* – the men who were the basis of their income – and sought Mr Bose's favours in order to discipline them. On the other hand, *majhis* in all their conversations sought to counter their moral and social inferiority. Love boat *majhis* were proud, for example, that during the Durga puja immersion ceremonies they helped the River Police direct the idols away from the ghat into the flow of the river, because this was '*sarkari kaj*' (state work). *Majhis* insisted that there was honour in their trade because they used the strength of their bodies and learnt skill to make their money on the river.

As soon as *majhi*s entered the office, Mr Bose switched demeanour and his other clients became uncomfortable. One day a love boat *majhi* and the love boat owner came to the office. The *majhi* explained that the police, who had stopped him because a man had been taken ill on his boat, had wrongly told him that his licence had expired. The *majhi* complained that the police were just taking advantage of him to get money. Mr Bose replied bluntly and with disgust, handing over a letter with his fingertips: 'I have given this paper. Take it back to them again and say I am supporting the *majhi*.' Everyone assembled in the room laughed uneasily and discussed the comedy of a love boat *majhi* and owner – two personifications of immorality – complaining of an illegality practised against them. The love boat *majhi* had asked for nothing more than most of the clients assembled there – a personal favour from Mr Bose – but access to Mr Bose's office was not as democratic as he claimed. River workers, who generated income for boat owners and entrepreneurs, were a valuable source of revenue for the state, but their place was beyond the lines of state patronage in an illicit, immoral space. Even though river workers now saw themselves as able to access the tokens and justice of the state via the SVLO, these social definitions meant they were marginalized, outside the lines of personal patronage through which state agents generated mutual prosperity for themselves and entrepreneurs. As less moral humans, river workers generated revenues for the state but did not benefit from either its personal patronage or the full protection of permanent, legal, unionized employment.

So what were the overall structural effects of Mr Bose's ambiguous modes of power on livelihoods and status on the river? The SVLO was now underwriting the unequal negotiations between *majhi*s, boat owners and *golabari*s. Mr Bose had lent the authority and tokens of the state to these relationships. On the whole, these were now increasing the power of *golabari*s and owners over *majhi*s. The Port Trust had granted the rights to excavation of sand in two key areas to *golabari*s, thus enforcing their middleman role in the business. Meantime, Mr Bose used all the methods he could to enforce the rights of sand boat owners over *majhi*s. Mr Bose's facilitation of the shipbuilding and fly ash trade multiplied the dangerous informalized working environments on the river, while his role as an inspector of these businesses protected a generic public from accidents. His reliance on multiple forms of legitimation had also made the SVLO a markedly Hindu space. It was no longer simply a place where the tokens of the state, its ledgers and licences held sway. Instead ritual idioms sealed the authority of Mr Bose's personal and state promises. *Majhi*s – the workers with least status on the river, whose labour generated the prosperity of both the state and entrepreneurs – had drawn closer to official state rights but were kept apart from lucrative lines of personal patronage and legal, permanent employment within the state. But most importantly, Mr Bose's office had become a central site for the negotiation of articulations between private informalized and public state networks. Here many different kinds of actors sought to appropriate state tokens, direct them towards their own profit-making projects and harness the strategies of the state to their own ends. This was the sign of Mr Bose's realisation of the ambitions of higher-level bureaucrats in the Port Trust. He had become a broker of governance beyond the state par excellence, stimulating the extraction of revenue and surplus value from informalized labour while still maintaining the legality and authority of the state.

Conclusion: State-Sanctioned Informality and Its Invisibility in State Textual Promises

In most neo-liberal settings where budgetary discipline and public-private partnerships constrain the actions of bureaucrats, they are faced with a contradictory task. They must make state projections into reality by maintaining relationships with private investors and entrepreneurs while safeguarding the public good. However, introducing such commercial partnerships and budgetary discipline into urban environments that, like Kolkata, are dominated by networks of informality creates particularly acute dilemmas. Middle- to lower-level bureaucrats must harness these networks, with their forms of illegality and exploitative labour practices, using personal lines of patronage and verbal promises to cut their budgetary expenses and raise revenues for the state. Yet they must also maintain the illusion that the formal networks of the state and its written projections remain apart from these as neutral, just sources of prosperity for all. Further comparative work is needed in other contexts where, as in Kolkata, informality is central to the private sector, but this case study suggests that in such a context, techniques and inequalities previously associated with the 'shadow state' or 'corruption' become central to the realization of state projections and revenues as a result of neo-liberal economic reforms.

This means that we have to radically rethink our discussions of corruption, patronage and the blurring of the boundaries of the state.[10] We can no longer assume that personal verbal promises, patronage and private agendas are used only to capture and divert the power and resources of state institutions. Bureaucrats now use these forms of power to further state projects and actively lend the insignia of state authority to informalized networks to cut public budgetary costs, realize plans or raise revenues.

The process of enfolding informality into state networks is facilitated and reproduced by ambiguous practices of polytonal authority among middle- to lower-level bureaucrats. The pursuit of personal gain and exploitation of casual, unregulated labour (including the pursuit of entrepreneurship by state agents themselves) is legitimized as productive of state ends.

In fact what is occurring is a state sanctioning and incitation of previously unofficial forms of brokering, patronage, personal gain and exploitation. The bureaucrat in liberalizing India has become Janus-faced, though not in the sense of Swyngedouw's use of this term to describe the mixed authoritarian and democratic form of the neo-liberal state (2005). Instead bureaucrats have taken on a central role in both rendering the distinctions between spheres of state and non-state action liminal and reinforcing them. This important dual role is likely to be manifest more widely across many forms of governance beyond the state. In addition, as demonstrated here, mixed, ambiguous personalizing and officializing modes of legitimacy, rather than simply a spread of calculative or audit rationales, are likely to be part of this mode of rule.

What is striking in the case of Kolkata (and may also be so in places where similar processes are under way) is that the articulations between neo-liberal state practices and networks of informality remain invisible to the wider middle- and working-class public. This makes comprehension of the reasons the urban landscape appears as it does difficult, and activism even less likely. Only after months of reading the minutes of Port Trust board meetings and a year of fieldwork was it possible for me to understand the fate of textual speculative projections and the forms of informality that had developed on the Hooghly. Central to this absence of public knowledge is the agency of the state document in all its forms, including the tender document, the licence, the contract and the textual state projection as publicized by public relations departments. The state tender, licence and contract conceal in their textual form the web of verbal promises and long-term relationships of brokering in which they are embedded.

The textual speculative promises of high-level bureaucrats work in another manner, reflecting the idealism of bureaucrats and their attempts to act for the public benefit and transform the city into a prosperous place. Certainly various Marine Department heads and chairmen of the port have attempted to remake the waterfront of the Hooghly, develop shipbuilding and revive inland water trade. The written state projection represents the hope of this transformation in a 'not-yet' temporal structure that has been identified as characteristic of neo-liberalism (Miyazaki 2003). It also helps to legitimize the project of liberalization by offering the possibility of transformation, while also simultaneously setting in motion decentralized practices of behind-the-scenes negotiation and planning between local-level bureaucrats and entrepreneurs.

The speculative state plan appears in the public domain and then inexplicably disappears without a trace. Its disappearance reflects the impossibility of realizing dreams of prosperity as long as extreme budgetary restrictions, resource grabs by other predatory bureaucracies and outsourcing to networks of informality continue. Meanwhile, on the waterfront and the river the liberalization state is built on extreme inequalities between citizens. At the heart of these inequalities is the agency of the verbal promises of state agents, which despite apparent ephemerality build the long-term networks of obligation that reproduce unequal access to the rights and resources of state institutions. This new agency of verbal and textual state promises and the decentralized forms of action they produce needs to be explored more widely.

Finally, it is important to recognize that these forms of micro-level bureaucratic action emerge from a broader sea change in the role of state institutions that is still a relatively neglected part of the story of neo-liberalism across the world. In India since the early 1980s, the state has gradually taken on an extractive rather than social investment role as it has become tied to international finance markets and relationships of debt. Its logics of public deficit, cost cutting and dis-investment are now spreading, in the era of first-world sovereign debt crises. It may well be that the experiences of places such as India can provide us with the theoretical language to analyse these transitions as well. In particular they may help us to understand what the changing role of the state plan may be in the future of Europe.

Notes

This chapter is based on two years of research funded by the Economic and Social Research Council from January 2008 to January 2010, including twelve months of continuous fieldwork on the Hooghly. I would like to thank the river workers who taught me their trades and welcomed me into their homes, motivated by the sense that the city of Kolkata had, as they put it, 'turned its back to them'. The essay has benefited from the fascinating, challenging questions raised by Simone Abram and Gisa Wezkalnys

 1. See Roitman (2005) on the productivity of debt.
 2. All fieldwork was carried out in Bengali by myself and involved extensive participant observation in the docks, with boatmen and river pilots on the river, in the SVLO and in a private shipbuilding firm. I also carried out archival work on Port Trust board meetings, covering the records from 1950 to the present.
 3. I checked the annual accounts from 1950 to 2006.
 4. Board Meetings of the Kolkata Port Trust, 4th meeting, 31 March 2000.

5. Board Meetings of the Kolkata Port Trust, 13th meeting, 13 November 1998, Appendix II, 54.
6. Board Meetings of the Kolkata Port Trust, 14th meeting, 28 December 1984.
7. Board Meetings of the Kolkata Port Trust, October–December 2001, 17 October 2001, p. 65.
8. Board Meetings of the Kolkata Port Trust, 3rd meeting, 24 February 2004. The jute mills were closed due to the declining demand for jute, which was replaced by plastics in the 1980s.
9. This was especially striking as most *majhi*s were Bengali-speaking Muslims.
10. This is, of course, the well-known phrase from Akhil Gupta's 'Blurred Boundaries' (1995).

References

Primary Sources

Board Meetings of the Kolkata Port Trust, 1950–2004, Port Trust Headquarters, Kolkata

Secondary Material

Adam, B. and C. Groves. 2007. *Future Matters: Action, Knowledge, Ethics*. Leiden: Brill.

Bear, L. 2008. *Lines of the Nation: Indian Railway Workers, Bureaucracy and the Intimate Historical Self*. New York: Columbia University Press.

Breman, J., I. Guerin and A. Prakash (eds). 2009. *India's Unfree Workforce: Of Bondage Old and New*. Oxford: Oxford University Press.

Corbridge, S. and J. Harriss. 2000. *Reinventing India: Liberalization, Hindu Nationalism and Popular Democracy*. Cambridge: Polity Press

Dash, K. 1999. "India's International Monetary Fund Loans: finessing win set negotiations within domestic and international politics", *Asian Survey* 13 (6), November–December: 884–907

Elyachar, J. 2005. *Markets of Dispossession: NGOs, Economic Development, and the State in Cairo*. Durham, NC: Duke University Press.

Gupta, A. 1995. 'Blurred Boundaries: The Discourses of Corruption, the Culture of Politics and the Imagined State', *American Ethnologist* 22(2): 375–402.

———. and A. Sharma. 2006. 'Globalisation and Post-colonial States', *Current Anthropology* 47(2): 277–307.

———. and K. Shivaramakrishnan. 2011. *The State in India after Liberalization: Interdisciplinary Perspectives*. London: Routledge.

Harriss-White, B. 2003. *India Working: Essays on Society and Economy*. Cambridge: Cambridge University Press.

Hibou, B. (ed.). 2004. *Privatising the State*. London: Hurst and Co.

Hull, M. 2003. 'The File, Agency and Autography in an Islamabad Bureaucracy', *Language and Communication* 23: 287–314.

Miyazaki, H. 2003. 'The Temporalities of the Market', *American Ethnologist* 105(2): 255–265.

Roitman, J. 2005. *Fiscal Disobedience: An Ethnography of Economic Regulation in Central Africa*. Princeton, NJ: Princeton University Press.

Roy, A. 2002. *City Requiem, Kolkata: Gender and the Politics of Poverty*. Minneapolis: University of Minnesota Press.

————. and A.S. Nezar. 2003. *Urban Informalities: Transnational Perspectives from the Middle East, Latin American and South Asia*. Lexington Books.

*Kolkata*Swyngedouw, E. 2005. 'Governance, Innovation and the Citizen: The Janus Face of Governance-beyond-the-State', *Urban Studies* 42(11): 1992–2006.

Van Gennep, A. 1960. *The Rites of Passage*. London: Routledge and Kegan Paul.

CONTRIBUTORS

Simone Abram is reader at the department of anthropology at Durham University, and at Leeds Beckett University and has worked in interdisciplinary planning departments at Sheffield and Cardiff Universities. Her books include *Culture and Planning* (Ashgate 2011), *Rationalities of Planning* with Jonathan Murdoch (Ashgate 2002) and *Anthropological Perspectives on Local Development,* co-edited with Jacqueline Waldren (Routledge 1998).

Richard Baxstrom is lecturer in social anthropology at the University of Edinburgh (UK). He is the author of *Houses in Motion: The Experience of Place and the Problem of Belief in Urban Malaysia* (Stanford University Press 2008), the co-author of *Evidence of Things Unseen: Benjamin Christensen's Häxan* (Fordham University Press, forthcoming) and the co-editor of *anthropologies* (Creative Capitalism, 2008).

Laura Bear is associate professor in the department of anthropology at the London School of Economics. She is the author of *The Jadu House* (Doubleday 1998) and *Lines of the Nation: Indian Railway Workers, Bureaucracy and the Intimate Historical Self* (Columbia University Press 2008). She has also made five films based on this fieldwork: *The Burning of the Stomach, Ma Ganga Navigation, Love Boat for Hire, Kolkata Riviera* and *Silver Sand.* She is the convenor of the ESRC research network Conflicts in Time: Rethinking Contemporary Globalization.

Åsa Boholm is professor of social anthropology at the School of Public Administration, University of Gothenburg. Research areas include cultural and organizational dimensions of risk, the communication and management of technological risks in public policy, land use planning, the role of science and technology in public administration and decision making. A recent publication is the *Earthscan Reader on Risk,* co-edited with Ragnar L. Löfstedt (Earthscan 2009).

John Gledhill is Max Gluckman Professor of Social Anthropology at the University of Manchester, co-managing editor of *Critique of Anthropology*, and Vice-President of the International Union of Anthropological and Ethnological Sciences. He has conducted ethnographic and historical research in Mexico and Brazil on a variety of issues including agrarian reform and indigenous autonomy movements, transnational migration, neo-liberalism and state transformations, urban social movements, elites and party politics and, most recently, securitization. His publications include *Power and Its Disguises: Anthropological Perspectives on Politics* and *Cultura y Desafío en Ostula: Cuatro Siglos de Autonomía Indígena en la Costa-Sierra Nahua de Michoacán.*

Deborah James is professor of anthropology at the London School of Economics. Her research interests, focused on South Africa, include migration, ethnomusicology, ethnicity, property relations and the politics of land reform, and popular economies. She is author of *Songs of the Women Migrants: Performance and Identity in South Africa* (1999) and of *Gaining Ground? 'Rights' and 'Property' in South African Land Reform* (2006).

Sarah Lund, emeritus professor at the department of social anthropology at the University of Oslo, began research in Peru in 1977 with a study of the land reform and its impact on traditional gender relationships. Subsequent work in Peru has focused on migration (*Lives Together, Worlds Apart: Quechua Colonization in Jungle and City*) and identity documents ('Bequeathing and Quest: Processing Personal Identity Papers in Bureaucratic Spaces [Cuzco, Peru]', in *Social Anthropology* 9[1]: 3–24). More recent research has focused on Norwegian American communities of the Upper Midwest (USA). In particular, agro-business and biodiversity are emerging as important topics relevant in the context of the departmental project 'Conceptualizing Nature: Environment, Climate and Culture'.

Halvard Vike is professor at the department of anthropology, University of Oslo. He has carried out extensive research on local politics, planning, public organizations, history, gender and cultural heritage in Norway, and is currently working on issues relating to comparative political culture. Recent publications include *L'état de la morale et la morale de l'État* (Ethnologie francaise 2009) and 'Cultural Models, Power, and Hegemony (A Companion to Cognitive Anthropology)' (Wiley-Blackwell 2011).

Gisa Weszkalnys is assistant professor in the department of anthropology at the London School of Economics. She has conducted ethnographic research on urban planning, interdisciplinary research practices and natural resource extraction in a range of geographical and cultural contexts. Her book *Berlin, Alexanderplatz: Transforming Place in a Unified Germany* (2010) tackles the intricate politics of place in contemporary Berlin. She is now working on a manuscript focused on her current research on the temporality and materiality of oil exploitation, specifically in West Africa.

INDEX